Perception, Hallucination, and Illusion

PHILOSOPHY OF MIND

Series Editor
David J. Chalmers, Australian National University and New York University

Self Expressions
Minds, Morals, and the Meaning of Life
Owen Flanagan

The Conscious Mind
In Search of a Fundamental Theory
David J. Chalmers

Deconstructing the Mind
Stephen P. Stich

The Human Animal
Personal Identity without Psychology
Eric Olson

Minds and Bodies
Philosophers and Their Ideas
Colin McGinn

What's Within?
Nativism Reconsidered
Fiona Cowie

Dreaming Souls
Sleep, Dreams, and the Evolution of the Conscious Mind
Owen Flanagan

Purple Haze
The Puzzle of Consciousness
Joseph Levine

Consciousness and Cognition
A Unified Account
Michael Thau

Thinking without Words
José Luis Bermúdez

Identifying the Mind
Selected Papers of U.T. Place
Edited by George Graham and Elizabeth R. Valentine

A Place for Consciousness
Probing the Deep Structure of the Natural World
Gregg Rosenberg

Three Faces of Desire
Timothy Schroder

Gut Reactions
A Perceptual Theory of Emotion
Jesse J. Prinz

Ignorance and Imagination
On the Epistemic Origin of the Problem of Consciousness
Daniel Stoljar

Simulating Minds
The Philosophy, Psychology, and Neuroscience of Mindreading
Alvin I. Goldman

Phenomenal Concepts and Phenomenal Knowledge
New Essays on Consciousness and Physicalism
Edited by Torin Alter and Sven Walter

Beyond Reduction
Philosophy of Mind and Post-Reductionist Philosophy of Science
Steven Horst

What Are We?
A Study in Personal Ontology
Eric T. Wilson

Supersizing the Mind
Embodiment, Action, and Cognitive Extension
Andy Clark

Perception, Hallucination, and Illusion
William Fish

Perception, Hallucination, and Illusion

William Fish

Oxford University Press is a department of the University of Oxford.
It furthers the University's objective of excellence in research, scholarship,
and education by publishing worldwide.

Oxford New York
Auckland Cape Town Dar es Salaam Hong Kong Karachi
Kuala Lumpur Madrid Melbourne Mexico City Nairobi
New Delhi Shanghai Taipei Toronto

With offices in
Argentina Austria Brazil Chile Czech Republic France Greece
Guatemala Hungary Italy Japan Poland Portugal Singapore
South Korea Switzerland Thailand Turkey Ukraine Vietnam

Published in the United States of America by
Oxford University Press
198 Madison Avenue, New York, NY 10016

First issued as an Oxford University Press paperback, 2013.

Library of Congress Cataloging-in-Publication Data
Fish, William, 1972–
Perception, hallucination, and illusion / William Fish.
p. cm.
ISBN 978-0-19-538134-4 (hardcover); 978-0-19-998113-7 (paperback)
1. Visual perception. 2. Perception (Philosophy)
3. Hallucinations and illusions. I. Title.
BF241.F565 2009
121′.34—dc22 2008030658

Printed in the United States of America
on acid-free paper

For Rowena

Preface

I suspect my future interests in the philosophy of mind may have been settled shortly after my birth when my father decided to name me after the Harvard psychologist/philosopher William James. Despite this, however, I didn't actually discover this fascinating area until I was a first-year undergraduate and was lucky enough to stumble upon two stimulating classes taught by Bob Kirk and Greg McCulloch. Since then, I have been fortunate enough to be able to go on to count both Bob and Greg as friends. I still communicate with Bob regularly and continue to learn a lot from our interactions. I still miss talking to Greg. I don't think he ever realized just how much I benefited from our discussions—often late at night, over a beer—or how much they shaped my thoughts. And while I don't think for a moment that he would have agreed with everything I say in these pages, I like to think that he would have concurred with its general direction.

My thinking about the nature of visual experience began to take its present shape when I discovered the works of John McDowell and Mike Martin. I still remember reading "Singular Thought and the Extent of Inner Space" and "The Transparency of Experience" in one (long) afternoon. It was a revelation. These papers opened my eyes to the potential of a disjunctive approach to visual experiences, an event that set me firmly on the path that resulted in this book. As I have walked that path, I have continued to benefit immensely from my conversations and interactions with many people, including David Bain, Stephen Barker, Robert Black, Ned Block, Bill Brewer, Stewart Brock, Berit Brogaard, Alex Byrne, Scott Campbell, Stephen Chadwick, Andy Clark, Eros Corazza, Tim Crane, Max Cresswell, Greg Currie, Pascal Engel, Nick Jones, Peter King, Bob Kirk, Heather Logue, Bill Lycan, Greg Mason, Cynthia Macdonald, Fiona Macpherson, Ed Mares, Mike Martin, Stephen Mumford, Paul Noordhof, Glen Pettigrove, Jonathan Schaffer, Susanna Schellenberg, Barry Smith, Paul Snowdon, Richard Spence, Daniel Stoljar, and Christopher Woodard, as well as comments and questions from audiences at Victoria University, the University of Waikato, the Australian National University's Centre for Consciousness, the Institut Jean Nicod, the University of Toronto's Cloak and Dagger Philosophy of Perception Reading Group, the Massachusetts Bay Philosophical Alliance, and the University of London's Institute of Philosophy. Many thanks to you all. If there is anyone I have failed to include in this list, please accept my apologies and trust that it is due to a failure of memory on my part, not a failure of gratitude.

I also owe special thanks to David Chalmers for his support and encouragement over many years. Having Dave and the other members of the Centre for Consciousness just a short hop across the Tasman Sea has been one of the best things about being in New Zealand. As anyone who has been there will know, it provides such a stimulating and challenging philosophical environment that you can't spend time at the place without significantly sharpening your thinking. I also owe Dave, together with Peter Ohlin, particular thanks for selecting OUP's readers for this book. These readers turned out to be Benj Hellie and Susanna Siegel. It is difficult to express just how valuable I found their contributions. Benj and Susanna provided an object lesson in just how the refereeing process ought to work. On two occasions, they both read the manuscript carefully and provided extremely detailed, thoughtful, and, most of all, constructive comments. Their input has improved this book considerably, and I owe them both a great debt.

Finally, I thank my children, Freya, Anya, and Finlay, for just being there to be acquainted with, and Rowena, without whom none of this would have happened.

Contents

Perception, Hallucination, and Illusion

1

Naive Realism: The Theory and Its Motivations

> In its purely phenomenological aspect seeing is ostensibly saltatory. It seems to leap the spatial gap between the percipient's body and a remote region of space. Then, again, it is ostensibly prehensive of the surfaces of distant bodies as coloured and extended.... It is a natural, if paradoxical, way of speaking to say that seeing seems to "bring one into direct contact with remote objects" and to reveal their shapes and colours.
>
> — C. D. Broad, "Some Elementary Reflexions on Sense-Perception"

In the epigraph above, C. D. Broad is explicitly attempting to spell out a natural, first-pass view of the purely phenomenological aspect of veridical visual experience or, as we might more normally say, the conscious character of *seeing*. I say the view is "first pass" to reflect the fact that Broad is trying to capture how seeing "appear[s] to any unsophisticated percipient, and [how it] inevitably *go[es] on appearing* even to sophisticated percipients whose knowledge...assures them that the appearances are largely misleading" (1951/1965: 30). Traditionally, the kind of philosophical theory that has attempted simply to take such a first-pass view at face value—a theory known as *naive realism* or *relationalism*[1]—has, as the end of the just-quoted text indicates, commonly been taken to be a philosophical nonstarter. I think, however, there is more to be said for naive realism than it has been given credit for, both in terms of its defensibility and in terms of its philosophical significance. This book is my attempt to explain why.

1. As theories of the conscious character of visual experience, I take naive realism and relationalism to be alternative names for the same thesis.

Broad's epigraphic passage is instructive because it illustrates a number of notable things: how natural this first-pass view seems to Broad (or us) *qua* perceiver, how paradoxical it seems to him (or us) *qua* philosopher, and how difficult it can be to articulate precisely just what it is that this natural view claims. This can be seen by the relatively unusual terminology Broad employs in attempting to draw our attention to two key ways in which seeing, as a primarily conscious episode, strikes us. The first of these features is that seeing seems to put us in "direct contact" with objects that are physically remote. This is the claim that vision is *saltatory*. It is not to say that vision makes the seen objects somehow proximal to us—it is not as if it makes it seem like they are *touching* us in a physical sense of direct contact—but rather to say that there is a special kind of immediacy to our visual awareness of them, despite this awareness placing them at a physical distance from us. The second feature, of *prehensivity*, is that vision, in putting us in what seems to be direct contact with objects, thereby appears to "grasp" or "reveal" their shapes and colors.

Despite Broad's choice of terminology, his point is nevertheless that conscious vision inevitably strikes the perceiver as both saltatory and prehensive, no matter how knowledgeable or philosophically astute that perceiver is. But even while acknowledging the naturalness of thinking about vision in these terms, as a philosopher he is not unaware that it is also deeply problematic. At the same time that we recognize how natural it is to say that sight reveals the shapes and colors of objects, for example, we also appreciate that one and the same object, which is in and of itself unchanging, can seem to be *different* shapes and colors at different times. But this looks to have the consequence that visual experience can seem to "reveal" the characteristics of the things it seems to put us in "direct contact" with when, in fact, it could not be doing so.

For this reason, cases of perceptual error—cases of hallucination and illusion—have played a monumental role in shaping philosophical thinking about sense experience. And the bite of these considerations is sharpened when we recognize that the difficulties raised by illusion and hallucination—the possibility that we sometimes seem to see objects as other than they are (illusion) or seem to see objects that are not there (hallucination)—are far from arcane or theoretical. Just as the conscious characteristics of vision highlighted by Broad are supposed to be those that the unsophisticated would recognize (even if not in Broad's terms), the force of the considerations that attempt to undermine the phenomenological evidence by highlighting our susceptibility to hallucination and illusion can likewise be felt by even the most nonphilosophical among us.

The aim of this book is to show both that the kind of first-pass view Broad articulates is in fact compatible with the possibility of hallucination and illusion, and that this is a philosophically significant result. In this opening chapter, I begin by providing a theoretical articulation of the naive realist conception of veridical visual experience. Let me note, at this point, that while this kind of theory is sometimes viewed as having a certain cachet inasmuch as it is a theory of the enigmatic 'common man'—as Broad's reference to the unsophisticated suggests—we shall see that this is not only a shaky motivation, but also far from the only reason that we have to endorse naive realism. Chapter 2 will then recount the reasons why perceptual error has been thought to render naive realism philosophically indefensible, how recent work in philosophy has suggested that these objections might be overcome, and the work that remains for the naive realist to do in order to complete the defense of the thesis. The final section of chapter 2 then outlines how this critical work will be done in the remainder of the book.

1.1 Formulating the Thesis

Before I begin to articulate naive realism,[2] let me make explicit an important restriction on the scope of this project. As I am aiming to provide a defense of what is a prima facie philosophically problematic thesis, in order to confine the project to manageable proportions I restrict my ambitions to a single sensory modality: vision. The choice of modality derives from the fact that, as the passage from Broad attests, it is the nature of conscious visual perception that underpins the first-pass characterization of perceptual experience. It is therefore the possibility of illusions and hallucinations in this modality that most threatens to undermine naive realism. But before I can embark upon explaining just how deceptive experiences threaten the position, let me first clarify precisely what claims the naive realist makes about the nature of the experiences we enjoy when we perceive the world.[3]

2. There is a sense in which this name is unfortunate: calling a view "naive" might seem to imply that it is simplistic, but as the reader shall discover over the course of this book, a successful defense of naive realism will be anything but simple.

3. Because there is room for confusion about this terminology, let me make it clear that I use the terms 'perception,' 'perceptual experience,' and their cognates to indicate that we are dealing with cases in which something is seen. I use 'visual experience' as a generic term that includes deceptive visual experiences together with veridical ones.

As far as the conscious character of visual perception is concerned, the core claim of naive realism is that, when we see,[4] external objects and their properties "shape the contours of the subject's conscious experience" (Martin 2004: 64), where the metaphor of 'shaping' is read in a constitutive rather than a merely causal sense. Consider the following scenario: looking down at a glacial valley, I say to you, "Can you see how the glacier shaped the contours of the landscape?" Here, 'shaping' is being used in a causal sense—the glacier shaped the contours of the landscape by causing the elements of the landscape to be the shape they are. On this reading of 'shaping,' the claim that external objects "shape the contours" of conscious experiences would in fact be compatible with *any* metaphysically realist theory of perception. But if I were to ask instead, "Can you see how the sides of the hills shape the contours of the landscape?" I would be using 'shaping' not in a causal sense but rather in a constitutive sense—on this reading, the hillsides shape the contours of the landscape by actually *being* the contours of the landscape. This, I suggest, is how we should understand the naive realist's claim that external objects and their properties shape the contours of the subject's conscious experience: they shape the contours of the subject's conscious experience by actually *being* the contours of the subject's conscious experience.

This claim—that naive realism takes a stand on the specific way in which external objects and properties feature in the conscious character of visual experience—is also apparent in the following characterizations of the thesis:

> [T]he phenomenal character of your experience, as you look around the room, is constituted by the actual layout of the room itself: which particular objects are there, their intrinsic properties, such as color and shape, and how they are arranged in relation to one another and to you. (Campbell 2002: 116)

> [T]he featuring of a quality or relation in the phenomenal content is... its external realization in the perceived item... made transparent to the mind—the external qualitative situation becoming experientially present. (Foster 2000: 60)

> [P]erceptual consciousness is, at least when veridical, an immediate registration of a normal physical object, in the sense that the sensory

4. Again, note the restriction to cases of *seeing*. Although common sense does acknowledge the existence of other cases of visual experience, as we shall see, the insight is not intended to cover such cases.

> character of your conscious state...is accounted for by the possession by that object of perceptible qualities, together with the fact that you stand in a relation of awareness, or receptivity, to it.... *[T]hat which gives sensory character to perceptual consciousness is a public quality of some physical object*. (Smith 2002: 43–44)

In order to enable us to reach a clearly defined characterization of the thesis, let us begin by clarifying some of the terminology that appears in these statements.

In these passages, as in the quote from Broad with which we began, naive realism is presented as a thesis about an experience's conscious character. Yet in the more recent quotes, various theoretical devices are used to signal this—"phenomenal character," "phenomenal content," and "sensory character," respectively.[5] Although some theorists do give the distinct variants different theoretical roles to play,[6] they have also been used interchangeably.[7] For the sake of clarity, then, I employ what is becoming the most commonly used of these devices—*phenomenal character*—and explain how the term is to be understood. The notion is often introduced with the claim that "the phenomenal character of a perceptual experience is what it is like to have that experience" (Chalmers 2006: 50) and, as an example of this 'what it is like'ness, Joseph Levine talks about the reddish character of an experience of a fire engine (2003: 57).

Of course, 'reddish' here is functioning as a piece of philosophical jargon. Inasmuch as there is an everyday property of reddishness, it is a property of *colors* (thus, certain shades of orange and purple might be said to be reddish), not a property of experiences. So when we say that an experience has a reddish phenomenal character, we are not intending to claim that the experience is *literally* reddish, but rather that it has

5. Further variants on this terminology include "qualitative character" (Shoemaker 1994: 22; Levine 2001: 7), "subjective character" (Metzinger 1995: 9; Davies and Humphries 1993: 9), "perceptual content" (Robinson 1994: 10), and "qualitative or sensational content" (Block 1990: 54).

6. See, e.g., nn. 12, 13, and 16.

7. A caveat: in recent philosophy, the claim that an experience has "content" has become deeply intertwined with the idea that this content will be something common to veridical and nonveridical experiences (e.g., Crane 1992: 139; Martin 1994: 464). But as will become clear in the remainder of this chapter, the first stage of a defense of naive realism consists in the *rejection* of the idea that veridical and nonveridical experiences share a common component. Given this, I forbear from employing the term 'content' in the present context in order to avoid the possibility of needlessly confusing the issues.

a property that is somehow correlated with what it is like to have the experience's being: *reddish*. As Alex Byrne puts it, "[T]he phenomenal character of an experience *e* is... that property [of *e*] that types *e* according to what it's like to undergo *e*" (2002: 9). A theory of the nature of this property, and how it relates to what it's like to undergo the experience that possesses it, is of course still required. But before I move on to discuss these issues, there are three further features of the notion of phenomenal character that it will be beneficial to discuss in more detail.

The first is that, in introducing the notion of phenomenal character, I have made use of Nagel's (1974/1979) terminology of *what it is like* for an organism to have conscious experience. This is closely related to the idea that there is *something it is like* to be a conscious being or to have a particular experience. As David Chalmers further explains: "We can say that a being is conscious if there is *something it is like* to be that being.... Similarly, a mental state is conscious if there is something it is like to be in that mental state" (1996: 4). And if there is something it is like to be a being, then there must be something specific it is like. This is where the notion of *what* it is like to be that being or what it is like to have that experience gets a foothold.

To head off any potential misunderstandings, let me take a moment to briefly say something about the relationship between there being something it is like to be in a mental state and there being something it is like *for the subject/organism* (see Nagel 1974/1979: 167) to be in that mental state.[8] For example, we should note that, at any one time, a subject will be likely to be in a range of different mental states, many or all of which may contribute to the overall matter of what it is like for that subject at that time.[9] So we should be careful not to confuse the question of what it is like to be in a particular mental state—the narrow contribution a particular mental state makes to the overall character of what it is like for the subject—with the more general question of

8. In using the terminology of 'mental state' to talk about the 'something it is like' locution, I do not mean to prejudge the question of what ontological category visual experiences fall into. Rather, in this kind of context, the notion of a mental state is used in a loose, catch-all sense, as including, among other things, states properly so-called and events.

9. Indeed, if Searle is right, the presence of a preexisting conscious field of which these different states are modifications may also contribute to what it is like to be that subject (2005: 37).

what it is like for the subject of that mental state. In addition, as I read it, if there is something it is like to be in a mental state, then there is thereby something it is like for the subject of that mental state—there is no philosophically significant difference between these two ways of putting the point. But this is not universally accepted.[10] It has been suggested that, even if there is, in a sense, something it is like to have an experience, for there to be something it is like *for the subject* to have that experience, the subject in question would need to be *aware of* its being that way for him or her, where 'awareness of' is taken to involve some kind of higher order perspective on that experience.[11] This has led some philosophers (e.g., Lycan 1999: 128) to complain that this terminology is irredeemably ambiguous. With this in mind, let me take this opportunity to simply stipulate that, even if there is an ambiguity here (but see Byrne 2004: §4.2 for an argument to the contrary), I use the what it is like/something it is like terminology in the sense according to which there being something it is like to be in a particular mental state entails that there is something it is like for the subject of that state. On this usage, questions about whether there is something it is like to be in a given mental state or what it is like to be in that state concern the nature and properties of the state itself, not any higher order perspective the subject may or may not have on that state.

The second feature of the phenomenal character terminology to note is that Byrne defines the phenomenal character of an experience as that property of the experience that types it according to what it is like to have it. This has the consequence that, if what it is like to have experience *e* differs in only the slightest regard from what it is like to have experience *f*, then *e* and *f* will differ in phenomenal character. On this

10. Lormand (2004) offers a dictionary definition–based semantic analysis of the 'something it is like' terminology, which he claims shows that the claim that there is something it is like to have an experience does indeed imply that the subject has some kind of higher order perspective on that experience. However, Lormand's semantic analysis has since been dismantled by Hellie (2007b), who shows that the dictionary definitions do not adequately support Lormand's claims.

11. Thus, e.g., we find Rosenthal claiming that "what it is like to be in pain, in the relevant sense of that idiom, is simply what it is like to be conscious of being in pain" (1990/1997: 733), where one is conscious of something "if one is in a mental state whose content pertains to that thing—a thought about the thing, or a sensation of it" (737). If we read the claim in this way, then for there to be something it is like *for the subject* to be in pain, the subject would not only have to be in pain—to be in a pain state—but would also have to have a higher order thought about or perception of that pain.

understanding, phenomenal character is a *"maximally determinate"* property (Byrne 2002: 9). Yet in such cases there may be ways in which what it is like to have *e* and what it is like to have *f* is the same or similar in some particular dimension. For example, we might want to say that what it is like to see the red of a fire engine is, as far as the experience of color goes, the same as what it is like to see the red of a London bus, despite the two experiences clearly not being identical in all respects. We can therefore use the familiar terminology of *phenomenal property* to give us a way of talking about particular aspects of what it is like to have experiences. So even though the experience of a fire engine and the experience of a London bus differ in their (maximally determinate) phenomenal character, we can nevertheless say they have a phenomenal property—the reddish character the two experiences share—in common. The two notions are then linked as follows: "[T]wo perceptual experiences share their phenomenal character if . . . the experiences instantiate the same phenomenal properties" (Chalmers 2006: 50).[12]

The final feature of this vocabulary we need to clarify is that Byrne's definition stipulates that the phenomenal character of an experience is properly understood as a property of the experience itself. Likewise, we have just seen both Chalmers and Levine talking about phenomenal properties as properties of experiences (see also Block 1995: 230). Yet when we look back at the quote from John Campbell in which a naive realist view is espoused, we find him stating that "the phenomenal character of your experience . . . is constituted by the actual layout of the room itself: which particular objects are there, their intrinsic properties," and so on. Such a view of phenomenal character is echoed in M. G. F. Martin's claim that "to know what one's experience is like is to know what properties, aspects or features are presented to one in having the experience" (1998: 174; see also Dretske 1993: 103). But, of course, a phenomenal character that was constituted by external objects and their properties could not be a property of an experience. Altogether, this can seem to suggest, in contrast to Byrne, Chalmers, and Levine, that "the features that define what it is like to have an experience are properties

12. It is worth noting that, sometimes, the terminology of phenomenal character appears to be used as equivalent to phenomenal property. Levine, e.g., identifies the qualitative character of an experience with a quale (2003: 57; see also Woodruff-Smith 1986: 152; Lycan 2004: 98) but also talks about experiences having a "complex qualitative character" (2001: 6). Given this, I prefer to use the terminology of phenomenal properties to talk about particular aspects of what it is like for a subject, and phenomenal character to name the complex totality of what it is like.

the objects we experience (not our experience of them) have" (Dretske 2003: 67; see also Tye 2000: 49; Lycan 2001: 32).[13]

There can therefore appear to be an ambiguity in the terminology, between phenomenal properties/phenomenal character understood as those properties *of experiences* that type the experiences according to what it is like to undergo them, and phenomenal properties/phenomenal character understood as properties (or, in the case of phenomenal character, collections of properties) *of objects* that, through being presented, or apparently presented, to the subject, characterize what it is like to have the experience. However, although some philosophers such as Michael Tye (2002) insist that it is therefore an open question whether phenomenal character is a property of an experience, I think we can make progress if we accommodate both points of view in the following way (see Chalmers 2004: 156). To do this, we need to draw a distinction between *phenomenal properties/phenomenal character*, understood as those properties *of experiences* that type the experiences according to what it is like to undergo them, and what I will call *presentational properties/presentational character*, understood as properties (or in the case of presentational

13. Other theorists have attacked the idea that the 'what it is like' aspect of an experience is exhausted by a catalogue of the properties that are presented to the subject in having that experience. Thus, Barry Maund, upon noting that it "is sometimes assumed that to speak of the 'what it is like' aspect of experiences is automatically to speak of the qualitative...features of experiences," suggests that this tendency is unfortunate, in part because it seems possible "that there could be intellectual experience, such as thoughts of certain kinds, without sensuous or qualitative character. It seems that they may have a feel to them, but a non-sensuous one" (2003: 57; see also Strawson 1994: 6–7; McCulloch 2003: 10). In making this claim, Maund suggests that, while there is something it is like to have both experiences and thoughts, what it is like to have the two types of state may differ with the former, but not the latter, involving the sensuous presentation of properties or qualities. This distinction is also made by Tim Crane, who uses "the word 'qualitative'...to describe those mental states whose conscious character is either sensory or like that of bodily sensations [which includes perception]. And...the word 'phenomenal' to describe those states...for which there is something it is like to be in them. Phenomenal character is thus the broader notion: conscious thoughts, perceptions, and other propositional attitudes, plus sensations and emotions, all have a phenomenal character" (2001: 75–76). On Crane's usage, some, but not all, phenomenal characters—those of bodily sensations and perceptual experiences—are also sensory, having to do with the way things feel or look or appear (compare Langsam 1997: 35, who, while also recognizing a distinction between what it is like to have experiences and thoughts, uses the term 'phenomenal character' to name the narrower, sensory type of what it is like). In what follows, I will continue to use the terminology of phenomenal character in the narrow way, but this should not be taken to imply that I reject the possible utility of a broader notion.

character, arrays of properties) that are, or at least seem to be, presented to the subject of experience and thereby characterize what it is like to be in the experiential state.[14] Importantly, unlike in the case of phenomenal properties, there is no restriction as to what presentational properties/ the properties that constitute presentational character are properties of. It is an open question whether *these* are properties of mind-independent material objects, properties of experiences (i.e., phenomenal properties), or maybe even properties of nonphysical objects.

Now that I have drawn this distinction, translations between the two notions can be provided. To see how, let us return to Fred Dretske's claim that what the subject is presented with in experience—what we are now calling the *presentational character* of the experience—is an array of mind-independent properties. Against the background of the claim that it is such mind-independent features that characterize what it is like to have an experience, the question we need to ask is this: *How* do these external features come to characterize what it is like to have the experience? Dretske tells us that the "experienced qualities... are—*all* of them—properties the experience represents things as having" (2003: 67; see also Lycan 2001: 18–19). So, on this view, these external features come to characterize what it is like to have the experience in virtue of the experience in question *representing* that those features are instantiated. This is the position known as representationalism or intentionalism. According to the representationalist thesis, then, for any given presentational character, the experience itself will have a corresponding property—the property of representing that the constituent elements of the presentational character are instantiated—that can then be identified with the phenomenal character. This is not only a property of the experience in perfectly good standing, but also (if the representationalist thesis is correct) that very property of the experience that types the experience by what it is like to have it.

So with the representationalist thesis filled out, translations can be set up between the notions of presentational and phenomenal character thus: for any presentational character, there will be a corresponding phenomenal character—the property of representing that the presentational character is instantiated.[15] In this way, we can retain the idea that the

14. Martin (1998: 174) draws essentially the same distinction using slightly different terminology.

15. Similar translations can, of course, be set up for other theories of perception.

phenomenal character of an experience is a property *of the experience*, while also making room for a theory to claim that the properties that we are presented with when we have an experience are not necessarily properties of the experiences themselves. This brings out an important consequence: once the distinction between presentational and phenomenal character has been made, we are no longer entitled to assume that the subject of experience is immediately presented with *phenomenal* character (or, indeed, phenomenal properties) either in normal experience or in introspection. The representationalist will be at pains to deny that, when we introspect, we are presented with the property of *representing that an external property is instantiated*. Rather, the claim is that we are presented with *the external property itself*, and that this is so in virtue of the experience having the property of representing that the external property is instantiated. So while we can follow Byrne and stipulate that phenomenal character is a property of experience, we must nevertheless bear in mind that it is the *presentational* character that the experience presents the subject with.[16]

With these clarifications made, if we think back to Campbell's claim that the phenomenal character of a visual experience just is the scene perceived, we can see that the naive realist is going to be broadly in agreement with Dretske when it comes to the constituents of presentational character. As Campbell says (translated into our terminology), on a naive realist view the presentational character of an experience—what we are presented with in experience—will be the perceived scene: the mind-independent objects, their properties, the relations they stand in, and so on.[17] However, the naive realist will differ from the representationalist when it comes to the *phenomenal* character of such experiences.

16. As I hope this shows, in making this distinction and allowing that phenomenal character is a property of experience, I am not saying anything that the representationalist need oppose (*pace* Tye 2002). Having said this, it is worth noting that Michael Tye actually uses the notion of phenomenal character in a *further* sense inasmuch as he actually identifies phenomenal character with the (right kind of) representational content (1995: 137; 2000: 48; 2003b: 166). This qualifies as a distinct sense because it is neither a property of experience nor something constituted by the external properties claimed to determine what it is like to have the experience. However, if we identify the phenomenal character with the property of representing that content, the representationalist can still maintain that the "content of [visual] experiences...*determines* their phenomenal character" (Byrne 2001: 204).

17. Because presentational character is not itself a property, there is no longer anything that need concern us in this claim.

The naive realist demurs at the representationalist account of phenomenal character because its claim that the "properties and situations one is aware of in having an experience... [are] properties things are represented as having" has the consequence that "the world needn't contain them in order to be represented as containing them" (Dretske 2003: 71). So, on the representationalist view, because the phenomenal character of an experience is its property of *representing* that a presentational character is instantiated, an experience could have the presentational character that it has—could present the subject with those worldly features—despite those features not being present, right then and there, in the subject's immediate environment. As a result, given the overall nature of the representationalist view, the contours of the subject's conscious experience will not be shaped by the *actual* layout of the world, but rather by the layout the world is represented to have.[18] This is why Martin claims that the representationalist will therefore be led to "deny that [the external objects and their manifest qualities] are constituents of the experience, or that their actual natures determine the phenomenal character of experience" (1997: 84–85). So, although naive realists will agree with representationalists that the constituents of presentational character are elements of the mind-independent environment, they cannot therefore endorse the representationalists' view of phenomenal character. Given this, let us return to our question: According to the naive realist, *how* do the external features that constitute the presentational character serve to characterize what it is like to have the experience?

The distinctive feature of naive realism lies in the claim that, when we see the world, the subject is *acquainted* with the elements of the presentational character—the mind-independent objects and their features—where 'acquaintance' names an irreducible mental relation that the subject can only stand in to objects that exist and features that are instantiated in the part of the environment at which the subject is looking.[19] Moreover, the naive realist also claims that it is the particular elements of

18. Of course, in veridical cases, the representationalist could argue that we represent the world to be a certain way *because* the world is that way, and thereby that the way the world is *does* shape the contours of the subject's conscious experience. But this is to read the metaphor of shaping in the causal way, which I have already discussed and rejected as inadequate to capture the naive realist claim.

19. The terminology of acquaintance derives from Russell (1912/1967: 25), but the key relationship has gone under many different names in the literature. These include "taking in" (McDowell 1994: 25), "awareness or receptivity" (Smith 2002: 43), "presentation" (Martin 2004: 38), and "appearance" (Langsam 1997: 36). As far as I can see,

the environment that the subject is acquainted with that shape the contours of that subject's conscious experience. Thus, for any given presentational character—the array of features that the subject is presented with in having that experience—the experience itself will have the property of *acquainting* the subject with that presentational character. Once again, this property is both a property of the experience and that very property of the experience that, if the naive realist is correct, types the experience by what it is like to have it. Why is it like *that* to have that experience? Because in having the experience, the subject is acquainted with thus-and-such objects and their properties. This acquaintance property can therefore be identified with the experience's phenomenal character. Similarly, we can also talk about an experience's 'phenomenal properties,' where a particular phenomenal property is the property the experience has of acquainting the subject with an individual element of the presentational character (known in turn as a presentational property).

To sum up: the naive realist claims, in accord with the representationalist, that when we see the world, the presentational character of the experience we have—the array of features that we are presented with and that characterize what it is like to have that experience—is constituted by features from the mind-independent world. Unlike the representationalist, however, the naive realist does not claim that the experience *represents* that the elements of this presentational character are instantiated, but rather that, in having the experience, the subject is *acquainted with* the elements of the presentational character, where the holding of this relation requires that the elements that constitute the presentational character actually exist and/or are instantiated in the part of the environment at which the subject is looking. So, according to the naive realist, the *phenomenal* character of the experience—the property of the experience that types the experience by what it is like to have it—is the property of acquainting the subject with such-and-such a presentational character. In this way, we can see how this thesis accommodates the idea that the very elements of one's environment can be said to shape the contours of one's conscious visual experiences.

---

nothing of significance hangs on the choice of terminology because, in each case, the relevant relationship is supposed to be irreducible or, in Williamsonian terms, "prime" (Williamson 2000: 65). The differences in names seem merely to reflect different attempts to convey the *immediacy* of the relation as the naive realist conceives of it. I say a little more about the relation in chapter 3.

Before we move on, let me take a moment to briefly recap where we have got to. I have suggested that the core feature of naive realism is a claim about the phenomenal character of veridical visual experiences. However, in response to a certain ambiguity in the way the notion of phenomenal character is used, I distinguished between the following two notions.

> *Phenomenal character*: A property of an experience that types the experience by what it is like to have it.
>
> *Presentational character*: A collection of properties (and maybe even objects) that the subject is presented with in having an experience and that thereby characterize what it is like to have it.

I then discussed the naive realist's claims about these features and concluded that, according to naive realism, the presentational character of a veridical visual experience is constituted by the elements of the material world that the subject is looking at,[20] and the phenomenal character of this experience is its property of acquainting the subject with this presentational character.

1.2 Subsidiary Formulations

This claim about the nature of phenomenal character is not the only thesis that has been presented under the heading of naive realism. Martin has also characterized naive realism as claiming that "some of the objects of perception—the concrete individuals, their properties, the events these partake in—are constituents of the experience. No experience like this, no experience of fundamentally the same kind, could have occurred had no appropriate candidate for awareness existed" (2004: 39). This formulation of naive realism does not mention the conscious character of perceptual experience at all. Rather, it is a more ontological characterization: it tells us that, according to naive realism, perceptual experiences essentially have mind-independent constituents, and thus, for any such experience, no experience of that ontological kind could have existed in the absence of appropriate objects of awareness.

20. I discuss the constitution of presentational character, and thereby the phenomenal character of veridical experiences, in detail in chapter 3.

Because this formulation does not mention the conscious character of perceptual experiences, it looks to qualify as a distinct version of naive realism, inasmuch as a theory might qualify as naive realist in this sense without allowing that external objects and properties shape the contours of the subject's conscious experience.[21] We can see how by briefly considering a position assayed by Byrne and Heather Logue in which visual experiences have representational contents that are partly particular (object dependent) and partly abstract (2008: 71–72; see also Soteriou 2000; Schellenberg 2008). With such a position, one might insist that, because any given veridical experience would have mind-independent constituents featuring in the particular contents, differences in (or the absence of) such constituents would therefore yield a difference in experiential kind. Yet this would be consistent with the further claim that the phenomenal character of such experiences would be determined by (e.g., would be the property of representing) the common abstract elements of the contents. While such a view could plausibly be claimed to qualify as naive realist in the ontological sense, it would not accommodate the claim that these objects shaped the conscious character of the subject's awareness, and would hence fail to qualify as naive realist in the initial phenomenal sense.[22]

Despite these two characterizations of naive realism not necessarily coming together, they are natural bedfellows. As we have seen, the naive realist about the conscious character of perception holds that phenomenal character is a special kind of relation between the subject and mind-independent elements of the subject's environment. If we also make the plausible assumption that experiences are typed by their phenomenal character, this will have the consequence that a change in these elements will yield a change in phenomenal character and hence a change in experiential kind. Martin's ontological characterization of naive realism therefore spells out the ontological commitments that are natural concomitants of the naive realist's claims about phenomenal character.

21. Chalmers also notes the possibility of two theories that differ in this way, calling them "disjunctivism about phenomenology" and "disjunctivism about metaphysics" in turn (2006: 53). I explain 'disjunctivism' in section 2.2.

22. Benj Hellie queried whether it might be possible to hold that what it is like on such a view could be determined by both contents in the veridical case, yet only the abstract content in the hallucinatory case. It seems that, while such a position would be possible, if the object-dependent content were to make a contribution to what it is like that is not present in the hallucinatory case, then such a view would fail to allow (as representationalists typically want to) that what it is like to hallucinate is the same as what it is like to perceive.

So the ontological formulation of naive realism, while potentially articulating a distinct thesis, can also be seen to be a further development of the theoretical commitments that one takes on in endorsing the naive realist's claims about phenomenal character.

For the sake of completeness, it is also worth noting that there is a metaphysical thesis that does business under the name of naive realism. This is the position according to which "unperceived objects are able to retain properties of all the types we perceive them as having" (Dancy 1985: 147). This is clearly a distinct thesis—one could be a naive realist in this sense without holding any view of the nature of visual experience other than the minimal claim that we perceive objects to have certain properties. Having said this, this theory is related to the naive realist claims about perceptual experience inasmuch as, if such claims were true, then metaphysical naive realism would have to be true, too. Given this conditional, the falsity of metaphysical naive realism would entail the falsity of naive realism about perceptual experience. And over the years, metaphysical naive realism has been subject to an important objection, the core of which is that advances in modern scientific understanding have shown us that some of the qualities we perceive objects to have are not really instantiated by material objects (for a recent version of this objection, see Foster 2000: 65). For present purposes, however, I am not going to detour into this metaphysical thesis (but see chap. 8 of Cornman 1975 for a detailed defense of the compatibility of what he calls minimal commonsense realism and minimal scientific realism). This is because, even if the world really were to be as vision presents it, most philosophers would still view naive realism as a nonstarter inasmuch as it is committed to an unworkable account of our visual access to that world. Now, because it is naive realism as a thesis about perceptual experience that is my present concern, the defense of the thesis to be presented here is, in a sense, somewhat partial—I argue that, *qua* theory of our visual access to the world, naive realism is defensible. I do not explicitly defend naive realism *qua* realist theory of the material world.

1.3 Phenomenological Motivations: A "Theory of the Common Man"?

As I noted at the outset, naive realism can be taken to have a certain cachet as the theory that legitimates a pretheoretical, 'naive' view of veridical visual experience: that it is to be preferred as it is the view of Broad's "unsophisticated" or of the 'common man.' However, as its opponents note, this is not the most stable of motivations. For one thing, inasmuch as the common man has a view of visual experience, it is likely to be a highly nebulous mix of phenomenological, epistemological, and metaphysical considerations that is lacking in specificity. This means that other theories of perception might well claim, with some reason, that they also adequately legitimate the view. For another, even if did turn out that the common man were to have an adequately specific view of veridical experience that only naive realism could legitimate, it is possible that he would also have views about other related situations—say, the nature of hallucination or the relationship between consciousness and the brain—that the naive realist will end up having to reject. So, a further reason to be skeptical of the force of this motivation turns on the fact that, if a 'naive' view is to be taken as our touchstone of correctness, then error may well have to come into the picture somewhere, so why not in the theory of veridical experience? Finally, even if there were to be a reasonably specific view that only naive realism could capture without locating error anywhere else, John Hawthorne and Karson Kovakovich argue that naive views shouldn't carry too much weight anyway, saying they are unable to "see much point in pursuing the philosophy of perception in a setting where it is assumed that [commonsense] commitments will survive philosophical and scientific reflection. After all, we shouldn't think that vulgar common sense has seen in advance how to handle various challenges to its commitments" (2006: 180). So, to think that naive realism can be adequately motivated purely by an appeal to the 'common man' is itself a somewhat naive position.[23]

While an attempt to motivate the theory in this way is undoubtedly problematic, it does gesture toward an important phenomenological point in favor of naive realism—that, as Martin puts it, it "best articulates how sensory experience seems to us to be just through reflection" (2006: 354). This motivation is also present in Broad's claim that sensory experience "appear[s in this way] to any unsophisticated percipient, and...*go[es] on appearing* [in this way] even to sophisticated percipients whose knowledge...assures them that the appearances are largely misleading" (1951/1965: 30). Yet rather than treat this claim as deference to the enigmatic common man, Benj Hellie (2007a) develops this insight

23. Thanks to Susanna Siegel, together with many of the 'common men' traveling through Sydney airport on 27 August 2007, for curing me of just such a case of naïveté!

into an argument by listing six passages in which philosophers make judgments about how perceptual experience seems to them at first pass.[24] The judgments Hellie lists include the quote from Broad with which this chapter began and Campbell's claim about the constitution of phenomenal character, as well as the following: "Mature sensible experience (in general) presents itself as...an *immediate* consciousness of the existence of things outside of us" (Strawson 1979/1988: 97), and "The ripe tomato seems immediately present to me in experience. I am not in any way aware of any cognitive distance between me and the scene in front of me.... The world is just there" (Levine 2006: 179).

Hellie's argument proceeds with the claim that these judgments qualify as having been made by people who we should consider experts at phenomenological study, under ideal circumstances for arriving at such judgments. The argument then turns on the premise that "a judgment about an experience to the fact that it is F based on phenomenological study [by experts, under ideal circumstances] will be accurate" (2007a: 267). Because, from these two premises, we can conclude that these judgments are accurate, what remains is to argue that the kinds of judgments that appear in these quotes attribute acquaintance properties to visual experiences. This is of course going to be open to dispute, but Hellie contends that the metaphors of 'prehension,' 'immediate consciousness,' and 'immediate presence' are all strongly suggestive of the kind of direct presence to the mind that the relation of acquaintance is intended to capture.

It is at this point that I would envisage the naive realist's opponent balking, and for two possible reasons. First, the claim that the relevant metaphors are intended to capture something as strong as acquaintance might be challenged. Perhaps, the thought might go, these experts didn't intend to assert something so specific. And second, even if they did, it might be objected that this was because they were unaware that other, non-acquaintance-based accounts of perceptual experience could adequately capture the phenomenological facts. So, even if the experts do intend their metaphors to be redolent of a relation such as acquaintance, this does not show that acquaintance is the only relation that can adequately account for the phenomenology. Rather, it shows a lack of

24. Hellie actually uses this argument to motivate a close relation of the naive realist view he calls "phenomenal naïveté," but he notes that the argument will be at least as strong, and maybe even stronger, as support for a naive realist view of the kind outlined here.

insight on the part of these experts in *thinking* that only such a relation could capture the phenomenology.

As to the first of these objections, that the relevant experts may not have intended their metaphors to be redolent of a relation as strong as acquaintance, we should bear in mind that many of these experts also go on to argue that this first-pass picture is straightforwardly refuted by the possibility of misleading experience. Broad, for example, argues that it "would be fatal to the prehensive account...if it could be shown that...the experience may arise even though no such body is then occupying the place in question" (1951/1965: 36). Such a possibility would only be fatal to the prehensive view if that account held the presence of the object to be a necessary condition of the experience. So, inasmuch as Broad holds that such a possibility would refute a view based on the metaphor of 'prehension,' it suggests that prehension is the kind of relation between a subject and an object that requires the existence of its relata in order for it to hold. This suggests that Hellie is right and that, in Broad's case, at least, the relevant metaphor is intended to capture a relation such as acquaintance.

Even so, as noted above, it could yet be argued that Broad was unaware of the possibility of doing justice to visual phenomenology without using a relation, like acquaintance, that requires the existence of its relata. As we have seen, representationalists can agree with the naive realist that the presentational character of an experience—the array of properties, aspects, or features that the subject is presented with in having that experience—is constituted by mind-independent objects and their features. It would thus seem possible for the representationalist to contend that, if the naive realist's take on presentational character is up to the task of capturing this phenomenological insight about the relationship between consciousness and the external world, then so, too, will be the representationalist's.[25]

25. Indeed, even some proponents of naive realism, such as Martin (2002: 397–398) and Campbell (2002: 120), accept that, when it comes to the phenomenology of perceptual experience itself, there will be no way of deciding between naive realism and representationalism. In the light of this, Martin instead develops a phenomenological motivation that turns on the phenomenology of sensory visual imagination rather than that of visual perception per se (2002: 402–419). In brief, he argues first for the dependency thesis—that imagining X = imagining *experiencing* X—and then for the claim that to imagine experiencing is to imagine how things would be immediately presented to us in such an experience. He then argues that the naive realist can give a much better account of this imagined immediacy than can a representationalist because, according to naive realism,

Yet things are not quite this straightforward. In allowing that an experience might have a presentational character of a certain kind even if the world is not as this character suggests, the representationalist constrains the way in which the properties of mind-independent objects can feature in presentational character in such a way that the resultant picture conflicts with elements of the phenomenologically motivated view just presented. To see this, note that Broad's quote incorporates the claim that seeing seems to "reveal [objects'] shapes and colours" and Campbell's quote holds that what we are now calling the presentational character of an experience contains objects *and their properties*. Even Tye has suggested that he has been "transfixed by the intense blue *of the Pacific Ocean*" (1992: 160, emphasis added), and Michael Loux likewise claims that, when focusing "on the colour of the Taj Mahal, I am not thinking of pinkness in general, but of that unique pinkness, the pinkness that only the Taj Mahal has" (2002: 86). All of these quotes suggest that, when we see an object—such as the Pacific Ocean or the Taj Mahal—it is not simply blueness or pinkness that we are aware of, but specific *instances* of blueness and pinkness: the blueness *of the Pacific Ocean* and the pinkness *of the Taj Mahal*.[26]

With this in mind, think of Tye seeing the Pacific Ocean and its blueness. Both the naive realist and the representationalist will agree that the presentational character of this experience will contain the Pacific Ocean and the property of blueness. Now, on the representationalist view, the phenomenal character of the experience is a matter of its representing that this presentational character is instantiated—of its representing that the Pacific Ocean is blue. And as the representationalist insists, an

---

the immediacy of a perceptual experience of X is explained by X's being presented to the subject. So, in imagining an experience of X, one thereby imagines X being presented to the subject and immediacy follows. The representationalist's account of perceptual immediacy, on the other hand, turns on the fact that the attitude the subject bears to the relevant content is stative—i.e., committal to the truth of the content—whereas, in imagination, one does not bear a stative attitude to the imagined content. One "is not thereby in a state whose attitudinative aspect would give rise to the phenomenon of immediacy" (415).

26. Although this claim is naturally read as introducing tropes into the picture, we need not take a stand on this particular metaphysical issue. As I discuss in chapter 3, when I develop the naive realist theory of veridical experience, I claim that we perceive *facts* (metaphysically understood), such as the fact of *a*'s being F. And this way of talking about particular properties—the Taj Mahal's being pink, say—is entirely compatible with a universalist picture of properties (Armstrong 1997: 16). However, to digress into this discussion here would take us too far from the present point, so I will continue to use this more tropish language.

experience could have this property even in cases in which the Pacific Ocean is not blue. Given the relationship between phenomenal and presentational character, this means that a presentational character of the same kind would be available in cases in which the ocean itself were not blue. In such a case, the blueness that features in the presentational character—the blueness that, according to the definition of presentational character, Tye is presented with in having that experience—while maybe being given as predicated of the ocean, could not actually be *the very instance* of blueness that is manifested by the ocean because there is no such instance (given that we are assuming Tye is presently misled). But then, because the same phenomenal and hence presentational character is also present in the veridical case, it seems to follow that the blueness that Tye is presented with in having the *veridical* experience will not be the very instance of blueness manifested by the ocean, either.[27] Thus, the wider commitments of representationalism preclude the theory from accommodating the idea, also apparently recommended by expert phenomenological study, that it is the very instance of blueness instantiated by the Pacific Ocean that Tye is presented with when he is transfixed by its intense color.[28]

1.4 Further Motivations

Although simply attempting to motivate naive realism as the theory of the common man is inherently unstable, Hellie shows that there are ways to develop a phenomenological motivation for the theory that

27. Hellie suggests that a representationalist might claim that veridical experiences possess a further content that is singular for properties as well as objects. While such a position would be possible, and may indeed allow for the claim that the very blueness of the ocean is *seen* by Tye (where seeing is a matter of veridical representation), as long as it is an abstract or general content that is identified with/determines phenomenal and hence presentational character, then the representationalist will be unable to hold that it is the very blueness of the ocean that Tye is *presented with*. And if a representationalist were to hold that this singular content determined phenomenal/presentational character, then such a phenomenal character would be unavailable in the nonveridical cases.

28. One may wonder how the claim that we see the very blueness instantiated by the Pacific Ocean lines up with the thought that in some cases it may be the same (in other words, *what it is like* may be the same) to have experiences with distinct phenomenal characters, as in cases of experiences of numerically distinct but qualitatively identical objects. Thus, to use an example suggested by Hellie, consider a subject who sees Tweedledee as fat. On the naive realist view, the presentational character of this experience

are not open to this charge. In addition to this, the growing literature on the topic provides other examples of potentially important considerations in favor of naive realism. For example, it has been argued that, if naive realism is correct, then Cartesian skepticism about the possibility of knowledge of the external world can be undermined before it even gets started (McDowell 1986/1998, 2008; see also Child 1994: 147–149; Johnston 2006: 286–299). John McDowell suggests that the skepticism in question gets a foothold only if we have to view perceptual experience in such a way that "even if we focus on the best possible case, [a subject's] experience could be just as it is, in all respects, even if there were no red cube in front of her" (2008: 378). It is against the background of such a view of experience that the skeptic can make a compelling case that empirical knowledge is thereby shown to be impossible and hence that we do not and cannot have knowledge of the external world. Given this, McDowell suggests that it would constitute a response to the skeptic if we could show that we can "make sense of the idea of direct perceptual access to objective facts about the environment" (379) where "direct perceptual access" names the kind of relation that, when it holds, *entails* that the fact to which one thereby has access obtains.

It is a relation of this kind that, as we have seen, is central to the naive realist picture of veridical experience. So if McDowell is correct, the defensibility of naive realism would "remove a prop on which skeptical doubt depends" (2008: 385). This would not, of course, show that we do know anything about the external world, merely that such knowledge is not impossible. Yet this would block the skeptic from using the

---

contains Tweedledee and Tweedledee's fatness, and the phenomenal character of the experience is the property of acquainting the subject with this presentational character. Yet in the case in which it is not Tweedledee and his fatness, but Tweedle*dum* and his fatness, that the subject sees, the presentational and phenomenal character will differ. So although *what it is like* to have the two experiences will plausibly be the same, they will differ in phenomenal character. We therefore need to recognize that different phenomenal characters (or, more accurately, different phenomenal properties) can be grouped into kinds (see McDowell 1984/1998: 220). Given the naive realist view of phenomenal character, this is merely a theoretical codification of the everyday platitude that different things can look the same. With this possibility in place, although the phenomenal character of the experience of Tweedledee as fat will not be identical with the phenomenal character of the experience of Tweedledum as fat, we can nevertheless allow that they are phenomenal characters of the same kind. And because phenomenal characters are those properties of experiences that type the experiences by what it is like to have them, what it is like to see Tweedledee as fat will be the same (of the same kind) as what it is like to see Tweedledum as fat.

impossibility of knowledge as a premise in an argument for this conclusion. With a naive realist picture of veridical experience in hand, we can deny that the very possibility of our being misled entails that, in cases in which I am not misled—that is, in veridical cases—my experience cannot support an adequate claim to knowledge.

This is not to say that naive realism allows us to show, on any given occasion, that we do have direct perceptual access to environmental facts. Any theory must accommodate the fact that experience can mislead, so it remains possible, of any particular case of visual experience, that it is one of the misleading ones. The point is, rather, that when I attempt to justify a claim to knowledge about some aspect of the world by claiming that I see it, I effectively point out or demonstrate a particular mental event as the one that justifies my knowledge claim. If the situation is indeed one of veridical perception, then given the view of experience offered by naive realism, my claimed justification will be secure—veridical experience will justify belief in a skeptic-proof way. If, however, I do turn out to be in one of the misleading scenarios, I do not demonstrate the same kind of mental event as I did in the veridical case, so I do not thereby show that the mental event that occurs in the veridical case cannot adequately support a claim to knowledge after all. Rather, my demonstrative *fails*, and consequently, my attempted justification fails—not because I demonstrate an event that is an inconclusive justifier, but because I fail to demonstrate a justifier altogether.[29]

With this in mind, consider the familiar skeptical claim that all of our experiences might have been just as they are even if we had been dreaming or in the clutches of Descartes's demon. Given a naive realist view on which veridical experiences are episodes of acquaintance with the world, this is no longer possible. If any of my experiences are veridical, then they could not have been the way that they are while being misleading. So the skeptic would need to reformulate the skeptical hypothesis. Suppose, then, that the skeptic were instead to claim that all of your experiences might simply have been of the misleading kind (as opposed to as they are *and* misleading). It seems that the right response to this would be to say, so what? As long as they are not of the misleading kind, then most of our empirical beliefs will be justified. For the skeptical

29. Perhaps the demonstrative doesn't simply fail—perhaps it succeeds in picking out a mental event that is completely different from the one picked out in the veridical case. Regardless of this, it remains the case that the demonstrative fails to pick out a justifier.

predicament to have force, then, the skeptic would need to claim, not that all of our experiences *might* have been misleading, but that all of our experiences are *in fact* misleading.

This is an interestingly different reformulation of the skeptical hypothesis. And, when considering such a reformulation, some philosophers have suggested that it is distinct enough to provide us with some traction in dealing with the skeptic. For example, Mark Johnston suggests that the claim that all of our experiences might actually be misleading is a "rather absurd dogmatic claim with nothing in particular to recommend it. Certainly [by suggesting this] the skeptic is no longer doing what David Hume so engagingly did. He is not drawing reasonable inferences from a subjectivist picture of our sensory awareness. He is just making odd claims about what is the case" (2006: 289). Similarly, McDowell suggests that, if this is what the skeptic claims, then the door is open for us to reverse the traditional skeptical order of things and claim instead that "our knowledge that [the skeptical] possibilities do not obtain is sustained by the fact that we know a great deal about our environment" (2008: 379).

Over the course of this book, I show that there are good reasons to think that all of our experiences could not be of the misleading kind. Despite this, however, I do not want to make the bold claim that naive realism offers an adequate response to skepticism—I think time, and the philosophical discussions that ensue, will be needed to determine whether this alternative approach to the skeptical issues does indeed issue a response. Having said this, though, I do think that the approach offered by naive realism is interesting enough and different enough to warrant pursuing it. And it also suggests that we have good reason to be interested in the question under discussion here: whether naive realism is a defensible thesis. Because if it is not, then any traction it may or may not offer regarding the skeptic will turn out to be irrelevant.

In addition to this antiskeptical motivation, Campbell (2002) has argued that something like naive realism is required to account for the fact that it is possible for us to have thoughts about mind-independent objects at all.[30] Campbell's argument is complex, but it begins from the idea that, ordinarily, if you are to know what my use of a demonstrative expression such as "that mountain" or "that building" refers to, you have to single out the relevant object visually. What is more, the relevant kind of visual singling out has to be *conscious*. To illustrate this, Campbell

30. Such a consideration is also present in McDowell (e.g., 1986/1998: 243).

uses an example of a party where you ask me questions about "that woman." When I look at the scene in front of me, all I am consciously aware of is a sea of faces—I can't consciously attend to the woman you are talking about—yet it nonetheless turns out that I can reliably point to the woman, make reliable guesses about what she is wearing, drinking, and so on (2002: 8–9).[31] Despite my having these abilities, Campbell suggests that if I cannot *consciously* single out the woman you are talking about, there is a very real sense in which I do not *know* to whom you are referring. If so, then conscious (visual) attention is ordinarily required for us to have knowledge of the reference of demonstratives. On the assumption that we can have knowledge of this kind, it therefore places a condition on an adequate account of visual experience—it must explain how it can be the source of this kind of knowledge. "This means," Campbell suggests, "that conscious attention to an object must be thought of as more primitive than thought about the object. It is a state more primitive than thought about an object, to which we can appeal in explaining how it is that we can think about the thing" (45).

He then argues that this consideration counts against a representationalist theory of visual experience. According to representationalism, experience is just one way among many of being related to an intentional content. But, Campbell suggests, this is just to say that experience is "merely one among many ways of grasping thoughts" (2002: 122). Yet if experience has to explain our capacity to think about objects—has to be more *primitive* than thought about objects—then it cannot be just another *kind* of thinking about objects, as the representationalist suggests. Instead, it must be more as the naive realist conceives of it—a kind of primitive relation of acquaintance with the objects in the world, a relation that can then serve to ground our more sophisticated capacity to have thoughts about these objects.

Campbell also asks: *What is it* about experience that enables it to play the role of grounding our knowledge of the reference of a demonstrative? He then suggests that, to *know* the reference of a demonstrative, rather than to merely have dispositions and abilities that are targeted on that object, we must take the demonstrative to be "referring to a categorical object, not merely a collection of potentialities" (2002: 145). To see why, consider the party example again: if I have the ability to reliably guess

31. These abilities are intentionally analogous to those possessed by a blindsight subject.

what the woman you are talking about is eating, drinking, and wearing, then if all there was to knowing the reference of a demonstrative was to be aware of the various potentialities that the object has, I could be said to know the reference of your use of "that woman." Yet as we saw, there is an important sense in which I *do not* know the reference of your demonstrative. Thus, being aware of the various potentialities an object has cannot suffice for the relevant kind of knowledge. What is missing, Campbell suggests, is experience of why these potentialities exist—experience of the categorical object that grounds these potentialities. So, if experience is to explain our knowledge of demonstrative reference, then an adequate analysis of experience must account for the fact that experience is experience of the categorical. Naive realist acquaintance with the object itself is perfectly placed to do this.

As with the antiskeptical motivation, I think that it is maybe a little too early to conclude that Campbell is right in his claim that naive realism is the only way of accounting for our ability to think about the mind-independent world. However, the question of how we have this ability is obviously an important one for philosophy to address, and Campbell does provide reasons to think that naive realism is well placed to account for it. Again, then, it makes the question of whether naive realism is defensible a matter of philosophical interest.

1.5 Conclusion

In addition to the motivations that are already present in the literature, I shall show, as we proceed, that there are further, as yet unidentified, considerations in favor of naive realism. Specifically, I will argue that naive realism offers new and potentially important insights into some long-standing problems from the philosophy and psychology of consciousness. At the end of chapter 3, I demonstrate how naive realism offers us the most plausible explanation yet of just how truths about consciousness supervene on physical/functional truths. In providing this potential explanation, naive realism thereby offers the outline of an answer to the hard problem of consciousness (Chalmers 1995/1997, 1997) that would also serve to bridge the explanatory gap (Levine 1983). In chapter 5 I also suggest a way in which naive realism can circumvent the binding problem from neuroscience. Given all of this, it is clear that the philosophical interest in naive realism goes far beyond the notorious claim that it is the view of visual experience of the 'common man.'

2

Naive Realism: Past and Future

Now that chapter 1 has explored the structure of the naive realist claim about veridical visual experience and the reasons for being interested in it, the question we turn to here is whether naive realism is a defensible thesis. And in order to answer this question, we need to fully explore the familiar contention that it is incompatible with the fact that experiences can be misleading.

2.1 The Fall of Naive Realism: Illusion and Hallucination

As we saw in chapter 1, the naive realist claims that the phenomenal character of an experience is its property of acquainting the subject with a particular worldly object and/or property. Given the nature of the acquaintance relation, if an experience is to have that character, that object must exist and/or that property must be instantiated. But as A. D. Smith notes, common sense also accepts that, sometimes, our visual experiences can mislead us as to the real nature of the world (2002: 22). This is why, in arguing for the falsity of naive realism, our attention is so often drawn to cases of perceptual error. Illusion and hallucination just are visual experiences in which we seem to see things to be a way that they are not and, as such, are in tension with the theoretical commitments of naive realism.

The philosophical arguments based around perceptual error—the argument from illusion and the argument from hallucination—exploit this tension. These arguments have often been employed in a dual role: to argue both *against* naive realism and *for* an alternative theory of perception. Paul Snowdon calls the first move (the rejection of naive realism) the *negative revision*, and the second move (the endorsing of a distinct positive thesis about experience) the *positive revision* (1992: 69). Because my main interest lies not in contesting the success of the arguments in establishing any particular theory of perception, but rather in challenging their success at the negative undertaking that must take place prior to the positive revision, I focus on the arguments' success at establishing the negative revision.

In addition to their dual role, Snowdon also points out that both of the arguments can be usefully broken down into two phases. Restricted to the negative revision, the two phases are these: an initial "base case" to show that naive realism is false in the particular focal case of perceptual error, and then a "spreading step" to the conclusion that naive realism is false in *all* cases, including the veridical ones (1992: 68). In outlining these arguments, I follow Howard Robinson's exposition of the argument from illusion (1994: 57–58), adapted so as to target the naive realist thesis as presented here. Once I have presented the argument from illusion, I then briefly indicate the key ways in which the argument from hallucination differs from this.

The base case of the argument from illusion begins with the premise that perceptual illusions—situations in which a perceived object (visually) seems to possess a property that it does not instantiate—are possible. Premise 2 then claims that, when it (visually) seems to the subject that an object possesses a certain property, that property—call it the illusory property—features in the presentational character of the illusory experience. But according to naive realism, a property features in presentational character through the subject's being acquainted with that property, and given the definition of acquaintance, this entails that the property is instantiated. Because the only plausible instantiator for the property seems to be the object, these claims therefore yield a contradiction: the illusory property both is and is not instantiated by the object. By identifying the naive realist claim that a property can feature in presentational character only if the subject is acquainted with that property as the culprit, we reach the conclusion of the negative revision for the base case of this argument: naive realism is false for those cases in which we are subject to illusion.

At this stage of the development of the argument from illusion, all that is claimed to have been established is that naive realism is false in the focal case of visual illusion. It remains compatible with the argument thus far that naive realism remains true of the veridical cases. This is where the spreading step of the argument comes in. It takes the conclusions of the base case and attempts to extend the results to cover all cases of visual experience, veridical and nonveridical alike. Where the argument from illusion is concerned, the central consideration in motivating the spreading step concerns the experiential continuity that can exist between those perceptual experiences that are veridical and those that are illusory. As A. J. Ayer puts it:

> From different angles [a] coin may appear a variety of different shapes: let it be assumed that only one of them is the shape it really is. There will be nothing to mark off this appearance from the others except a difference of aspect which may be extremely slight.... But, since only one of the appearances can fail to be deceptive, we must allow that in all but one of the instances it is not the physical object that is directly perceived. And if we are willing to admit that the instances are all sufficiently alike for it to be reasonable to hold that an object of the same type is directly perceived in every case, it will follow that the physical object is not directly perceived in the remaining instance either. (1956: 88–89)

The base case of the argument from illusion provides the support for Ayer's interim conclusion that in all the deceptive instances (i.e., "in all but one of the instances"), it is not the physical object that is directly perceived. The spreading step then appeals to the fact that there is only an "extremely slight" experiential difference between these cases and the case in which the coin appears "the shape it really is." Given this, the argument proceeds, we should be willing to admit that all the instances are sufficiently alike for it to be the case that what is true of one is true of the others. As C. D. Broad puts it, "[I]n view of the continuity between the most normal and the most abnormal cases of seeing, [to claim that veridical cases are naive realist while nonveridical cases are not] would be utterly implausible and could be defended only by the most desperate special pleading" (1951/1965: 36–37). So, because naive realism is false for the illusory cases (from the conclusion of the base case), the spreading step concludes that it is false for the veridical cases, too.

With the negative revision in place, the positive revision can then take place. This will, of course, take a different form depending upon the theory to be established. So, for example, a sense-datum theory will treat the base case as indicating that, because there are no appropriate elements of the mind-independent environment for the subject to be acquainted with in deceptive cases, the subject must in fact be acquainted with mind-*dependent* entities—sense-data. The representationalist, on the other hand, will see the base case somewhat differently—as demonstrating that the relevant relation between the subject and the mind-independent elements of the presentational character cannot be a relationship such as acquaintance, which carries a commitment to the present existence or instantiation of its relata, but must rather be a relationship such as representation, which does not. When it comes to the positive revision for the spreading step, all theorists will unite in taking this to show that the particular theory that is favored for the illusory cases also holds true in the veridical cases.

The argument from hallucination is very similar: the most significant difference appears, as we shall see, when it comes to the spreading step of the negative revision; the negative revision of the base case differs only slightly. As in the case of the argument from illusion, the base case of the argument from hallucination begins by defining the problem cases—hallucinations being situations in which it (visually) seems to subjects as if they see objects when no appropriate external objects exist to be seen—and claiming that these problem cases are possible. The most important feature of this premise, at least when it comes to pushing through the spreading step, is that it is hallucinations that are, from the point of view of the subject of experience, *indiscriminable* from veridical perception that are claimed to be possible. The second and third premises then follow the argument from illusion: the second claiming that the hallucinated elements will feature in the presentational character of the hallucinatory experience; the third, that this is inconsistent with naive realism and hence that naive realism is false for such cases.

The critical difference between the two arguments is that, where hallucinations are concerned, it is not so straightforward to present a compelling continuity case in which a hallucination shades into a veridical perception by experientially small degrees with which to push through the spreading step (see Smith 2002: 195).[1] For this reason, an alternative means of motivating the spreading step appeals to the first-person

1. That is not to say that it would be impossible to contrive such a case. For example, Robinson presents a case in which an electric probe is introduced in order to keep a subject's brain activity constant while the putative objects of perception are hidden and contends that this would provide an experientially seamless transition from veridical

similarities in perceptual and hallucinatory experience (hence the importance, noted above, of the possibility of *indiscriminable* hallucinations). This is how Ayer describes the move: "[A]n experience of this sort [i.e., an indiscriminable hallucination] is like the experience of seeing a real physical object.... But in so far as the experiences are alike, their analysis should follow the same pattern" (1956: 90). So the claim is that the experiential similarities between veridical perceptions and those hallucinations that are indiscriminable from them give us reason to conclude that, if naive realism is false for one case, it will be false for the other. And because the base case claims that naive realism is false for the hallucinatory cases, the spreading step therefore concludes that it is false for the veridical cases, too.[2]

2.2 The Rebirth of Naive Realism: Disjunctivism

So these are our classic arguments against naive realism—the argument from illusion and the argument from hallucination. The purported refutation of naive realism proceeds in two stages. First, naive realism is shown to be false in the base cases of perceptual error. Second, the spreading step generalizes this conclusion to cover the veridical situations, too. Yet despite the power of these arguments, there has recently been a resurgence of interest in naive realism, and some philosophers have even suggested that naive realism can be defended from these attacks, at least for the central cases of veridical perception. The initial key to this defense lies in the adoption of an approach to visual experience known as *disjunctivism*. The response to the arguments embodied in disjunctivism does not dispute the conclusions of the base case phase of the arguments, so it accepts that naive realism is false in cases of perceptual error, but aims to block the spreading step from going on

---

perception to hallucination (1994: 151–152; see also Valberg 1992: 10–11). My point here is merely that, in the case of illusion, the existence of continuity cases are an undeniable fact about our everyday visual access to the world; in the case of hallucination, they are more speculative and rely on certain assumptions about the role of the brain in experience (discussed in section 2.3).

2. There are other ways in which theorists have attempted to push through the spreading step of the argument from hallucination. A particularly important attempt, which turns on the possibility in principle of replicating the neural activity that underpins a particular veridical experience, is discussed in section 2.3 after I have outlined the naive realist response to the spreading step in its present form.

to generalize this conclusion to the case of veridical perception. The endorsement of disjunctivism is therefore the first step to explaining how, in those cases in which we are not misled by experience, worldly objects and their properties can continue to shape the contours of consciousness in the way envisaged by the naive realist.

When we look at the appearance of disjunctivism in the philosophical literature, we find that the thesis has been introduced primarily as a response to the argument from hallucination. As described above, one crucial way in which this argument differs from the argument from illusion is that the absence of natural continuity cases makes the spreading step look less obviously compelling where hallucination is concerned. With this in mind, Ayer notes that, while the argument turns on the assumption that "if veridical and delusive perceptions were perceptions of objects of different types, they would always be qualitatively distinguishable," he accepts that this assumption "could be denied without self-contradiction" (1940: 12). The possibility of such a move is also highlighted by J. L. Austin, who asks, in characteristically exasperated fashion, "[W]hy on earth should it *not* be the case that, in some few instances, perceiving one sort of thing is exactly like perceiving another?" (1962: 52). So, in their own different styles, these two thinkers highlight the logical availability of a certain way of responding to the argument from hallucination: when faced with the fact that we may be unable to tell whether we are perceiving or hallucinating, we can nevertheless hold firm and insist that the objects of the two states are ontologically distinct.

This approach gives us our first sighting of disjunctivism: Ayer and Austin both highlight the possibility of being disjunctive about the *objects* of visual experience. Thus, where the spreading step of the positive revision of the argument from hallucination takes the indiscriminability of perception and hallucination to show that there is only *one* kind of object we can perceive—usually a sense-datum—the disjunctive response aims to resist this and hold instead that the objects of visual experience might be of one kind *or* of another, it is just that objects of different kinds might yet be indiscriminable (recall Austin's soap that looks just like a lemon [1962: 50]). On this particular way of responding to the argument from hallucination, there is one type of experiential relation—Ayer and Austin call it 'perception'—but two ontologically distinct types of object that can be perceived.

The development of disjunctivism as a thesis is given a further important dimension in the writings of J. M. Hinton (1967, 1973). Hinton proposed that a sentence such as "I seem to see a flash of light" is simply "a more compact way of saying" something like this: "Either I see a flash of light, or I have an illusion of a flash of light" (1967: 217). An illuminating way of understanding what Hinton is trying to achieve here is to view him as offering an alternative way of understanding how a statement such as 'I seem to see an F' might be true in both veridical and non-veridical situations. If we assume, as can be quite natural, that such a statement would be made true by the obtaining of the same kind of state of affairs in both cases, then the state of affairs that makes it true would have to be compatible with the nonexistence of an F. Hinton's proposal is therefore to treat the seems-statement as elliptic for a disjunctive statement of the form: *either* I see an F *or* it merely seems to me as if that were so. This statement—and hence the original seems-statement that goes proxy for it—can be made true in *two* distinct ways: either by its being true that I *actually do* see an F, or by its being true that I don't see an F but that it is for me *as if* I did.

Where Ayer and Austin offered a picture in which we could be disjunctive about the objects of visual experience, the way Hinton characterizes disjunctivism leaves the way open to another way of being a disjunctivist—a way that seems to have become the more common form of disjunctivism in the contemporary literature.[3] Hinton's disjunction—between seeing a flash of light, on the one hand, and, on the other, having the illusion of a flash of light—leaves it open that having an illusion of a flash of light *might* be a matter of perceiving an unusual type of object (a flash of light sense-datum, say), but it does not *restrict* us to that explanation. It is compatible with Hinton's disjunction that having the illusion of a flash of light is a completely different kind of mental episode from actually seeing one—a mental episode that does not involve the *perception* of anything whatsoever.

Hinton's insight, then, was to see that disjunctivism would allow us to disjoin two psychologically different kinds of *experience*, rather than merely two ontologically different kinds of *objects* of perception. This

3. Having said this, John McDowell has been cited as a recent proponent of object disjunctivism (by Thau 2004: 195) in virtue of his claim that "an appearance that such-and-such is the case can be *either* a mere appearance *or* the fact that such-and-such is the case making itself perceptually manifest to someone" (McDowell 1982/1998: 386–387). I have omitted McDowell from the main text, however, because there is dispute over whether this interpretation is correct. For example, Scott Sturgeon offers two distinct readings of McDowell, both of which interpret him as endorsing a version of disjunctivism about visual experiences (2008: 118–119), and Alex Byrne and Heather Logue offer a reading of McDowell on which he comes out as *neither* (2008: 65–68). Yet while there is dispute on

more inclusive characterization of the position seems to be that adopted by the majority of recent disjunctivists. Consider the following three characterizations of the critical disjunction:

> [I]t looks to S as if there is an F [if] there is something which looks to S to be F [or] it is to S as if there is something which looks to him (S) to be F. (Snowdon 1981: 185)

> [A]ny case of its looking to S as if something is F will be... *either* a case of something's looking F to S, *or else* a case of its merely being for S as if something looked F to her. (Child 1994: 144)

> Either the subject is genuinely perceiving a pig, or it is with them just as if they were perceiving a pig. (Martin 2002: 394)

For each of these theorists, the key distinction is between a perceptual state of affairs in which something (a mind-independent object) is perceived by the subject (Martin) or looks to the subject to be a certain way (Snowdon and Child), and a second, nonveridical state of affairs in which it is for the subject merely *as if* this is the case. This way of characterizing the nonveridical disjunct leaves it open to offer different kinds of accounts of the deceptive cases. One might explain its being for subjects merely as if they perceive mind-independent objects in the way envisaged by Ayer and Austin: because the subject *actually* perceives an ontologically different kind of object that is indiscriminable from a mind-independent one. But it also leaves the door open for another kind of explanation, one that doesn't treat the deceptive cases as involving the perception of anything at all, but rather as a different kind of mental state that the subject falsely takes to be a perception.

The core idea behind disjunctivism is that the mental state involved in a case of veridical perception is of a different fundamental kind[4] from that involved in an indiscriminable hallucination, or alternatively, that

---

precisely how we should understand McDowell's disjunctive commitments, there are good reasons to think that McDowell wants to use the logical space opened up by the position to defend a version of naive realism given his complete rejection of the "Cartesian picture" of the mind wherein a subject's "inner life takes place in an autonomous realm, transparent to the awareness of the subject" (1986/1998: 236; see also his discussions of the possibility of acquaintance with ordinary objects at 231).

4. The 'fundamental kind' terminology derives from Martin (2004: 60–61). It is employed to allow for the fact that veridical perceptions (of Fs) and indiscriminable hallucinations of such will both fall under the kind *indiscriminable from a veridical perception of an F*, while denying that, in the case of veridical perceptions at least, this is its most fundamental kind— "the kind in virtue of which the event has the nature it does" (60).

there is no mental state common to cases of both veridical perception and indiscriminable hallucination. As M. G. F. Martin puts it, disjunctivism

> claims that we should understand statements about how things appear to a perceiver to be equivalent to a disjunction that either one is perceiving such and such or one is suffering a...hallucination; and that such statements are not to be viewed as introducing a report of a distinctive mental event or state common to these various disjoint situations. (2004: 37)[5]

The formulation of naive realism presented in chapter 1 claims that, when we see the world, the visual experience we enjoy is a matter of the subject's being acquainted with elements of the mind-independent environment, where a relationship of this kind would not hold were the subject's environment not to be as the experience presents it as being. Thus, naive realism entails disjunctivism: if naive realism is true, then the kind of mental state that is involved in a veridical perception—a mental state that relates the subject to elements of the mind-independent environment—could not be involved in a hallucinatory situation. The hallucinatory state must therefore be of a different kind. As it has been outlined thus far, however, disjunctivism makes no positive claims about the nature of the mental states involved in veridical perception and hallucination, other than to say that they are not of the same fundamental kind. Thus, disjunctivism does not entail naive realism—this formulation of disjunctivism does not preclude theories of the veridical state that are not naive realist in nature; it only insists that the nature of the veridical state must differ in kind from that of the hallucinatory state.[6]

5. The ellipsed section of this quote removes a reference to illusion. I discuss such cases independently in section 2.4.

6. For example, consider Byrne and Logue's "moderate view" discussed in chapter 1, according to which veridical perceptions and hallucinations "are different in significant mental respects, despite having a common mental element" (2008: 71). As examples of the kind of common element they have in mind, Byrne and Logue mention qualia and/or representational content. The question, then, is whether one's individuative criteria for mental states has the consequence that similarity in these aspects suffices to make it the case that the subjects are undergoing the same experience in both cases. If not, then such a theory could qualify as a version of disjunctivism on the restricted formulation. Yet because naive realism additionally states that the phenomenal character of the experience involves acquaintance with mind-independent objects, then on the assumption that these common elements feature in the moderate view as determinants of phenomenal character, such a view would therefore be an example of a disjunctivism that is not naive realist.

For this reason, other theorists have incorporated a positive naive realist claim about the veridical disjunct into the definition of disjunctivism. Snowdon, for instance, takes disjunctivism to claim the following:

> The experience in a genuinely perceptual case has a different nature to the experience involved in a non-perceptual case. It is not exhausted, however, by the simple denial of a common nature, but involves also the characterisation of the difference between the perceptual and non-perceptual in terms of the different constituents of the experiences involved. The experience in the perceptual case in its nature reaches out to and involves the perceived external object, not so the experience in other cases. (2005: 136–137; for a similar formulation, see Sturgeon 2006: 187)

The first part of Snowdon's claim connects disjunctivism with the basic thesis outlined above, but the second part goes beyond this in explicitly incorporating something like naive realism about the perceptual case into the very definition of disjunctivism.[7]

Nothing of substance seems to hang on whether we restrict the thesis called "disjunctivism" to the denial of a common nature or expand it to include naive realism about the veridical disjunct. Because the major motivation for endorsing disjunctivism would be to sustain naive realism, restricting disjunctivism to the denial of a common nature would likely be a principled rather than practical decision. Yet because there are taxonomic reasons for making the restriction,[8] I will employ the more restrictive definition of disjunctivism, which claims only that the mental state involved in a case of veridical perception differs in

7. When John Campbell defines disjunctivism, he incorporates into the thesis the yet more specific claim that the seen object "is a constituent of the *proposition* which gives the content of the experience" (2002: 123, emphasis added). He then rejects disjunctivism, thus understood, but goes on to endorse a view he calls the "relational view," which would qualify as disjunctivism on either of the formulations just presented. With this in mind, I treat Campbell as a naive realist disjunctivist.

8. These reasons emerge when we consider the kind of theory that results from *accepting* the spreading step of the argument from hallucination—the 'common kind' theory—which holds that both veridical perception and hallucination have a kind of mental state in common. As the history of the subject has shown, there is scope for there to be many different theories of that common mental core. Resisting the spreading step of the argument from hallucination opens up space for a similar range of theories in which the theory of veridical perception *differs* from the theory of hallucination. Because all of these theories would treat general statements about how things seem or appear to a subject as equivalent to disjunctive statements that the subject is in either one kind of state or another, calling such a collection of theories "disjunctive theories" would be apt.

fundamental kind from the mental state involved in an indiscriminable case of hallucination. Although, strictly speaking, this opens up the possibility of variants of disjunctivism that are not naive realist, I do not consider them here. For present purposes, defending disjunctivism and defending naive realism should be understood as the same project.

Regardless of whether we restrict our definition of disjunctivism to the denial of a common element or also incorporate a substantive claim about the nature of the veridical disjunct, a notable feature of the thesis is how little it has to say about the nonveridical disjunct. Because we are employing disjunctivism in the service of naive realism about veridical perception, all we know about the hallucinatory cases is that naive realism is not true of them, but we already knew this from the base case of the argument from hallucination. So, effectively, disjunctivism alone has nothing new to say about hallucination at all. This has led many commentators to find the theory exasperating. A good example of this kind of frustration can be found in Scott Sturgeon's paper "Visual Experience." Here, Sturgeon discusses a view he calls "disjunctive quietism," which, although he doesn't cite any particular sources of the view, he seems to see as representative of the disjunctivist literature. Disjunctive quietism, then, offers a broadly naive realist account of veridical perception and a "purely negative treatment" of hallucination according to which hallucination is defined simply as *not* being naive realist (1998: 183). This conception of the basic disjunctivist claim about hallucination is echoed by Jonathan Dancy, who states that, in "the standard formulation of the account,... this is explicitly the way in which the second disjunct is characterized: we characterize it solely by saying that it is like what it is not" (1995: 436).

Sturgeon complains that such a purely negative characterization of hallucination precludes the theory from explaining those very things we need a theory of visual experience to explain and that it should therefore be rejected. And I think many people would share Sturgeon's obvious frustration with the doctrine. This said, however, Sturgeon does allow (in a footnote) that it is "theoretically possible... to remove Quietism while preserving Disjunctivism" (1998: 186), and Dancy likewise continues by suggesting:

> Presumably, however, there may be available a more direct characterization of the second disjunct, and in a totally explicit version of the theory it would indeed be characterized in that better way. The current characterization is just a sort of place-holder, showing what has

> to be said about the relation between the first and second disjunct. (1995: 436)

The challenge that these theorists raise for the disjunctivist is to provide an adequate fleshing out of the theory—to present a fully explicit characterization of hallucination with which to replace the current second-disjunct placeholder. Only then, the thought would go, can disjunctivism be adequately considered at all. To an extent, I agree: the disjunctivist does need to say more about hallucination. Yet having said this, as we shall see in chapter 4, what is said may not be quite what Sturgeon and Dancy had envisaged. Nevertheless, it is true to say that merely asserting the truth of disjunctivism is not enough; rather it is simply the first step of a much longer journey—a journey that occupies the rest of this book.

2.3 Naive Realism and Local Supervenience

Before I get ahead of myself, there is an apparent oversight in our discussions of the argument from hallucination that must be addressed. When the argument was introduced, the spreading step was presented as being motivated primarily by the indiscriminability of certain cases of perception and hallucination. As I noted in introducing disjunctivism, however, this attempt at generalizing is not as compelling as it was in the case of illusion because, where illusions are concerned, the plausibility of the spreading step can be enhanced by building continuity cases such as Ayer's twisting coin case, discussed in section 2.1 above, in which veridical and illusory experiences of a coin shade into one another as the coin turns around. But in the case of hallucination, it is not so easy to develop an uncontroversial continuity case with which to link the veridical to the deceptive cases. This is the chink in the argument's armor that is then exploited by the disjunctivist.

In light of this, a number of recent exponents of the argument from hallucination have augmented the spreading step of the argument with considerations concerning the relationship between neural activity and a subject's experiences. Robinson, for example, suggests that when a subject looks at

> a brown table stood against a green wall . . . a certain brain state is induced in them . . . and they have the experience of seeing the table against the wall. Now suppose that their brain is fixed, in the relevant areas, in this

> state, and the table and wall hidden from them....[I]f such fixing took place the subject would continue to have an experience exactly similar to that of seeing the table and wall—they would "see" a brown table-shape against a green background. (1994: 151–152)[9]

Similarly, Smith argues that "it is surely not open to serious question that [the principle of same proximate cause, same effect] does apply with respect to the merely sensory character of conscious states" (2002: 203), and John Foster asserts that "given any genuine visual perception... we can envisage a situation in which... by electrically stimulating the optic nerves... the subject would have a visual hallucination which was, as an experience, exactly like it" (1985: 148).[10]

The common thread that unites these contentions seems to be an appeal to something like the following two (putatively empirical) claims:

1. That it is possible in principle to recreate the proximal neural conditions that occur when one perceives an object
2. That if the proximal neural conditions that occurred when one perceived an object were created in the absence of that object, the subject would have an experience with the same phenomenal character as the original perceptual experience

9. Strictly speaking, Robinson's argument is a little more complex than this may suggest, but in ways that need not concern us for present purposes. When Robinson claims that the nonveridical experience would be "exactly similar," he intends to assert that the subject will be presented with the same array of properties in both cases, but to leave open the possibility that, in the veridical cases, the properties the subject is presented with are properties of mind-independent objects while, in the nonveridical case, they are properties of sense-data. He then argues from exact similarity to ontological similarity as follows: "If the mechanism or brain state is a sufficient causal condition for the production of an image... when the table and wall are not there, why is it not so sufficient when they are present? Does the brain state mysteriously know how it is being produced; does it, by some extra sense, discern whether the table is really there or not and act accordingly, or does the table, when present, inhibit the production of an image by some sort of action at a distance?" (1994: 153–154). These considerations are important, and I discuss them in chapter 4. They need not, however, concern us at present.

10. I suspect that something like this principle also forms a background assumption for many scientists working on vision. Although I can't find any direct endorsements of the principle, one can sometimes find scientists saying things that look like an explicit acceptance of the weaker claim that neural activity alone suffices for phenomenal character. Take, for example, neuroscientist Christof Koch's remark that "if there is one thing that scientists are reasonably sure of, it is that brain activity is both necessary *and sufficient* for biological sentience" (2004: 9, emphasis added).

If these claims are correct, and neural replication would produce a mental state with the same phenomenal character as a veridical perception in the absence of appropriate objects, then this can be used to spread the conclusion of the base case of the original argument from hallucination to the veridical case. Recall that when I presented the naive realist thesis, I claimed that the phenomenal character of an experience is its property of *acquainting* the subject with particular mind-independent elements of the environment, where it is not possible for a subject to be acquainted with something that does not exist/is not instantiated. With this in mind, consider an experience, E, with the property of acquainting the subject with mind-independent object, O. According to the definition of acquaintance, E could not have this property unless O existed. Yet given (1)—the possibility in principle of artificially replicating neural activity in a laboratory context (a theoretical possibility that I cannot see any reason to deny)—then, given (2), it would be possible in principle to create an experience with this property in the absence of any suitable material objects. But because E could not have this property if O did not exist, this neural activity would also have to suffice for the existence of O, which conflicts with the requirement that O be mind independent. So a theory that accepts (2)—a principle I will call the 'local supervenience' principle—will by that very fact be unable to adequately accommodate the various components of naive realism as defined here.

In attempting to defend naive realism, I therefore *reject* the local supervenience principle. Now, I have no doubt that this will strike some as a preposterous course of action; I suspect that many will assume that if a theory is shown to be incompatible with a claim of this kind, this will thereby function as a *reductio* of that theory. But over the course of this book, I hope to show that rejecting local supervenience is not as outlandish as it may first seem. In arguing this, my approach is *not* to try to prove that local supervenience is false, but rather to show that many of the reasons given for thinking it to be true are not as compelling as they are often assumed to be. To achieve this, I will consider the central considerations that have been cited in support of local supervenience and will argue that none of them prove (or, indeed, even come close to proving) the thesis. But the nature of this approach means that I currently find myself in somewhat of a precarious position.

To understand why, consider the fact that Robinson argues that neural activity must be sufficient for phenomenal experience by posing the following problem: "[I]f it were not the case that perceptual processes, however stimulated, were sufficient to generate experience, it would be a mystery why [veridical-seeming] hallucinations should occur" (1994: 152). At present, what is important about this claim is that Robinson cites the capacity of local supervenience to explain the very occurrence of real-seeming hallucinations as a point in its favor—indeed, he suggests that if they were not explained by local supervenience, then their existence would be a mystery. So, in order to try to undermine this consideration, we would need to offer an alternative way of thinking about veridical-seeming hallucinations in order to dispel Robinson's sense that local supervenience is the only way of explaining the occurrence of such experiences. But we will be in a position to do *that* only if I continue to present the positive accounts of perception and hallucination in the face of the fact that I have not yet adequately dispatched local supervenience. For this reason, I will have to continue without further argument on this point at present. Rest assured, however, that I fully recognize the scale of the debt I am incurring here: chapter 5 deals with these issues in detail, and there I offer a full defense of the current rejection of local supervenience.

2.4 Naive Realism, Disjunctivism, and Illusion

At this point, one could be forgiven for wondering whether I had somehow contrived to *forget* the argument from illusion in the preceding discussions of the reappearance of naive realism in the literature. It is true that, both in the account presented here and in the literature more generally, the introduction of disjunctivism as a way of revitalizing naive realism has focused predominantly on the fact that it enables us to resist the spreading step of the argument from hallucination. Yet there is still another major argument against the thesis waiting patiently in the wings. What is more, there is at least one recent opponent of naive realism who has claimed that it is the argument from illusion, not the argument from hallucination, that clinches the case against the thesis (Foster 2000: 61). So, even if we were to discover that developing a disjunctive theory enables us to deflect the force of the argument from hallucination, we still have to ask: How does disjunctivism help in drawing the sting of the argument from illusion?

Sadly, and possibly even surprisingly, I don't think that disjunctivism, as it stands, is any help whatsoever in avoiding the conclusion of the argument from illusion. If we look at the way contemporary disjunctivists have treated illusion, we find that the standard approach is to place illusion into one of the two disjuncts that were created in order to evade the argument from hallucination. For example, consider

John McDowell's statement of the key disjunction: "[A]n appearance that such-and-such is the case can be *either* a mere appearance *or* the fact that such-and-such is the case making itself perceptually manifest to someone" (1982/1998: 386–387). Because McDowell's veridical disjunct contains those cases in which a 'fact' makes itself manifest, and given that there is no such thing as a nonobtaining fact, then any scenario in which it appears to the subject that such-and-such is the case when it is *not* could not be a case of a fact making itself manifest. Thus, illusions look to fall into the category of cases in which it merely appears as though a fact is made manifest along with hallucinations.

Yet there are reasons to be dissatisfied with classifying illusions alongside hallucinations. Robinson protests that, "if all non-veridical perceptions were treated in the same way as hallucinations, then every case of something not looking exactly as it is would be a case in which one was aware of some kind of subjective content. Only perfectly veridical perceptions would be free of such subjective contents" (1994: 159). This would present certain difficulties for the naive realist. For one thing, it seems natural to think it is possible to veridically perceive certain properties of an object—its shape, for example—while misperceiving other properties, such as its color. But at least in normal cases, our capacity to perceive an object's shape appears to depend crucially on our ability to discriminate its color from that of the background. So, if we were to treat illusions as on a par with hallucinations while treating hallucinations as involving "awareness of some kind of subjective content," then we would need an account of how it would be possible to successfully perceive an object's shape, where this involves a relation to the shape itself, in virtue of *failing* to be related to its color and being related instead to a subjective content.[11] Moreover, recall the kinds of continuity cases discussed above in which an illusion shades into a veridical perception by experientially small degrees. If such illusions are as prevalent as Ayer suggests, then the naive realist would be forced to concede that, most of the time, we have experiences that fail to put us in contact with the mind-independent world; only occasionally do we enjoy a fundamentally different kind of experience in which we are granted a direct glimpse of reality. As Smith lampoons it, the "picture of our daily commerce with the world through perception that therefore emerges is one of a usually indirect awareness of physical objects occasionally interrupted by direct visions of them glimpsed in favoured positions" (2002: 28).

11. Thanks to Susanna Siegel for convincing me of the importance of such issues.

In the light of difficulties such as these, perhaps we would be better served bringing illusion under the perceptual, rather than the hallucinatory, disjunct. The key disjunctions offered by both Snowdon and William Child suggest they are thinking along these lines because they both characterize the perceptual disjunct as containing cases in which something *looks to S to be F*. Illusions, of course, involve situations in which something *does* seem to be F, but where that thing—the thing that seems to be F—is not *really* F.[12] So these disjunctivists appear to place illusion in the same category as veridical perception. But if this is the case, then adopting disjunctivism has got us precisely *nowhere* when it comes to the argument from illusion. The point of endorsing disjunctivism was to enable us to provide a broadly naive realist account of the veridical perceptual disjunct. As we have seen, to accommodate the phenomenal aspects of naive realism, such a theory insists that what it is like to have a veridical perceptual experience is a matter of the subject's being acquainted with the properties or qualities that are possessed by the mind-independent objects that are seen. So, if illusions—situations, recall, in which a perceived object is experienced as possessing a property or quality that it objectively *lacks*—are to be counted in with veridical perceptions, then the key challenge raised for naive realism by the argument from illusion is still in force. Going disjunctivist hasn't helped one bit.

The problem here lies in the fact that the disjunctive nature of disjunctivism—the fact that it operates by cleaving the class of 'appearances that such-and-such is the case' in two—has a tendency to make us think that every instance of an appearance that such-and-such is the case must fall on either one side or the other of this great divide. But cases of illusion simply will not fit in such a scheme. If we view them as falling on

12. Interestingly, Martin is the only one of the above disjunctivists who explicitly sets out to employ disjunctivism as a way of resurrecting naive realism. (Snowdon and Child are primarily interested in disjunctivism as a way of thinking about perception that is an alternative to the causal theory of perception and, as we have seen, McDowell's main interest is epistemological.) But if you look again at the details of Martin's key disjunction, you will see that it doesn't explicitly cover seeing an object to have a certain property, so it doesn't thereby give us any way of seeing what Martin's response to the problem of illusion would be. Having said this, Martin does discuss illusion in a footnote where he explicitly acknowledges that he is "glossing over" the question of what to do with illusion and suggests that "the most significant form of disjunctivism will actually fall somewhere in between these two approaches: not simply focussing on the contrast between when an object is present and when it is not, but focussing on whether some apparently perceived feature or aspect is present or not" (2002: 395n24).

the same side of the rift as hallucination, then we are saddled with the problems just noted. Yet if we treat them as falling in with veridical perceptions, then it remains the case that we cannot give a consistent naive realist account of all the cases on that side of the divide.

Perhaps, then, the solution would be to bring out our disjunctive axe and cleave once again on the side of veridical perception, thereby separating veridical perceptions from illusions. But while adding further disjunctions into the picture is a possibility, the different cases that go under the name of "illusions" form such a diverse group that it will not be plausible to offer one unique treatment that will apply to each and every case of illusion (I discuss this further in chapter 6). Given this, rather than accept a proliferation of disjunctions,[13] my preference is to stick with the original two disjuncts. However, rather than assume that disjunctivism operates by dividing the class of appearances that such-and-such is the case into two mutually exclusive classes, I suggest that the disjunctive move serves to highlight two *poles* or *boundary points*, where perfect veridical perception is one pole and total hallucination is the other. By focusing attention on these outermost cases, I will be able to tell two stories: one about what is involved when we veridically see that such-and-such is the case, and another about what is going on when we hallucinate that such-and-such is the case. These are the stories that are told in chapters 3 and 4, respectively.

The advantage of using the metaphor of poles or boundary points is that it no longer implies a chasm, on one side or the other of which every individual case must fall. Instead, it implies a continuity of ground *between* these two points. If we are at one extreme, the first story will be the only story to tell; if we are at the other, the second story will be the only story to tell. But if we are dealing with a visual experience that is located at some point *between* the two poles, then both stories will feature in an explanation of that experience, but to varying degrees. The closer we are to the veridical pole, the more the perceptual story will be the principal explanatory story, and the more the case of illusion will resemble a case of veridical perception. Likewise for the hallucinatory pole: the closer a case of illusion is to that, the more the alternative story will take over as the primary explanation and the more comparable the

13. Some of Hinton's claims suggest he would have been comfortable with such an approach. Although he initially employs a disjunction of the form ($A \vee B$)—"Either I see a flash of light, or I have an illusion of a flash of light" (1967: 217)—he later explicitly states that both of the disjuncts A and B are themselves "implicitly disjunctive" (219).

illusion will be to a case of hallucination. Thus, the suggestion—briefly hinted at here, but developed in detail in chapter 6—is that illusion is not a further, mutually exclusive disjunct, nor is it really a special case of either existing disjunct. Rather, illusion occupies the vaguely defined mid-ground *between* the two primary disjuncts or poles.

2.5 The Way Forward

I have now presented an overview of the philosophical work that needs to be done if a naive realist view of veridical visual experience is to be defended. Chapter 1 showed that the naive realist claims that when we see the world, the subject enjoys an experience in which he or she is acquainted with elements of the mind-independent environment. The phenomenal character of such an experience—that property of the experience that types the experience by what it is like to have it—is therefore its property of acquainting the subject with those particular elements of the mind-independent environment. In the light of this, this chapter has considered the arguments from illusion and hallucination, primarily in their negative role as arguments *against* naive realism. Then, focusing on the argument from hallucination, we saw how endorsing disjunctivism can enable us to embrace the powerful first stage of the argument, which shows that hallucination cannot be naive realist, while nevertheless refusing to accept that this has any consequences for the theory we can give of veridical perception.

The first stage of my project is to flesh out the naive realist account of veridical perception—this occupies chapter 3. Because endorsing disjunctivism allows us to refuse to accept that the first stage of the argument from hallucination has any consequences for the theory we can give for the veridical cases, we find ourselves in the refreshing position of being able to provide a theory of perception without constantly having to ensure that the account can also hold true of hallucination. The real work then begins in chapter 4. Endorsing disjunctivism affords the space in which to offer a naive realist account of veridical perception, but it comes at a cost. I attempt to meet that cost in chapter 4 by offering an account of the ontologically different state of hallucination. The key component of this account is an explanation of how a subject might confuse a situation that involves a radical failure to be in touch with the world—a situation that therefore lacks phenomenal character as outlined here—with the very *different* case of veridical perceptual contact with that world. The most significant feature of this account is that it does not proceed by attempting to find an alternative source of phenomenal character for hallucinations, but rather embraces the claim that hallucinations lack phenomenal character and explains how hallucinations, thus understood, can nevertheless be indiscriminable from veridical perceptions.

As I have already foreshadowed, the positive accounts of veridical perception and hallucination proceed against the background of a rejection of the local supervenience principle. In chapter 5 I therefore return, having laid out the positive theses, to the question of whether the phenomenal character of an experience is wholly determined by processes in the subject's brain and central nervous system. Because I am unable to *refute* local supervenience, what I attempt to show is that the reasons given for accepting local supervenience are not as strong as they are often assumed to be and that not only *can* local supervenience be resisted, but there are actually good reasons to resist it. Then, having laid down and defended the theories of the boundary points of veridical perception and hallucination, in chapter 6 I provide an analysis of those cases that occupy the ground *between* these two poles: cases of illusion. As I have already explained, this does not take the form of a further theory, but rather explains how different kinds of illusion can be accounted for by varying the admixture of the two core theories.

3

Perception

When it comes to the task of theorizing about the veridical perceptual disjunct or 'pole' (see chapter 2), my primary purpose is to develop a more substantive account of the phenomenal character of veridical visual experience that will serve as a touchstone of naive realism. But this account also has another critical role: it must function as a foil against which to present the theory of the complementary disjunct of hallucination. So, while the adoption of a broadly disjunctive approach does allow us to stop worrying about hallucination to some extent—because we don't need this particular theory to also hold true in hallucinatory cases—we do need to bear in mind that, when it comes to hallucination, the objective is to show how hallucinations can be indiscriminable from veridical perceptions, where veridical perceptions are understood as presented here.

As discussed in chapter 1, the central feature of visual perception that the naive realist is trying to codify is the idea that, when we see the world, the objects that inhabit the environment, together with their properties and other features, shape the contours of the subject's conscious experiences. I then developed this intuition into the philosophical thesis of naive realism with two related claims: first, the presentational character of visual perception—the array of properties, aspects, or features that are presented to the subject of experience—is constituted by the seen objects and their properties; second, the phenomenal character of a perceptual experience—that property of the experience that types it by what it is like to have it—is its property of acquainting the subject with the elements of the presentational character, where the nature of acquaintance has the consequence that an experience's having this property entails that the elements of the presentational character exist and/or are instantiated.

Because the phenomenal character of an experience is its property of acquainting a subject with a particular presentational character, our understanding of an experience's phenomenal character proceeds via our understanding of its presentational character—to know what the phenomenal character of an experience is, we need to know the constitution of the presentational character that it acquaints the subject with (see Martin 1998: 174). What is more, given that the focus in this chapter is solely on the case of veridical perception, we can, for present purposes, take it for granted that those objects and properties that the experience acquaints the subject with—those objects and properties that feature in the presentational character of the experience—will exist or be instantiated in the mind-independent world. In order to provide a more substantive account of the phenomenal character of veridical experience, then, we need to address *how* we can flesh out the core claim that elements of the environment feature in presentational character.

We might initially suppose that the job of providing this kind of theoretical gloss is relatively straightforward. As discussed in chapter 1, the naive realist wants to say that, in veridical perceptual experience, the layout of the environment shapes the contours of the subject's conscious experience. A natural suggestion would therefore be simply to hold, as John Campbell does, that the presentational character of your experience is constituted by the scene you are facing. That way, all the objects and properties that inhabit that tract of the environment would be sure to feature in the presentational character of the experience and, in turn, to determine the experience's phenomenal character. As it turns out, however, things are far more complex than this suggests. Over the course of this chapter, I describe how the presentational character (and hence phenomenal character) of a specific veridical experience is conditioned by an array of different factors, ranging from the obvious (e.g., the layout of the environment) to the not so obvious (e.g., the degree and focus of a subject's attention). The challenge for the naive realist is to explain just how these considerations affect the presentational character of a subject's experience in a way consistent with the underlying principles of naive realism.

3.1 Properties, Objects, and Facts

On the assumption that a particular object or property features in the presentational character of a veridical experience, let us start by asking how it so features. To begin with such a question may seem puzzling. If we accept that an object or property features in presentational character, what more need we say? Consider, then, that it would be entirely compatible with this claim to suppose that a particular object or property appears in the presentational character of an experience *simpliciter*—on its own, as it were. But in the case of objects, it simply is not clear what sense we could make of the idea that an object might appear in presentational character alone. Whenever we have a perceptual experience, we never simply experience an object in splendid isolation; rather, when we experience an object, we also experience some of the properties that the object instantiates. This gives us reason to think that objects are not constituents of presentational character per se, and similar claims have been made about the supposition that properties or qualities might appear in presentational character *simpliciter*. Roderick Firth, for example, argues that "the qualities of which we are conscious in perception are almost always presented to us, in some obvious sense, as the qualities *of physical objects*. We are not conscious of liquidity, coldness and solidity, but of the liquidity of water, the coldness of ice, and the solidity of rocks" (1949/1965: 222).

Mohan Matthen has also argued that certain empirical results are adequately explained only on the assumption that we do not see properties or qualities *simpliciter*, but rather see objects bearing properties. To give a brief idea of the kinds of empirical results Matthen appeals to, consider an experiment in which subjects viewed a display of two Gabor patches—circular, striped patches—superimposed upon one another. The patterns on each Gabor patch were different, and over a period of time each patch "dynamically changed its orientation, spatial frequency and colour, but never its spatial location" (Blaser et al. 2000: 196). Yet despite these two patches occupying the same region of space, "observers saw these patterns as distinct objects in the same location, and were able to track them independently.... These results show that these observers were attending to features by attending to the objects to which these features were attributed, and not by attending to the features directly" (Matthen 2005: 281).

For present purposes, these empirical considerations are adduced as further support of the idea that the basic constituents of presentational character are not objects and properties per se. Instead, they provide additional reasons to think that to see a property is to see it as inhering in some object or other. When we combine this with the thought that we never simply see an object but always see it by seeing one or more of the properties it possesses, it suggests a general theory of what the fundamental constituents of presentational character are. Take a given tract of the environment that I visually perceive. This tract of the environment contains an array of objects and surfaces that possess a vast assortment of properties. Given that, when we see an object in our environment, we don't "just" see that object, when we see an object what we see must be, at a minimum, that object's bearing a property. Likewise, given that we always see a property as inhering in an object, when we see a property what we see must be, at a minimum, an object's bearing that property.

Taken together, these considerations suggest that the basic units that feature in presentational character are not properties and objects *simpliciter*, but rather object–property couples. This is, I take it, the view outlined by Mark Johnston, who holds that "I sense—am aware of—. . . exemplifications of properties by objects or quantities of stuff (the snubnosedness of Socrates, or the astringency of calvados)" (2006: 281). Johnston calls these external spatiotemporal particulars "truthmakers," but I prefer the more metaphysical term 'facts' (Olson 1987: 2; Kirkham 1992: 73; Armstrong 1997: 113).[1] In their most atomic form, such facts have one of two basic structures: either "*a's being F*" (Armstrong 1997: 142) or "*a's R*-ing *b*" (Mulligan et al. 1984: 297). So when we see an object (a) by seeing one of its properties (its F-ness), we can say that we see a particular fact—the fact of a's being F. Likewise, when we see a property (G) as instantiated in an object (b), we see the fact of b's being G.

This generates a view of the perceptible environment according to which a particular tract of the environment contains an array of facts that, through featuring in the presentational characters of a subject's

1. A closely related term in metaphysics is 'state of affairs.' However, this term has been used in such a way that a state of affairs can be said to exist but not obtain (Plantinga 1976). Employing this term would therefore threaten the picture's claim to legitimate the commonsense intuition that the way things *actually are* shapes the contours of the subject's conscious experiences.

conscious perceptual experiences, can shape the contours of those experiences. Although there are clear similarities between this view of the perceptible environment and the view of the world Wittgenstein outlines in the *Tractatus* (1921/1961), there is an important way in which the Tractarian view of the world goes beyond anything we need to claim here. The Tractarian view is about the fundamental ontological structure of reality: when Wittgenstein claims that the world is a world of facts, not of things, I take it that he is asserting that facts, rather than objects, are ontologically fundamental. The view of the perceptible environment outlined here is not a claim about the fundamental ontological structure of reality. Because of this, I do not need to make a claim as to the ontological priority of facts and objects. My key claim here is that, whatever the basic ontological structure of the world, our fundamental mode of perceptual contact with that world is with facts—with things bearing properties—not directly with either properties or things *simpliciter*.

Because it is critical that this position can be seen to incorporate the idea that the layout of the environment shapes the contours of a subject's conscious experiences, let me be absolutely clear that I am *not* using the term 'fact' in its more linguistic sense, wherein a fact is a true proposition—something that is only contingently true and hence might have been false.[2] I am completely in agreement with Johnston when he claims that, on such an understanding of the term, the claim that sensing is directed at facts would "not earn the right to the metaphor of the senses taking in *concrete* reality... [because] concrete reality does not consist of items that could have been false" (2006: 269–270). As I am using the term, however, facts are not things that could have been false—they are necessarily *actual*—and there is no such thing as a false or nonobtaining fact. So, as understood here, facts are *not* true propositions. Where propositions are our model truth *bearers*, facts are pieces of reality—indeed, they are precisely those pieces of reality that Johnston takes to be the truth*makers* of propositions.

When we take on board this metaphysical conception of facts, we can also see that the claim that all perception is fact perception is not

2. Johnston hesitantly suggests (2006: 269n9) that this is the core of the view presented in John McDowell (1994). I'm not so sure, however—for an interpretation of McDowell that sees him as offering a picture more along the lines of Johnston's and the one presented here, see Fish and Macdonald (2007). That paper also explains how this metaphysical conception of fact can be made consistent with the term 'fact' connoting something involving a mode of presentation.

committed to an implausible analysis of what it is to see an object. Fred Dretske has argued (e.g., 1969: 11; 1990: 132) that, if to see a fact is to come to know, on the basis of perception, that the fact in question obtains, then a subject can be said to see an object only if the subject comes to know something *about* that object. But this is implausible, Dretske contends, because it would imply, for example, that subjects who carefully read a page of text must come to believe or know something about each and every one of the hundreds of different objects (the letters) that they see. To avoid this implausibility, Dretske suggests, we should acknowledge a more basic mode of object perception on which fact perception is based.

When it comes to the way I am using the term, however, to claim that we see facts is not to claim that we come to know, on the basis of perception, that the fact obtains. Instead, facts, as I am using the term, correspond to what Dretske calls "states of affairs" (1990: 131)—the cat's being black, for example—and there is no claim here that, to see such a fact, a subject must come to know that the fact in question obtains. My claim that all perception is fact perception is not, therefore, compelled to offer the kind of analysis of the reading case that Dretske rejects. Instead, my account would claim that we see a given object by having facts in which that object features figuring in the presentational character of our visual experiences. So, in having facts feature in the presentational character of one's experience, one is thereby acquainted with objects and their properties; in seeing the fact of the cat's being black, one sees the cat and its blackness.[3] There is thus no obligation to appeal to a lower level of perception to account for our intuitions about when objects are perceived.

3.2 Veridical Perception and Visual Acuity

The claim that facts are the basic constituents of presentational character suggests that we might begin delineating the naive realist account of presentational character as follows: when a subject is conscious of a particular tract of the environment, it is not the tract of the environment per se that features in the presentational character of that subject's visual

3. This aspect of the claim enables the naive realist to accommodate the intuition, appealed to in chapter 1, that it is the very instance of blackness exemplified by the cat that we are aware of when we veridically see a black cat as such.

experience, but rather the array of facts that inhabit that tract of the environment. Yet it would be implausible to hold that, when we perceive a tract of the environment, we perceive *every* fact from that environment. For one thing, the position or perspective from which the subject perceives the environment will affect which of the facts from that environment the subject can become aware of. So, for example, the distance from which a subject views a particular object will usually affect which of the facts concerning that object the subject is able to see, as will the distribution of objects in that environment. From certain points of view, some objects will occlude others, and this will usually prevent the subject from seeing facts in which the occluded object features. These considerations are not in any way arcane or theoretical: they are all truistic components of an everyday conception of perceptual experience. Therefore, we can accommodate the truism that not every fact from the relevant tract of the environment is seen by explicitly including the claim, within our theory of veridical experience, that the facts that feature in the presentational character of the subject's experience are constrained by such things as the layout of the environment and the subject's position in/perspective on that environment.

Even when modified in this way, the claim that the presentational character of a given perceptual experience is constituted by the facts that inhabit a particular tract of the environment (restricted in the kinds of ways noted above) is unacceptable. This claim would yield the prediction that the presentational characters of two experiences of the same tract of the environment (from the same place) would be constituted by the same set of facts. Given the connection between phenomenal and presentational character, this is simply to say that the phenomenal characters of the two experiences would be the same and hence that "two ordinary observers standing in roughly the same place, looking at the same scene, are bound to have experiences with the same phenomenal character" (Campbell 2002: 116). Yet such a prediction looks to be falsified by the everyday observation that subjects who have different levels of visual acuity can have experiences of the same tract of the environment from the same position that differ in their phenomenal character.

For example, as I sit here now, I can make out the different shapes and colors of the book spines on my bookshelf and the rectangles corresponding to the different days on my wall planner. But my eyesight is not good enough to enable me to see any of the titles of the books or to see what I have written in any of those rectangles. Yet if I were to ask my colleague to sit in the same chair, she would be able to make out the titles of the books and what engagements I have without any difficulty. To that extent, what it is like for her and what it is like for me to see my room while sitting in my chair differs. But that is just to say that the phenomenal characters of our visual experiences differ, despite its being the case that we are both open to the very same tract of the environment. Therefore, simply identifying the presentational character of an experience of a particular environmental expanse with the facts present in that region, even when those facts have been restricted in the kinds of ways discussed above, will fail to account for the fact that the phenomenal characters of different experiences of the same part of the environment can differ.

Because these two experiences of the same part of the environment differ in phenomenal character, it would, of course, be open to one who endorses disjunctivism to hold that one of the two experiences—mine, probably, as the inferior one—is thereby revealed to be nonveridical. In this way, a disjunctivist could reject the call to treat this case within the theory of veridical experience. Yet while it is true that my colleague can see things that I cannot, a theory of veridicality that held that experiences are veridical only if they are the most detailed experiences possible would surely be implausible. The implausibility of such an account of veridicality would be transmitted to the claim that my visual experience is nonveridical in the case just described. But if the naive realist declines the disjunctive option just described, an account of how two veridical experiences of the same tract of the environment from the same position might differ in phenomenal character is still owing.

In discussing problems of this sort, Michael Tye suggests that, "when one unfocuses one's eyes or takes off one's glasses…one simply loses information.…Some information that was present…is now missing" (2003a: 18). This is also true in the kind of two subject case we are discussing. When I look up at my bookshelf, I can see that the book on the top left of my bookshelf is small, thin, and a blue-green color, but I can't make out the title. When my colleague views the same scene, she can still see all of the details I can, but she can also make out more; for example, she can see that the book is H. B. Acton's *Kant's Moral Philosophy*, and that the top corner of the spine has been damaged. As I sit here, then, I am not aware that the top of the book's spine is damaged. Now, the book really does have the property of having a damaged spine—there is a fact of the book's having a damaged spine—it is just that, due to my inferior visual acuity, I am not visually aware of that fact from where I am sitting. My colleague, on the other hand, is aware of that fact when sitting in the same place. One difference between our experiences, then, is that the presentational character of her experience—the array of features that she is acquainted with in her experience—contains a fact that mine does not.

Appreciation of this feature of the situation points us in the direction of a general resolution to the problem at hand. More generally, we might suggest that what distinguishes the phenomenal characters of my colleague's experiences from mine is that, due to her higher levels of visual acuity, the presentational characters of her experiences are more detailed or incorporate more facts. This accounts for the differences in what it is like for us to have experiences of the same tracts of the environment. This explanation of the difference between our experiences is fully compatible with the natural view that the contours of our conscious experiences are shaped by the layout of our environment. In this case, the difference between us is that there is a perfectly objective element of our shared environment—the fact of the book's having a damaged spine—that contributes to shaping the contours of her conscious experience but does not contribute to shaping mine.[4]

We can therefore deal with the difficulties raised by subjects with different visual acuity by extending the scope of our initial response and acknowledging a further constraint on the facts that can feature in the presentational character of perceptual experience. We started out with the claim that, in veridical perception, I am directly aware of a tract of the environment. We then refined this claim to allow that, while I can be said to be presented with a tract of the environment when I perceive it, it is not the relevant tract of the environment per se that I am presented with (i.e., that features in the presentational character of my perceptual experience), but rather a range of the facts that populate that tract of the environment. The present suggestion is that this is further refined as follows: when we see a tract of the environment, our position in that environment together with the limitations of our visual systems serves to constrain the facts from that environment that shape the contours of

4. This resolution of the problem parallels a basic claim of the representationalist thesis, that "there can be no difference in phenomenal character without a difference in [representational] content" (Byrne 2001: 204). In effect, I am suggesting that the naive realist is committed to a counterpart of this principle: any difference in what it is like for a subject to enjoy a veridical perceptual experience will be accompanied by a difference in the facts featuring in the presentational character of that experience. So, for any two veridical experiences that differ in phenomenal character, the naive realist must hold that these experiences will be experiences of a different set of facts.

our conscious experience. This modification allows us to account for the differences we find in the phenomenal characters of experiences of the same scene. When we visually perceive a particular scene, it is a specific array of facts from that scene that features in the presentational character of our visual experience. If our visual acuity increases, then the number of facts that we are aware of increases, and thus the phenomenal character of our perceptual experience changes accordingly. Likewise (as those of us whose eyesight has gotten worse over the years can testify), as our eyesight deteriorates, the number of facts that we can pick up on through vision reduces and the phenomenal character of our perceptual experiences reflects this.

3.3 The Role of Attention: Sighted Blindness

Given the picture of our perceptual interaction with the world presented thus far, we might suppose that the phenomenal character of any given perceptual experience can be determined as follows. First, we catalogue the facts that exist in the tract of the environment a subject is viewing; then we jettison all of those facts that are not accessible to vision given the subject's visual acuity, their position in that environment, and so on. The facts that then remain are the facts that the subject perceives, or that feature in the presentational character of the subject's experience. The phenomenal character is then the property that this experience has of acquainting the subject with this presentational character. However, this picture is in tension with the results of psychological research into two areas: change blindness and inattentional blindness. Because these are quite similar phenomena, I bring them together under the rubric of 'sighted blindness' (see Mack and Rock 1998: 14).

Sighted blindness cases are situations in which normal subjects fail to see some aspect of their immediate environment that we would have antecedently expected them to see. Consider change blindness first. In the most easily accessible (and therefore well-known) change blindness experiments, subjects view a computer screen on which an image depicting a natural scene is presented. After the scene has been presented for a short time—say, 240 milliseconds (Simons and Levin 1997: 265)—the scene "flickers" off (is replaced by a blank screen) for 80 milliseconds and then reappears containing a significant change. The purpose of this flicker is to prevent transient signals in the visual system from immediately alerting subjects to the change. The kinds of significant change that occur during the flicker are such things as large objects appearing and disappearing, or moving, or changing color; for example, in one such experiment, a picture of an airplane disappears and reappears without its engines, and in another, a picture of a house disappears and reappears without its garage. After the changed image has been displayed for 240 milliseconds, the display flickers off again (80 milliseconds), and the original scene reappears. The images then cycle while the subject searches for the change.

What is initially surprising about these experiments is that, even though viewing conditions are optimal and subjects are primed to search for changes, subjects can take a long time to see what the changes in the scene are. "Experiments using the flicker paradigm found that almost none of the changes were detected during the first cycle of alternation, and many changes were not detected after nearly one minute of alternation" (Simons and Levin 1997: 263). The flickers are not an essential part of the experiment, however. John Grimes describes versions of the change blindness experiments in which changes are made during subject saccades. In these experiments, the changes that took place included two men exchanging hats of different colors and styles, and a parrot, occupying about a quarter of the picture space, changing color from brilliant green to brilliant red. And even though subjects were told that they were studying the images for a memory test (to ensure they are concentrating on features in the image) and also informed that the scenes depicted may change (so changes are expected), Grimes reports that, overall, two out of three changes still went undetected (1996: 102).

What is perhaps even more surprising is that such results are not limited to the laboratory context. In a later paper, Daniel Simons and Daniel Levin published results showing that change blindness was also present in real-world interactions. They set up two experiments in which a pedestrian (the subject) was approached by an experimenter asking for directions. After the subject had interacted with this individual for 10–15 seconds, two other experimenters passed between them carrying a door. During the period the conversation was thus interrupted, the experimenter who had initially asked for directions switched places with one of the experimenters carrying the door. In one of the two versions of the experiment, the experimenters were both dressed as construction workers, but the substitute differed in both height and voice and wore a black as opposed to light blue shirt, an unbranded as opposed to branded safety hat, and a large tool belt as opposed to no tool belt. Yet in 66% of trials (8 of 12), subjects continued the conversation and, when asked if they had noticed anything unusual, did not report noticing the change of experimenters (1998: 647).

Equally interesting results have been returned in experiments investigating the closely related phenomenon of inattentional blindness. In these experiments, subjects are given a task to perform that requires their attention. A well-known "real-world" example is one in which subjects are shown a recording of two teams of basketball players—one team in black, one in white—and asked to count the number of passes made by members of the white team to one another, whereas a typical laboratory experiment will require subjects to engage in an attention-occupying task such as reporting which arm of a briefly displayed cross is longest. Then, while the subject's attention is occupied by the assigned task, a further event occurs that the subject is not expecting. In the cross case, a "critical stimulus" such as a small colored square appears close to the point at which the subject's eyes are fixated; in the basketball case, someone dressed in a gorilla suit walks across the court.

As is the case with the change blindness experiments, we would normally expect these events to be seen quite easily. Yet the fact that subjects' attention is otherwise engaged means that they will often fail to see the unexpected event. For example, a startling 46% of subjects fail to see the gorilla cross the basketball court (Simons and Chabris 1999). In the cross experiments, if both the cross and the critical stimulus are presented at fixation, then 25% of subjects fail to see the critical stimulus. Probably the most surprising result, however, is that when the subjects were directed to fixate on a point and to attend to a cross to be presented parafoveally (at the periphery of the visual field), a staggering 85% of subjects failed to see a critical stimulus that was presented at the very point of fixation (Mack and Rock 1998: 15).

These sighted blindness results are relevant to our present concerns inasmuch as they suggest that a fact's being present in the tract of the environment one is currently facing, together with one's having the kind of visual acuity that would enable awareness of that fact, nonetheless does not suffice for one to be acquainted with that fact or, alternatively, for that fact to feature in the presentational character of one's experience. If we accept this interpretation of these results, then the account of the presentational character of visual experience presented here requires further modification. Of course, we could refuse to accept this reading of the situation. Strictly speaking, all that these results show is that subjects don't *report* having seen the stimuli, not that they haven't actually seen them. This leaves the way clear for a reading of the sighted blindness results according to which, while perception "provides a rich source of high-fidelity information about one's immediate surroundings [it is only] if that sensory information is integrated, through attention, into stable knowledge structures, [that] it will be remembered. Without such integration, it exists only in the moment of perceptual experience" (Pani 2000: 110). So John Pani proposes a position according to which subjects do see the stimulus—in our terms, that the fact in question does, after all, make it into the presentational character of the visual experience—but that because of the lack of attention, this particular fact "exists only in the moment of perceptual experience": it is not remembered and is hence not reported as having been seen.

I am sure that the seen-but-not-remembered response will have a role to play in providing explanations of a number of cases of sighted blindness. But even if it is available in some cases, it is unlikely to be true across the board: as Simons points out, "it is somewhat hard to imagine seeing a gorilla that was visible for up to 9 seconds, and then forgetting it immediately after the task" (2000: 153).[5] What is more, although the sighted blindness cases do surprise us with just quite how "big" are the facts that we can fail to see under conditions of change or inattention, given the sheer volume of facts out there in the world, it should not surprise us that there may be some visible facts that we see only when we attend to them. This suggests that there is an independent need to consider why certain visible worldly facts may not make it into the presentational character of a subject's visual experience.

Let us take the inattentional blindness results first, because these cases are most impervious to the seen-but-not-remembered mode of explanation. If we accept that, in these cases, the stimuli are not seen, then we will need to explain why a stimulus presented under conditions of inattention may go undetected. As we have seen, a condition of inattention is created when a subject is given an attention-demanding task to complete. This suggests that attention is a finite resource and that, in creating a condition of inattention, some of the attentional resources that would have been devoted to certain areas of the visual field have to be reallocated to the area in which the attention-demanding task is taking or will take place. This reduction in attentional resources, then,

5. Of course, in saying that the gorilla went unseen, we are not necessarily claiming that the object—the gorilla—was not seen at all, but merely that its gorillaness—the fact of its being a gorilla—was not seen. This is compatible with other facts about that object—including, say, the fact of its being black—having been seen.

has the consequence that the subject might be blind—inattentionally blind—to stimuli presented in those areas. We might, therefore, modify our account to accommodate the phenomenon of inattentional blindness in the following way. For the claim 'attention is a finite resource,' read 'the subject can be aware of only a finite number of facts at any one time.' In a normal experience of the world, we are aware of an array of relatively fine-grained facts in the part of the visual field that we are foveating and, outside this, facts that are somewhat coarser in their grain. When we attend to something, this distribution of attentional resources is altered in such a way that we become aware of an increased number of fine-grained facts concerning the object or area attended to, and a decreased number of facts across the rest of the field of view. Then, because what is left of one's attentional resources during a condition of inattention would enable one to pick up on only coarse facts at best where the rest of the field of view is concerned, it would be no surprise that one sometimes fails to register the presence of a stimulus in those areas.

We should not assume, however, that it is only *where* we attend to that is important: *what* we attend to might also lead to certain kinds of sighted blindness. Consider a further experiment, by George McConkie and David Zola, in which subjects were directed to read text in which the cases of letters alternated. For example, they were asked to read:

> In ThE eStUaRiEs Of ThE fLoRiDa EvErGlAdEs ThE rEd MaNgRoVe

While subjects read, researchers tracked the subjects' eye movements, and during some saccades, the case of every letter in the sentence was switched. That is, the sentence the subject was reading would be switched to

> iN tHe EsTuArIeS oF tHe FlOrIdA eVeRgLaDeS tHe ReD mAnGrOvE

and then switched back on a later saccade. McConkie and Zola found, again somewhat surprisingly, that not only did subjects succeed in reading the changing sentences—suggesting that all the constituent letters are seen—they did so without these changes producing any abnormal patterns of eye movement (e.g., shorter saccade distances, longer fixation times, or increased numbers of regressive saccades) and without subjects reporting that these changes were taking place. Indeed, McConkie and Zola report that they themselves underwent the experiments and, even with full knowledge that these changes would be occurring, totally failed to detect them (1979: 224).

This suggests that, although the letters were seen (a claim supported by the fact that successful reading took place), the specific shapes of the letters were not. The account I have outlined provides us with a plausible way of explaining how this might be. We might hypothesize that, in honing one's ability to read English, a subject would learn to abstract away from irrelevant information concerning the particular shapes of the letters—because these can change quite dramatically between different texts—and to focus their attentions on determining which letter they are looking at, because this information is most important when it comes to determining which words are presented. If this were the case, then we would not be shocked to find that a competent reader of English was relatively inattentive to the fact that a letter has a certain shape while being attentive to the fact that the letter is of a certain kind, say, the fact of a particular letter's being a t. If competent readers were to be inattentive to facts about the shapes of the letters, we might therefore expect them to be inattentively blind to changes in those shapes. Correlatively, if competent readers were to be attentive to facts about which letter is which, we would expect them to notice changes in those facts. But, of course, these are precisely those facts that are held constant in this experiment. In this way, we can explain how the letters are seen (in virtue of facts in which they are constituents being seen), how successful reading takes place (in virtue of facts about which letters are which being seen), and how the changes are nonetheless missed (in virtue of the subject being inattentive to facts concerning the specific shapes of the letters).

Finally, consider how this modification to the thesis would account for another bizarre reading experiment described by Grimes (1996: 94). In this study, subjects are placed in front of a computer screen and directed to read lines of text. As before, the subject's eye movements are being monitored, but in this experiment, the eye tracker is used to ensure that, wherever subjects are looking, they will see coherent text. Outside of this the computer fills the screen with Xs, as shown below (the underline indicates the point of fixation):

xxx xxxxx xxxxxxx th<u>u</u>ndered inxx xxx xxx xx x xxxxxx xx xxxxx.

xxx xxxxx xxxxxxx xxxxxxxed in<u>t</u>o the sky xx x xxxxxx xx xxxxx.

Because the computer ensures that subjects always find sensible text whenever they saccade to a different part of the line, the experimenters found, as in the alternating case experiment described above, that these changes yielded no irregularities in subjects' eye movements during reading, nor any effect on subject awareness: subjects reported an experience of a solid, stable page of text—just like the page you are reading now.

The theory I have been developing would offer the following explanation of this phenomenon. When subjects fixate on a particular letter, they become aware of fine-grained facts concerning the letter fixated as well as fine-grained facts concerning some of the letters that fall either side of that letter. As far as the remainder of the line is concerned, the subject picks up on a much more coarse fact—perhaps the fact of the line's containing *more text* or some such—rather than picking up on fine-grained facts about which actual letters appear.[6]

3.4 How the World Features in Experience

This explanation of Grimes's findings can still seem surprising: when you look at the page in front of you, it seems as though you see that the entire page contains legible text, not just the 18-character window you are currently foveating. But if the results of these experiments are sound, you could be wrong—the rest of the page could contain an array of Xs. So how can we explain our confidence that this is not how things are—that we *can* actually see that the whole page is filled with readable words?

> [The reason] why our visual phenomenology is of seeing everything in front of us, derives from the fact that since the slightest flick of the eye or attention allows any part of a visual scene to be processed at will, we have the immediate feeling of availability about the whole scene.... Suppose you should ask yourself, "Am I currently consciously seeing *everything* there is to see in the scene?" How could you check that you were seeing everything? You would check by casting your attention on each element of the scene, and verify that you have the impression of consciously

6. If this sounds like an odd fact for the visual system to pick up on, consider a further experiment (reported by Dennett 1996) that suggests that it is possible for a subject to take an area to contain text without thereby taking it to contain any specific letters. In this experiment, subjects are presented with a screen full of text save for a blank area designed to fall under the subject's blind spot. Subjects report that they see text in that area, but "of course the words were not readable, the letters were not identifiable" (168–169). In such a case, subjects report being aware (wrongly, in this case) that an area of the screen contains text, without being aware that it contains any particular letters.

> seeing it. But obviously as soon as you do cast your attention on something, you see it. Conclusion, you will always have the impression of consciously seeing everything, since everything you check on, you see. (O'Regan and Noë 2001: §4.2)

This explanation of the feeling of richness available to us in a given perceptual experience fits perfectly with the account just provided: a perceptual state makes us aware of rich, detailed facts concerning the particular part of the visual scene to which we are attending, and just *enough* facts concerning the rest of the scene—the fact of the page's containing more text, for example—to enable us to garner more detailed information by shifting our attention.

Alva Noë develops this suggestion using the metaphor of *virtual presence*: "[W]e have the impression that the world is represented in full detail in consciousness because, wherever we look, we encounter detail. All the detail is present, but it is only present virtually, for example, in the way that a web site's content is present on your desktop" (2004: 49–50). According to this metaphor, there are two ways in which detail can be present. It can be *literally* present, in the way the news story you are reading is present on the Web page you are looking at—in virtue of being explicitly represented. Or it can be *virtually* present in the way that the other, linked news stories could be said to be present in virtue of being available to be looked at. Because virtually present detail is not literally present, virtually present detail is not represented explicitly, but we can still say it is present, argues Noë, inasmuch as there are repositories of this further information that will make this additional detail literally present when probed. This analogy would suggest, in the case of perceptual experience, that detail can likewise be present in two ways: by being literally present in experience or by being virtually present. And because virtual presence is not literal presence, the virtual presence of detail in experience would not require the experience to literally contain that detail; it would require only there to be a repository of this detail that can supply it when probed. This further repository of detail is usually taken to be the external world itself (O'Regan 1992: 461; Clark 2002: 185; Noë 2004: 50).

Given the importance the external world plays in this picture, one would expect that the kind of intrinsically world-involving theory of perception I have been developing would sit well alongside it. However, I suggest that the relationship is stronger than this: the adequacy of the virtual presence metaphor actually necessitates a naive realist conception of the perceptual state. To see why, suppose that perceptual experience is not intrinsically object involving. The picture of experience thus yielded would then look like this: any literally present detail would be explicitly represented in the experience (perhaps in virtue of the experience involving qualia, sense-data, rich representational content, or some such); the virtually present detail would not. As the Web page analogy suggests, this detail would be virtually present in virtue of there being "links" to that information—links that, when selected, would instantaneously replace the link with literally present information (and at the same time replace the information that had previously been literally present with a further link). Now, if the external world is assumed to be the repository of this extra detail, then if perceptual experience were not object-involving, the repositories of detail would not themselves be present in the experience. So, what component of a perceptual experience would be analogous to the links? Perhaps the links would be ill-defined sense-data (which contrive to look like text without looking like any text in particular) or relatively nonspecific representational content (representing the presence of text but not the presence of any text in particular). But if we were to conceive of the links in this way, it becomes difficult to see on what grounds "virtual presence" would qualify as a kind of *presence* at all. When I look at a page from the *New York Times* on my desktop, I am aware of the "detail" of the story I am currently looking at in the main part of the screen, and I am aware of the links to the other stories that appear in the borders of the screen. But although the links themselves are doubtlessly present, there is no real sense in which the *detail* of those stories is present on that very page, even if it can quickly be made (literally) present. So a conception of the perceptual experience as non-object-involving leaves virtual presence not looking much like presence at all.

If we adopt the kind of view of phenomenal/presentational character being developed, we can see how virtual presence could be a very real kind of presence after all. As outlined above, this view claims that when we have a perceptual experience, the presentational character of that experience is constituted by an array of facts: relatively fine-grained facts where the parts of the world we are foveating/attending to are concerned, and relatively coarse-grained facts in the other areas. What is important about this picture when it comes to the metaphor of virtual presence is that the objects that feature in coarse-grained facts are themselves the repositories of the fine-grained detail we become aware of when we attend to those objects. The object-involving aspect of this theory therefore enables the repository of fine-grained detail itself to be literally present in the experience in virtue of being a constituent of a coarse-grained fact.

Suppose I am peripherally aware of a car on the street. Because I am not attending to this vehicle, I may be aware only of coarse-grained facts in which the car features, such as the fact of its being a car, and maybe also a car of a certain shape and/or color. Yet this rudimentary awareness of the car gives me enough information to determine whether it is something I want to ignore or attend to. And if I do choose to turn my attention to it, I would then become aware of a range of fine-grained facts such as the facts of its having a dent on its door, its being made by Ford, its having a broken aerial, and so on. In such a case, the particular that is present in my experience when I look closely is one and the same particular that was present in my experience when it was only seen peripherally: the physical car itself. Even when it is only peripherally seen, then, the repository of the additional detail is literally present in my experience. In this way, we can make sense of why the virtual presence of as-yet-unseen detail qualifies as a type of presence—because the repository of that detail is present in the experience. In many ways, then, the claim that in veridical perception different subjects can pick up on different facts concerning one and the same particular enables *the world itself* to play the role that has normally been reserved for qualia, sense-data, or nonconceptual contents in a philosophical theory of perception. The very tract of the environment that we are open to in perceptual experience can do the job of providing the rich backdrop to our attentive experiences that is usually reserved for nonconceptual contents and the like.

3.5 Having the Capacity to Be a Perceiver

The preceding sections have described a number of different ways in which our awareness of worldly facts can be restricted, ranging from our perspective on the environment together with the way that environment is laid out, through to our visual acuity and the current distribution of our attentional resources. There is still a final constraint to be introduced: in order for one to become acquainted with a particular fact, or to have a particular fact feature in the presentational character of one's experience, one must have the *capacity* to see that fact or, more broadly, facts of that kind.

On the face of it, this constraint is apt to seem truistic. But it is a truism that points us in the direction of some interesting questions. To see how, consider Tim Crane's example of a scientist and a child looking at a cathode ray tube. Crane highlights this example because it is one in which our intuitions are pulled in two different directions. Because the scientist has knowledge and experience of cathode ray tubes that the child lacks, Crane suggests that there is a sense in which "the [scientist] will see it while the [child] won't.... On the other hand," he says, "it is [also] plausible to say that the child and the scientist have something perceptually in common" (1992: 136–137). The position I have been developing would account for our conflicting intuitions in such a case as follows. Both the scientist and the child "see" the cathode ray tube, and thereby have something visually in common, inasmuch as certain facts concerning the cathode ray tube—perhaps including shape facts, color facts, and so on—feature in the presentational character of both of their experiences. And then a natural explanation of the differences between the two experiences would be that there is (at least) one fact about the cathode ray tube that features in the presentational character of the scientist's, but not the child's, experience: the fact of the object's *being* a cathode ray tube. This difference will account for the sense in which we find it natural to say that the scientist sees the cathode ray tube—she sees the fact of the object's being a cathode ray tube—while the child does not.

In light of our truistic constraint, for this explanation to be available we need to accept that, while both the scientist and the child have the capacity to see certain basic facts involving the object, only the scientist has the capacity to see the fact of the object's being a cathode ray tube. Our first interesting question, then, is this: What do the scientist and the child have in common in virtue of which they both have the capacity to see certain simple facts? The second question reciprocates: In virtue of what does the scientist, but not the child, have the capacity to see the fact of the object's being a cathode ray tube? Focusing on the latter question first, we might answer, at least partly in virtue of possessing the *concept* of a cathode ray tube. If a subject's possession of the capacity to pick up on or recognize facts of certain kinds is conceptually fostered in this way, I will call such a capacity a *conceptual-recognitional* capacity.

The difference between the scientist and the child is that the former has a conceptual-recognitional capacity that the latter lacks—the capacity to pick up on the fact of the object's being a cathode ray tube. This is a recognitional capacity (indeed, strictly speaking, a *visual*-recognitional capacity) because it is a capacity to recognize, through vision, certain features in the world; it is a conceptual capacity because possession of the capacity requires the subject to possess the relevant concept. However, it is worth noting that the mere introduction of concepts does not yet serve to clarify exactly what is required to possess such a capacity, because the question of what is involved in possessing a concept is itself a matter of much debate. For instance, philosophers have often tied the very possession of concepts to the resources afforded subjects in virtue of their mastery of a language. If we were to find such a view compelling, we might therefore postulate that a subject has the concept of a cathode ray tube—and thereby the conceptual-recognitional capacity to see the fact of an object's being a cathode ray tube—if and only if she is master of the term "cathode ray tube" (or a translation thereof). In other words, the thought would be that a subject has the capacity to *see* things as cathode ray tubes only inasmuch as she has the capacity to *think of* things as cathode ray tubes.

Of course, mastery of the term alone is not sufficient for having the capacity to see facts of certain kinds. One obvious reason is that, to have the ability to *see* a fact, a subject will additionally need to have a functioning visual system. But there are other, philosophically more interesting reasons to suppose that knowing the term alone will not suffice. For example, Gregory McCulloch has developed a picture according to which "our having the experience-informing concepts we do have is constituted...by our abilities to move around and engage with the things in our surroundings" (1995: 140), and likewise, Noë has argued that part of what it is to have certain concepts is to have a range of tacit expectations as to how the appearances of certain objects will change under movement (2004: 77). On such an account, to see something *as a tomato* is to see it as something whose visual appearance will vary in certain predictable ways as we move around it; in our terminology, when we perceive the fact of an object's being a tomato, we implicitly take that object to fall under a particular pattern of sensorimotor contingencies, which in turn explains why we experience the three-dimensional nature of that object.

It may be, of course, that in reality a perceiver would not acquire mastery of the term without simultaneously mastering these sensorimotor contingencies, but this serves merely to highlight the difficulty of the task of trying to provide anything approaching a set of necessary and sufficient conditions for when a subject possesses a certain concept. This difficulty is compounded when we consider that subjects with different capacities may be said to possess a given concept to greater or lesser degrees, or perhaps in a particular sense. So, for example, one might hold that while both a scientist and a lab technician could be said to possess the concept of a cathode ray tube, the scientist's additional mastery of the equipment means that she has it to a "greater degree" than the technician. Or take the concept of redness possessed by one who cannot see; we may feel that a suitably knowledgeable blind subject could have *a* concept of redness but, being blind, could not have the concept of redness "in the same sense" as a sighted subject. Judgments of such kinds arise because, in each case, a subject possesses some of the capacities that we think important to the question of whether they possess a certain concept, while lacking others.

In discussing J. J. Gibson's theory of information pickup, Jerry Fodor and Zenon Pylyshyn argue that to answer the question, "how do people perceive that something is a shoe?" with the claim that they do so by picking up on the property of the thing's being a shoe would be to offer not an explanation, but a pseudo-explanation (1981: 142).[7] But it is important to be aware that, in the present context, this is far from all the explanation I am envisaging. For a start, I have already insisted that a subject has the capacity to pick up on the fact of something's being a shoe only if the subject has the concept of a shoe, and as the preceding discussion indicates, there is going to be a substantive story to tell about what is required for a subject to possess that concept. And while this is not the appropriate time to detour into full-blown theorizing about concepts, for the kinds of reasons laid out above I would expect that story to appeal in part to the highly specific interactions with the environment that the subject has enjoyed. So, having acknowledged that there are these big explanatory questions waiting in the wings, it is clearly far from trivial to say that

7. If, however, we were to read the objection as claiming that we do not perceive higher order properties of this kind *at all*, then I would be unconvinced—on the face it, we *do* pick up on properties of this kind. For example, it looks as though I can just see that the machine in front of me has the property of being a computer. Why might we think we do not pick up on such properties? One significant reason would be that we could be wrong—that we could conceivably see an identical box and have an identical experience, but fail to pick up on the fact of its being a computer because the box is merely a fake and there is no such fact to pick up on. Yet while I acknowledge the force of this motivation, in line with the general disjunctive approach being taken here, the fact that things can go wrong in deceptive cases will not be allowed to constrain the successful cases. In later chapters, I present an account of how to make sense of such mistakes without supposing that we cannot perceive such facts in the veridical cases. Inasmuch as that theory is successful, it would then remove the force of this motivation for thinking that higher order properties of this kind cannot be perceived in the first place.

the fact of something's being a cathode ray tube is enabled to feature in the presentational character of a subject's experiences only if the subject has the capacity to pick up on such facts, given that having this capacity requires the subject to possess the concept of a cathode ray tube.

There is also the question of what determines *which* of our many conceptual-recognitional capacities might be exploited in any given experience. Again, I do not have much to say about this issue, but one thing I can say is that the deployment of such capacities in experience is not in any sense an *activity*—something that we, as agents, *do*. As John McDowell says when defending a similar claim: "In experience one finds oneself saddled with content. One's conceptual capacities have already been brought into play, in the content's being available to one, before one has any choice in the matter" (1994: 10). Substitute "presentational character" for "content" here, and I fully endorse McDowell's claim. So the claim that conceptual-recognitional capacities are operative in experience should not be taken to commit us to the claim that the subject chooses or decides which of these capacities to deploy; experience can remain, in essence, a passive occurrence. Of course, this serves only to highlight the absence of a positive answer to the question of what, if not the choice of the subject, determines which conceptual-recognitional capacities are passively deployed on any given occasion. Inasmuch as I have a substantive claim to make about this, it will be that the conceptual-recognitional capacities that are deployed in veridical perception will be primarily determined by the nature and layout of the environment the subject is facing, together with the subject's mental makeup and learning history (possibly including recent visual encounters).[8] And although I do not further defend this claim here, I will clarify it as I present the theories of hallucination and illusion in chapters 4 and 6, respectively.

8. I include "recent visual encounters" to account for phenomena such as perceptual priming and stabilization, which occur when prior processing of a visual presentation has measurable effects on a subject's performance in subsequent tasks. For example, in classical priming models, a subject who has already been exposed to a picture of a cup will more quickly recognize that a fragmented picture they are asked to identify is also a picture of a cup (Srinivas 1993), and a subject who is presented with the word "happy" will be more likely to classify a term subsequently presented as pleasant (Greenwald et al. 1996). Importantly, where classical perceptual priming need not be conscious—it can occur even when the priming stimulus is effectively rendered invisible by backward masking (Bar and Biederman 1998)—the closely related phenomenon of stabilization, which occurs when previous conscious interpretation of an ambiguous stimulus makes a subject more likely to resolve a subsequent ambiguity in a particular direction, seems to occur only when there is conscious awareness of the stimulus (Kanai and Verstraten 2006).

If the possession or otherwise of conceptual-recognitional capacities is the critical *difference* between the scientist and the child, could we offer a comparable answer to the first question of what the scientist and child have in *common* in virtue of which they can both see certain basic facts? Because conceptual-recognitional capacities are capacities that subjects can have only if they have the right kinds of concepts, to do so would be to claim that a subject only has the capacity to see facts *at all*—in other words, to have conscious perceptual experiences at all—inasmuch as that subject possesses concepts. Given this, the plausibility of this line depends on how demanding a criterion one places on the possession of concepts. As we have seen, one might place demanding language-based requirements on concept possession. If the capacity to see any fact at all were to be a conceptual-recognitional capacity, then the resultant view would therefore be one on which a subject only has the capacity to see facts at all inasmuch as that subject has a mastery of a language. This is the kind of view held by McDowell. He argues that, for the kinds of recognitional capacities that are operative in our perceptual sensitivity to the environment to underpin conscious experience, those same capacities "must also be able to be exercised in judgements, and that requires them to be rationally linked into a whole system of concepts and conceptions within which their possessor engages in a continuing activity of adjusting her thinking to experience" (1994: 47). And as he later makes clear, McDowell conceives of these capacities as ones that nonlinguistic creatures such as animals and infants lack (114–125). If we were to follow McDowell in placing demanding language-based requirements on the ability of a subject to have facts feature in presentational character—indeed, to have experiences with presentational character at all—we would thereby be compelled to deny that nonlinguistic creatures such as animals and infants have perceptual experiences as we understand them.

It is important to note that the naive realist does not *have* to be so demanding in response to the more general question of what the scientist and child have in common in virtue of which they both have the capacity to see facts of certain kinds. It would be entirely consistent with naive realism to hold that our capacities to see certain rudimentary facts are not *conceptual*-recognitional capacities at all, and instead that subjects have the capacity to see such facts simply in virtue of having, say, a fully functional visual system. If such a position were adopted, then the naive realist could claim that a range of basic facts—perhaps including shape and color facts—could be perceived without placing any conceptual requirements on the subject whatsoever. This seems to be the general line taken by Johnston, who argues that "in order to see an F I need not conceptualize, classify, or think of it as an F. This is the sense in which visual experience can be *conceptually undemanding*" (2006: 283).

While I have sympathy with Johnston's claim, I also have some sympathy for McDowell's contention that, for a subject to have conscious perceptual experiences, the capacities that underpin that subject's ability to perceive facts must be integrated into his or her cognitive systems in a way which at least enables subjects to, in some sense, "adjust their thinking to experience." My reason for this derives from the thought that our having the capacity to perceive any given fact seems to go hand in hand with our having the capacity to think about that very fact. This, it seems to me, is the intuition that McDowell is attempting to capture with his claim that, in any experience that presents a shade of color for which we appear to lack a concept, "one can give linguistic expression to a concept that is exactly as fine-grained as the experience, by uttering a phrase like 'that shade,' in which the demonstrative exploits the presence of the sample" (1994: 57). This example highlights the way in which we can think about anything we see, even though we may only be able to linguistically articulate what we are seeing/thinking about using a demonstrative expression (that shade, that shape, that pattern, etc.).

This consideration suggests that all of our recognitional capacities—all of our capacities to have facts of certain kinds feature in the presentational characters of our visual experiences—are, to some extent, *conceptual*-recognitional capacities; they are the kinds of capacities that allow us to think about what is seen, and therefore that require the subject to possess concepts. However, there is a way in which we can accommodate the claim that we can think about anything we can see without thereby making language a prerequisite for conscious experience. Robert Kirk argues that, to qualify as a conscious perceiver—in our terms, to be able to have experiences with phenomenal character—a system must be able to "(i) *initiate and control* its own behaviour on the basis of incoming and retained information: information that it can use; (ii) *acquire and retain information* about its environment; (iii) *interpret* information; (iv) *assess its situation*; (v) *choose* between alternative courses of action on the basis of retained and incoming information; [and] (vi) *have goals*" (2005: 89). There are clear similarities between this requirement and McDowell's—both Kirk and McDowell require the deliveries of a discriminatory capacity to be suitably linked up with other general cognitive systems—but Kirk goes to great lengths to "desophisticate" his framework and show that it can be understood in a way that does not presuppose that the possessor of these capacities is also a language user. Such a theory could thereby explain how it is that we can think about anything we see without thereby precluding animals and infants from being perceivers.

With a theory of this kind, we can allow that any capacity to perceive a fact—to have a fact feature in the presentational character of one's experiences—is a conceptual-recognitional capacity without thereby binding our very ability to have conscious visual experiences to the possession of language. Yet having said this, such an approach does not come at the cost of making higher cognitive functions such as language irrelevant to the facts we can perceive. Indeed, a theory that maintains that rich, sophisticated facts (such as the fact of an object's being a cathode ray tube) can feature in presentational character ought surely to insist that we are not aware of all these facts from the outset, but rather that our capacity to become aware of facts can increase. As Johnston is keen to emphasize, even if "some of what we sense requires little if any in the way of deploying our conceptual sophistication, the totality of what we sense, and so the totality of [facts] with which we are presented, is immensely richer thanks to our conceptual sophistication" (2006: 283).

The foundation against which this proliferation occurs would, of course, be a subject's ability to perceive a certain array of basic facts, and I have tentatively endorsed the idea that a subject might have the capacity to see such rudimentary facts simply in virtue of possessing fully functional visual systems that are suitably connected to a cognitive system of the kind described by Kirk. This could be what the scientist and child share in virtue of which they can both perceive basic facts. Then we can "conceive our maturing perceptual selves as becoming... progressively refined instruments for detecting more precisely features that await discovery" (Vision 1997: 20). As the subject acquires a more complex behavioral repertoire and/or learns a language, further sophistication is added that in turn provides the subject with capacities to perceive various *new* facts—such as the fact of something's being a cathode ray tube—to which it had previously been blind.[9]

9. Johnston is also keen to stress, as am I, that "to admit this is crucially not to grant that *the exemplifications themselves are the product of an antecedent synthesis under concepts....* Conceptually refined sensing does not *constitute* its objects. It is just that having certain concepts requires certain abilities, and that among these abilities are characteristic refinements of the capacity to sense what is there in the environment anyway" (2006: 283–284).

3.6 Conclusion: Naive Realism and the Problems of Consciousness

We have now reached the point where we can draw together the different elements of the naive realist account of veridical perception developed in this chapter. The point from which we began was that, when we have a visual experience, we are consciously acquainted with a particular tract of our environment. The theoretical gloss I have given to this over the course of the chapter is that the phenomenal character of a visual experience is the property of acquainting the subject with a selection of the facts that inhabit the tract of the environment the subject perceives. The particular array of facts that the experience relates the subject to—and hence the phenomenal character of the experience itself—is determined by

- the distribution of objects and properties in the environment,
- the subject's position in/perspective on that environment,
- the nature of vision in general and the idiosyncrasies of the subject's visual system,
- the current distribution of the subject's attentional resources, and
- the subject's conceptual resources.

Taken together, these considerations enable us to make sense of the many different ways in which veridical experiences of the same tract of the environment may differ in phenomenal character.

This view of experience also offers us new insights into some familiar and long-standing philosophical problems of consciousness. Take, for example, the following expression of Joseph Levine's contention that there is an explanatory gap between consciousness and the underlying physical/functional processing:

> Let's call the physical story for seeing red "R" and the physical story for seeing green "G." ...When we consider the qualitative character of our visual experiences when looking at ripe McIntosh apples, as opposed to looking at ripe cucumbers, the difference is not explained by appeal to G and R. For R doesn't really explain why I have the one kind of qualitative experience—the kind I have when looking at ripe McIntosh apples—and not the other. (1983: 357–358)

If naive realism is correct, then the reason that Levine cannot find the answer he is looking for is because he is searching in the wrong place. The difference in what it is like to see a ripe McIntosh apple and what it is like to see a ripe cucumber is not explained by the differences in the underlying processing—instead, it is explained by the different color properties that the two objects possess. When we see a ripe McIntosh apple, the phenomenal character of our experience is its property of acquainting us with the fact of the object's being *red;* when we see a ripe cucumber, it is the experience's property of acquainting us with the fact of the object's being *green.* This is where the difference between what it is like to have the two experiences is to be found.[10]

What this story doesn't tell us is why it has to be like *anything at all* to be a system undergoing the kinds of physical/functional processing characteristic of R and G. This is a second dimension to the explanatory gap and is also the central plank in David Chalmers's contention that there is a special "hard problem" of consciousness: "Even when we have explained all the cognitive and behavioral functions in the vicinity of experience—perceptual discrimination, categorization, internal access, verbal report—there may still remain a further unanswered question: *Why is the performance of these functions accompanied by [a conscious] experience?*" (1995/1997: 12).

Naive realism alone doesn't offer an answer to this question. However, it can be employed as a supplement to a certain thread in the pro-functionalist literature of the past 30 years which has attempted to argue that, in fact, the physical/functional truths do entail that we are conscious subjects. This thread begins with Sydney Shoemaker (1975), who argues that if we can have knowledge of the phenomenal character of an experience, as he thinks we surely can, then that phenomenal character must have causal consequences. He thereby concludes that a creature whose states lacked phenomenal character could not be functionally identical to one of us. If this were so, then all the functional truths about us would in fact entail that we were phenomenally conscious. Although Ned Block (1980) pointed out some serious flaws in Shoemaker's original argument,[11] Tye (2006) has defended a version of this contention by

10. Of course, this is not to say that the physical stories R and G are irrelevant. On the contrary, this kind of story is crucial when it comes to explaining what is involved in a subject's having the capacity to be acquainted with a particular fact. More on this in chapter 5.

11. Block countered with the claim that, even if, in us, phenomenal character is necessary for an experience to have the causal consequences it does, it is possible that something else may have those causal consequences in a different system (1980). Shoemaker replies in his (1981), but my purpose here is not to address these issues in detail, merely to show the presence of this line of thought.

asking us to imagine that we perform an "exchanger operation" on him and his putatively nonconscious yet functionally identical twin, NN. This operation has the consequence that Tye loses all his phenomenal states other than his phenomenal memories and has them replaced by NN's ersatz phenomenal states. Correspondingly, NN loses his ersatz phenomenal states and has them replaced by Tye's true phenomenal states. Because Tye and NN are, *ex hypothesi*, functional duplicates, an exchange of functionally equivalent states should leave them functional duplicates still. But as Tye points out, while it is reasonable to suppose that he will mourn the loss of his phenomenal states for merely ersatz ones, it is implausible to suppose that NN would mourn the loss of his ersatz phenomenal states given that he has acquired real conscious states! If this is coherent, it suggests that the presence or absence of phenomenal consciousness does indeed have functional consequences as Shoemaker originally suggested, and hence that the functional truths will indeed entail the presence of phenomenal consciousness.

In addition to this kind of contention, which argues that functional duplicates of conscious subjects will necessarily themselves be conscious subjects, Andy Clark (2000) and Kirk (2005) focus on specific functional capacities that, they argue, imply the presence of phenomenal consciousness. Clark contends that if a system has the capacity to know, noninferentially, that it *sees* the difference between, say, a red cup and a green cup, rather than hearing or feeling the difference, then this entails that there will be something it is like for the system. Likewise, Kirk suggests that if changes in a system's environment are forced upon the system in such a way that it is enabled to respond instantly and appropriately to those changes—that is, respond without having to *act* (e.g., guess or probe) to discover what has changed regardless of whether these changes are related to its current plans and goals—then there must be something it is like to be that system.

When these considerations stand alone, they fail to adequately address all the concerns that motivate those who think that there is a hard problem/explanatory gap. The problem is, even if these arguments do show that there has to be *something it is like* to be a system performing the right kinds of physical/functional processing, they do not answer Levine's concern as to why processing of a particular kind should be accompanied by the particular phenomenal character it is. Thus, Tye accepts that his argument "does not fully close the explanatory gap—in particular, it does not explain why, once a particular functional organization is in place, an experience is like *that* and not like something else" (2006: 164), and Clark suggests that "we must be humble. The argument…shows only (at best) that…it must look like something when, for example, we judge that one cup is red and the other green. Why then…does it look *like this*? Our story doesn't say" (2000: 36).

For this reason, even if these considerations are felt to be somewhat compelling, they are nonetheless unlikely to convince the proponent of the hard problem/explanatory gap. Yet when this kind of story is supplemented with a naive realist view of experience, the functionalist component of the picture is thereby released from the problematic responsibility of having to explain *what* it is like to have an experience. When placed alongside naive realism, the role of the functionalist considerations is merely to explain why there is something it is like rather than nothing at all—and the kind of story given above is far better placed to do this than to explain the specifics of what it is like to have an experience. In essence, then, we can see the functional story as telling us what kinds of functional underpinnings are necessary for a subject to be acquainted with elements of his or her environment. What it is like to have the experience can then be explained by the elements of the environment with which the subject is thereby acquainted.[12]

This approach therefore offers to provide the most intelligible, transparent explanation yet of just how it could be that the truths about phenomenal consciousness supervene on the physical/functional. In fixing the physical facts, the facts about how the objects in the environment

12. Could the representationalist appropriate this motivation by arguing that, if acquaintance with worldly redness can account for what it is like to have an experience, then representation of worldly redness should also suffice? Not as things stand, for two related reasons. First, most extant representationalist theories do *not* claim that the representation of redness by a state alone suffices for there to be something it is like to be in that state; they generally claim that the state with content also needs to play the right functional role (e.g., Tye 1995: 143–144; Dretske 1995: 19; Lycan 1996: 11; for more on this objection, see Kriegel 2002). I think there is a reason for this, which in turn points us toward the second problem for a representationalist in trying to appropriate this motivation: the account of what is required for a state to represent a property. A functional account of acquaintance, along the lines of the above, is supposed to make it transparent why there has to be *something* it is like to be acquainted with a property; *what* it is like then being supplied by the property itself. But equivalent naturalistic theories of representational content—say, that a state represents *P* if it has been selected by evolution to covary with *P* (Tye 1995: 153; Dretske 1995: 15)—do not even attempt to claim that there has to be something it is like to be in a state that represents *P* (for more on this kind of concern, see Maund 2002: §1.6; Thompson 2008). So, as things stand, naive realists are in a much better position than representationalists to use this as a motivation for their respective theories.

are located, shaped, colored, and so on are thereby fixed; in fixing the functional facts, the facts about which environmental elements the subject is acquainted with are thereby fixed. And because the phenomenal character of an experience is its property of acquainting a subject with certain worldly features, this is just to say that the phenomenal characters of the subject's experiences are thereby fixed. In this way, naive realism offers us new and exciting insights into some traditional problems of consciousness. Of course, this is not to say that naive realism *solves* these problems. Naive realism as presented here is a theory about veridical visual consciousness, while the hard problem/explanatory gap considerations pertain to consciousness in all its many forms, visual and otherwise, veridical and otherwise. But it is nevertheless an interesting enough result to make it worthwhile to consider whether naive realism can be defended from the arguments from hallucination and illusion. I will begin this task in chapter 4.

4

Hallucination

Now that I have laid out the naive realist theory of veridical perception, the shadow of the argument from hallucination looms large. In hallucination, we are in a state that seems to us just like a veridical perception of a worldly fact or facts, yet in which there are no suitable facts for the hallucinatory state to acquaint us with.[1] Because adopting a broadly disjunctivist approach puts us in a position to provide an account of the hallucinatory state that doesn't have to follow that of veridical perception, the absence of appropriate worldly facts does not mean that we have to endorse some kind of strange realm of objective nonfacts for the subject to be acquainted with in hallucination (contra Dodd 1995: 163). But it does serve to counterpoint the magnitude of the task that still awaits us—that of providing a theory of hallucination that accounts for the possibility of a nonveridical mental event being indiscriminable from a case of acquaintance with the world. This is the task of the present chapter.

1. One slight complication: many hallucinations actually occur against a background of experience of the world. This suggests that a state might be, at the same time, part hallucination and part veridical perception. For the present, however, I propose to treat of the limiting case of pure hallucination. Chapter 6 considers mixed cases in more detail.

I begin by discussing the concept of indiscriminability and considering what kinds of constraints the very fact of indiscriminability places on the hallucinatory state or event. I will then go on to discuss M. G. F. Martin's work on these issues, beginning in section 4.2 with his contention that the naive realist must also take care to avoid presenting an account of hallucination that 'screens off' the naive realist aspects of veridical perception from playing an explanatory role in shaping the contours of the subject's conscious experience. The following section then outlines Martin's accounts of indiscriminability and hallucination and considers some problems that his position faces. In the light of this, I then go on to present an alternative theory of hallucination and show how this can explain everything that needs to be explained while avoiding the difficulties that face Martin's theory. As we shall see, the most striking feature of the theory I defend is that it incorporates the claim that hallucinations lack phenomenal character altogether.[2] Before I explain and defend this surprising claim, let me begin by clarifying precisely what theoretical commitments we take on when we endorse the datum that hallucinations can be indiscriminable from veridical perceptions.

4.1 Indiscriminability and Identity

In his definition of the everyday conception of indiscriminability, Timothy Williamson highlights some features of the concept that are relevant to our purposes. He defines indiscriminability as follows: "*a* is indiscriminable from *b* for a subject at a time if and only if at that time the subject is not able to discriminate between *a* and *b*, that is, if and only if at that time the subject is not able to activate (acquire or employ) the relevant kind of knowledge that *a* and *b* are distinct" (1990: 8). I say more about the right-hand side of this biconditional in due course, but for now, I focus on a feature of the left-hand side: Williamson is explicitly defining a notion of indiscriminability that is doubly relative—it is relative *to a subject* and it is relative *to a time*. The subject relativity is there to

2. Interestingly, Scott Sturgeon, whom I cast as an opponent of disjunctivism in chapter 2, has more recently suggested that there will be "plenty of dialectical settings in which [a disjunctivism that maintains that hallucinations lack phenomenal character] is the best motivated version of disjunctivism. There may even be some in which it is the best motivated view of visual experience full stop" (2008: 142).

account for the fact that you may be able to discriminate between two things where I cannot—perhaps because you have sharper eyesight than I do or know what you are looking for. The temporal relativity is there to account for the possibility that I may be unable to distinguish between two things at one time, yet be able to distinguish between them at a different time. For example, if I am looking at two people at a distance or in half-light, I may well be unable to make a discrimination. According to this definition, those individuals are therefore indiscriminable (by me, at that time). But bring them closer to me, or turn up the lights, and I may then be able to tell one from the other. So at this later time when the conditions under which I am attempting the discrimination have improved, the individuals are now discriminable (again, by me, at that time).

With these sources of relativity made explicit, we can see that there are a number of different factors that could go to determine whether two things are found to be indiscriminable. The most conspicuous factor lies, of course, in the similarity of the things to be discriminated: as a general rule, the more similar two things are, the more difficult they will be to tell apart, and indeed, in the limiting case, two qualitatively identical objects will be impossible to tell apart. In addition to the similarity of the two objects, however, the double relativity of the notion of indiscriminability makes it clear that a range of other relevant factors relating to the 'discriminatory context'—the context under which the discrimination is attempted—can affect whether two things are discriminable. The discriminatory context includes such things as the subject's discriminatory capacities and the observation conditions in which the discrimination is attempted. When this is taken into account, we can see that it is not necessary that, for two things to be found to be indiscriminable, they must be the same in some intrinsic way.

This leaves open the logical room for the naive realist to deny, as Martin contends they must do (see section 4.2), "that two experiences, one of which is indiscriminable from the other, must share phenomenal character" (2006: 367). Yet this does run counter to a tempting line of thought: that the indiscriminability of hallucinations from veridical perceptions is one of those special cases in which indiscriminability is grounded in a certain kind of identity—identity in phenomenal character, or what we might call phenomenal identity. Indeed, A. D. Smith (2008) goes so far as to claim that hallucinations, at least as the term is used in philosophical contexts, are phenomenally identical to veridical perceptions as a matter of definition. So if we are to render plausible the denial that indiscriminability entails phenomenal identity, we need to offer a diagnosis of why this misleading line of thought can seem so tempting. One reason for this, I suspect, lies in the assumption that neural replication could produce a hallucinatory experience with the same phenomenal character as a veridical perception. But as noted in chapter 2, this assumption turns on a premise that the naive realist is committed to rejecting. A possible second reason turns on the thought that it is simply a conceptual truth about phenomenal character that, if two states are indiscriminable, they must therefore share phenomenal character.

When we bear in mind the specifics of our employment of this terminology, we can see that it has no such consequence. When these terms were introduced, we discussed Lycan's contention that the 'something it is like' terminology is incurably infected with ambiguity and, in response to this concern, determined to restrict the use of the terms to the sense in which there being something it is like to be in a given mental state is solely a matter of that state and its properties, and not a matter of the subject's having any higher order thoughts, beliefs, or experiences that are directed at that state.[3] So, with the way we are using the 'something it is like' terminology, there is no straightforward entailment from one's *thinking* or *judging* that there is something particular it is like to be in a mental state, to its actually *being* like that to be in the mental state, as the reasoning above would require.[4] For example, imagine being hypnotized to think that what it is like for you, right now, is peculiar in some way or another. There is no reason to assume that, to make you think such a thing, the hypnotist would have to proceed by altering the phenomenal character of your experiential state in some special, peculiar

3. Importantly, this claim does not beg the question against those who hold a higher order theory of consciousness. Lycan, for example, allows that a mental state might have redness as its phenomenal character, yet that this mental state will not be a conscious mental state unless it is monitored by a faculty of inner sense (1996: 76; see also Rosenthal 1992: 198, who allows that a mental state can have sensory character without being conscious for the same kind of reason). Higher order theorists will therefore view the present discussion as simply developing a theory of (mere) first-order phenomenal character rather than phenomenal consciousness in (their) full-blooded sense.

4. At least, this cannot be assumed without further theoretical commitments. For example, if one were to "attribute to responsible subjects potential infallibility about the course of their experiences" (Martin 2004: 51), one could thereby insist that indiscriminability entailed phenomenal identity. The point I am trying to make here is merely that, given the way we are using the terms—with phenomenal character as a metaphysically robust property of experiences—it is not a *conceptual* truth that indiscriminability entails identity of phenomenal character.

way.[5] With the way I am using the terms, it is possible for one to think that what it is like to have one's experience is thus-and-so without its actually being like that. Indeed, as David Rosenthal notes in his discussions of his higher order thought theory of consciousness, when the terminology is used in this way it leaves open the possibility of having a higher order thought that we are in a first-order mental state in the absence of any first-order state at all (1990/1997: 744).

4.2 The Problem of Explanatory Screening Off

If we do not take it for granted that indiscriminability entails identity in phenomenal character, then the question of what to say about the phenomenal character of hallucination remains open. One constraint, of course, is that whatever we say must be shown to be compatible with the indiscriminability of hallucination from veridical perception. In his discussions of these matters, Martin raises another:

> Suppose we do get a further specification of the kind of mental event that occurs in the non-privileged [i.e., nonveridical] circumstances. If what marks these cases out in the first place is just that they involve the absence of perception, then one may worry that whatever fixes what they have in common with each other will apply equally to any case of perception.... Now if the common element is sufficient to explain all the relevant phenomena in the various cases of illusion and hallucination, one may also worry that it must be sufficient in the case of perception as well. In that case, disjunctivism is threatened with viewing its favoured conception of perception as explanatorily redundant. (2004: 46)

This has become known as the "problem of explanatory screening off" (Martin 2004: 71). To see how it plays out, suppose that the naive realist supplies a positive account of the mechanisms that suffice for a hallucination to have a property, P, that in turn suffices to explain "all the relevant phenomena." The concern is that, if these mechanisms are also operational in the case of veridical perception, then this would likewise suffice for property P, which would, *ex hypothesi*, explain everything that needs to be explained. This common property would thereby threaten to 'screen off' those properties that are unique to the veridical

5. Interestingly, Smith agrees (2008: 185). Martin also makes the same point using an example of delusion (2006: 389).

case—in our case, relational properties of acquaintance with elements of the mind-independent world—from having the kind of role in explaining our experience of the world that is so central to the naive realist picture.

One option would be to bite the bullet and accept that there is massive, systematic overdetermination in the veridical cases, but this would seem to be a last, and somewhat desperate, resort. Another option that may seem available would be for the naive realist to deny that the mechanisms that suffice for the explanatory property in the hallucinatory case are also operational in veridical experience. The concern with this proposal is that, given the nature of hallucination, it would seem that whatever mechanisms suffice for the explanatory property in the case of hallucination would be physically internal to the subject. Yet at least in the limiting cases of neural replication, there need be no internal physical differences between a perceiving and a hallucinating subject, so any account of how these mechanisms could possibly fail to function in the veridical case runs the risk of looking implausibly ad hoc. As an example of this, Howard Robinson considers what options might be available if the positive proposal were that neural activity would cause a mental image in the case of hallucination:

> If the mechanism or brain state is a sufficient causal condition for the production of an image... when the table and wall are not there, why is it not so sufficient when they are present? Does the brain state mysteriously know how it is being produced; does it, by some extra sense, discern whether the table is there or not and act accordingly, or does the table, when present, inhibit the production of an image by some sort of action at a distance? (1994: 154)

An adequate naive realist account of hallucination therefore faces at least the following two constraints. First, it should be compatible with the indiscriminability of hallucination from veridical perception. Second, it should ensure that the acquaintance properties that are unique to the veridical case should not be screened off from playing the critical explanatory role that the naive realist assigns to them.

A key aim of Martin's theorizing about indiscriminability and hallucination is to provide a way of thinking about hallucination that avoids the screening off concern without falling into the kind of implausibility Robinson outlines. I explain this shortly, but to set the scene for these discussions it will be instructive to first return to the right-hand side of Williamson's definition of indiscriminability and highlight the ways in which it fails to provide an adequate way to conceive of the indiscriminability of perception and hallucination, because this will help to clarify some of the details of Martin's approach.

The first concern is that, as we saw, Williamson suggests that objects *a* and *b* will be indiscriminable for a subject if and only if "the subject is not able to activate (acquire or employ) the relevant kind of knowledge that *a* and *b* are distinct." Yet while defining indiscriminability in this way may suffice for our everyday notion of indiscriminability—in which discrimination is essentially a comparative act that requires the discriminator to consider two things, which may be presented either simultaneously or consecutively, and reach a judgment about whether they are the same or different—when we endorse the claim that a hallucination is indiscriminable from a veridical perceptual experience, we should not be taken to be asserting that the hallucination will be indiscriminable from a particular token experience. Moreover, we should not be taken to be committing ourselves to the claim that a hallucinating subject will have actually had a veridical perceptual experience of the kind that the hallucination is claimed to be indiscriminable from. And even in cases where the subject can be taken to have had such an experience, we are certainly not intending to claim that they have this experience at the same time as the hallucination, nor that the experiences are had in anything like the kind of temporal proximity that might underpin an attempt at consecutive discrimination as we usually understand it.

This raises the question of exactly how we should interpret the assertion that a hallucination is indiscriminable from a veridical perception if we are not thereby intending to assert that there are two events—one perceptual and one hallucinatory—that the subject undergoes and then fails to tell apart. Now it might be tempting to read the claim counterfactually, as claiming that *if* the subject were to have had a perceptual experience of the relevant kind and the hallucinatory experience (presumably in close temporal succession), *then* the subject would have been unable to tell one from the other. But this would seem to introduce extraneous considerations concerning the role of memory (Farkas 2006: 211–213; Siegel 2008: 209); what is more, if we do bracket the claim that neural replication will bring about phenomenally identical experiences, it is not even clear that this counterfactual would be true. If we don't simply *assume* that we are dealing with a phenomenally identical hallucination (of a certain kind), what other reasons do we have for assuming that, if *this* hallucinatory experience either followed, or was followed by, a veridical perception of that very kind, the subject would not notice any difference? This is not the case for dreams, for example. Even though dreams can seem quite real while one is dreaming, the vast majority of people have no difficulty in distinguishing between dream experiences and perceptual experiences once they have woken up. So, even if a hallucination is mistaken by a subject for a veridical perception of a certain kind, we should not thereby simply assume that, if a subject were to suddenly find his hallucination supplanted by a veridical perception of the relevant kind (or vice versa), he would be unable to tell the difference between the two experiences.

If we do not read the indiscriminability claim counterfactually, then we need to explain what it means to say that a hallucination is indiscriminable from a veridical perception when (1) there is no implication that the subject of the hallucination has actually *had* a perceptual experience of the kind the hallucination is claimed to be indiscriminable from, and (2) there is no implication that, *if* the subject were to have (had) such a perceptual experience, he *would* find it indiscriminable from the hallucination he is actually having. To do this, Martin suggests that, rather than employ a straightforward *de re* notion of indiscriminability as Williamson does, we should instead employ a *plural* notion of indiscriminability, such that a hallucination of an F "is such that it is not possible to know through reflection that it is not one of the veridical perceptions [of an F]" (2006: 364).

This notion of plural indiscriminability, however, is potentially ambiguous.[6] To say that it is not possible to know that mental event, *e*, is not one of the *V*s could be interpreted as claiming that it is not possible to know that *e* is not *V1*, and that it is not possible to know that *e* is not *V2*,...and that it is not possible to know that *e* is not *Vn*. The problem with this reading is that Martin makes it clear, in a footnote (2006: 364), that he wants to resist the claim that a veridical perception of an F is indiscriminable from a hallucination of an F (in other words, that the indiscriminability relation is symmetrical). But because *de re* indiscriminability is symmetrical—to say that *x* is indiscriminable from *y* entails that *y* is indiscriminable from *x*—each conjunct of the plural indiscriminability claim would seem to be symmetrical as well, thus rendering the plural indiscriminability claim itself symmetrical. An alternative reading, which avoids this difficulty, is suggested by Scott Sturgeon, who characterizes Martin's position in *predicative* form, such that the indiscriminability claim is taken to assert that "what one cannot

6. Thanks to Benj Hellie for pointing this out to me.

know by reflection...is...that the episode does not have the feature of being" a veridical perception of an F (Sturgeon 2006: 195). This interpretation seems to both do the job Martin requires of it—in particular, it avoids the implications outlined above—and enables him to hold that the indiscriminability relation is not symmetrical. With such a conception of indiscriminability in hand, Martin then tells us that, "when it comes to...the hallucinatory experience, nothing more can be said than the relational and epistemological claim that it is indiscriminable from the perception.... [I]t is nothing but a situation which could not be told apart from veridical perception" (2004: 72).[7]

On Martin's view, the property that a hallucination has in virtue of which it has the effects that it does is a *negative epistemic* property—it is the property of not being knowably distinct from (being indiscriminable from) a veridical perception of a certain kind. "Why did James shriek like that? He was in a situation indiscriminable from the veridical perception of a spider.... [W]ith no detectable difference between this situation and such a perception, it must seem[8] to him as if a spider is there and so he reacts in the same way" (2004: 68). So the negative epistemic property of being indiscriminable from a veridical perception of an F can explain everything that needs to be explained.[9]

Because veridical perceptions are indiscriminable from themselves, this property is common to both the veridical and the nonveridical

7. Strictly speaking, Martin restricts this claim to causally matching hallucinations—hallucinations with the same proximal causes as veridical perceptions—but this restriction need not concern us here.

8. As Martin notes, "seems" talk can sometimes be used to "talk of sensory states or events and sometimes simply to indicate a subject's evidential position or inclination to believe" (2004: 66). In the present context, "seems" is to be understood in the purely epistemological sense.

9. The reader may be wondering why, in characterizing Martin's views, I have not done so using the phenomenal character terminology I have employed thus far. This is because I am not confident in my interpretation of Martin's take on the question of the phenomenal character of hallucination. As I understand it, his position is that there is something it is like to hallucinate, that it is the hallucination's indiscriminability property that would type the experience by what it is like to have it, and that we can therefore identify the indiscriminability property as the phenomenal character of the hallucination. This interpretation is supported by claims such as these: "Surely the condition of introspective indiscriminability guarantees that phenomenal consciousness is present" (2006: 375); "there is nothing more to the character of the...hallucination than that it can't be told apart through reflection from the veridical perception" (370). However, because I am not confident in this interpretation, nor is it crucial to this discussion, I mention this only in a footnote.

scenarios and the screening off concern thereby comes into play. But Martin suggests that, when we pay attention to the relation that such a negative epistemic property bears to the property unique to the veridical situation, we see that the screening off problem does not apply in such cases. To see why, consider the following analogy. The property of being an unattended bag in an airport will cause a security alert despite there being nothing intrinsically threatening about an unattended bag. So why does this property cause a security alert? Because of the relation it bears to the property of being a bomb in an airport. Whatever explanatory potential the property of being an unattended bag in an airport has in explaining why there is a security alert is inherited from the property of being a bomb in an airport due to the relationship the two properties bear to one another. The same goes for the negative epistemic property of being indiscriminable from a veridical perception of an F. Whatever explanatory potential this property has is inherited from the property of actually *being* a veridical perception of an F. In the case of James and the spider just discussed, the indiscriminability property only explains James's shrieking because he is scared of spiders and therefore actually *seeing* a spider is a reason for fear. So to explain James's shrieking, we need not only to appeal to his situation's being indiscriminable from a veridical perception of a spider, but also to the fact that a veridical perception of a spider constitutes, for James, a reason to shriek. So, as Martin concludes, "cases of inherited or dependent explanatory potential offer us exceptions to the general model of common properties screening off special ones" (2004: 70).

While Martin's account of hallucination does avoid the screening off concern, it faces other problems. Recall the relevant conception of indiscriminability: x is indiscriminable from a veridical perception of an F if and only if x is such that it is not possible to know through reflection that it is not a veridical perception of an F. There are two key features of the right-hand side of this definition that cause problems for Martin: first, the restriction to the relevant knowledge being acquired 'through reflection'; second, the question of how to interpret the modality present in "not possible to know." I discuss these difficulties in turn.

The appeal to 'through reflection' is introduced into the picture to rule out the possibility that a hallucinating subject might come to know that his experience is not a veridical perception of an F from testimony. As Martin says, "If I... subject you to an expensive visual-cortical stimulator so as to induce in you the hallucination of an orange, it seems quite conceivable that I should put you in a situation which in a certain respect is just like seeing an orange" (2006: 364). But, of course, if you have been told that this experiment is going to be performed on you, then you know something that enables you to know that your situation is not a veridical perception of an orange. Yet, suggests Martin, there is still an important sense in which this experience should qualify as indiscriminable from a veridical perception of an orange. This means that "we need to bracket the relevance of the additional information you have acquired through testimony. This is what the appeal to 'through reflection' is intended to do" (2006: 364–365).

Sturgeon (2006: 208–210) argues that it is far from straightforward to spell out just what information should be disqualified by not being available 'through reflection.' To illustrate this, he discusses a real-life case in which, over a number of evenings, he would have an auditory hallucination of his daughter crying. After repeated visits to check the child and discover that she was fast asleep, Sturgeon eventually came to the conclusion that the apparent cries were in fact hallucinatory. The relevance of a case of this kind turns on the fact that, although it was not acquired through testimony, Sturgeon's knowledge of the experience's hallucinatory character is such that it ought not to be allowed to rule out the possibility that the hallucination should nevertheless qualify as indiscriminable from the relevant kind of veridical experience. Sturgeon concludes that the appeal to 'through reflection' therefore needs to rule out knowledge acquired from this kind of source, as well as knowledge acquired by testimony. Indeed, he suggests that, once we generalize this to other possible cases, we will see that the 'through reflection' restriction must in fact be strong enough to rule out any of the routes by which hallucinating subjects might "figure out" that they are hallucinating. As a result, Sturgeon suggests, the 'through reflection' clause must be taken to stipulate that the "information involved in background beliefs cannot be generally available to reflection.... Otherwise the possibility of everyday knowledge of [hallucination] will slip through the net [and] count as knowledge obtainable by reflection" (2006: 209).

As Sturgeon goes on to point out, however, when one hallucinates an F—say, an orange—one is thereby in a position to know a vast array of things. Because a hallucination of an orange is *not* indiscriminable (i.e., *is* discriminable) from veridical experiences of bananas, blowflies, and bass guitars, Martin's definition of indiscriminability will require that, for each case, a subject hallucinating an orange can know, by reflection alone, that his experience is not one of these veridical experiences. As Sturgeon says, "[T]hat is a huge amount of knowledge to be got solely by reflection... and *not* by reflection on the visual character of [the hallucination], recall.... The only way that could be true, I submit, is if background beliefs were generally available to reflection on context" (2006: 210). So we have a problem. On the one hand, to rule out the possibility we might simply use our background beliefs to work out that we must be hallucinating, the 'through reflection' clause must restrain us from making use of background beliefs. Yet on the other hand, to make sense of all the knowledge Martin's theory allows that we are in a position to get through reflection, Sturgeon maintains that the 'through reflection' clause must *allow* us to make use of background beliefs. But this is just to say that Martin cannot give an adequate account of the 'through reflection' restriction.

In addition to the problem with spelling out the 'through reflection' condition, Martin's theory also faces difficulties with the 'not possibly knowable' condition. To see why, we need first to consider the "dog problem" (Siegel 2008: 213). The dog problem begins with the objection that, in virtue of its essentially cognitive nature, Martin's theory faces difficulties when it comes to accounting for hallucinations in creatures such as dogs that lack cognitive sophistication.[10] To see why, recall that, on Martin's view, a hallucination is indiscriminable from a veridical perception of a certain kind if it is not possible for the subject to know that the hallucination is not a veridical perception of that kind. Given the centrality of the notion of knowledge in this definition, the problem appears in the guise of the concern that, if a dog is incapable of making judgments, then it will be incapable of making judgments of difference. Thus, all experiences will be such that, for the dog, the dog cannot *know* them to be distinct, and hence all will qualify as indiscriminable on Martin's account. And

10. Of course, as was noted in chapter 3, claims about the experiences of such creatures are to some extent up for grabs. If you are happy that animals that lack the right kinds of cognitive capacity would thereby lack the capacity for sense experience, then you will be happy that such animals cannot hallucinate, either. But standing against this is some fairly compelling empirical evidence that lower animals (e.g., rodents) can have hallucinations (e.g., Corne and Pickering 1967; Florio et al. 1972; Siegel et al. 1974; Yamamoto and Ueki 1980), as well as strong intuitions that such creatures would lack the kind of cognitive sophistication required to engage in reflection or make judgments about their own experiences. Of course, given that such animals are incapable of describing their experiences to us, the evidence for animal hallucinations will never be demonstrative, so it will always be possible to simply deny that they occur. Yet if we do find these claims compelling—if we accept that some animals lacking in cognitive sophistication can nevertheless suffer from hallucinations—then this possibility raises problems for Martin's account of indiscriminability.

although this conclusion might be resisted when it comes to dog perceptions—differences in those being taken to be a matter of differences in dog phenomenal character—this line cannot be taken in the case of dog hallucinations. The threat, therefore, is that on Martin's account of indiscriminability, any dog hallucination will qualify as indiscriminable from each and every kind of dog perception (see Siegel 2004: 98).

In responding to the dog problem, Martin retains his original cognitive notion of indiscriminability but insists that we should not conceive of indiscriminability in a subject-relative manner. He says that while "a dog might fail to discriminate one experience from another, making no judgment about them as identical or distinct at all, that is not to say that we cannot judge, in ascribing to them such experience, that there is an event which would or would not be judgeably different from another experience" (2004: 76). Essentially, then, Martin contends that we should understand the modality present in his account of indiscriminability in an impersonal way, such that, when we say the hallucination is not possibly known to be distinct from a veridical perception of a certain kind, we do not mean not possibly known *by the subject* but rather, not possibly known *in some impersonal sense*.[11] The answer to the question of whether a creature's mental state will be indiscriminable from a veridical perception will therefore not be constrained by any incapacities on the part of the putative hallucinator.

This response also faces objections. Susanna Siegel argues that it faces the crucial problem of explaining how we can pick out the hallucinatory "experience"—the state or event that is reflected upon—in an appropriate yet non-question-begging manner (2008: 212). Given Martin's view, the state or event cannot be picked out in virtue of its having any robust features because this would conflict with the claim that nothing more can be said of the hallucination than that it is indiscriminable from the veridical perception. Yet we cannot pick out the relevant state in virtue of its indiscriminability property, either. We are trying to explain what it is for a state of the dog's to have the indiscriminability property in the first place, so we cannot get a fix on which state we are talking about by appeal to its being the one that has that property. This dilemma

11. "In some impersonal sense" clearly stands in need of further unpacking. Martin discusses some ways *not* to understand this (2006: 396), and Siegel also offers some possible unpackings (2008: 212). Because I do not follow Martin in attempting to resist the problem of unsophisticated hallucinators by appeal to an impersonal notion of indiscriminability, I do not pursue these details here.

highlights the problems that an appeal to impersonal indiscriminability will face in picking out exactly what it is that is claimed to be the object of impersonal reflection.

4.3 Defining Hallucination

In the remainder of this chapter I present and defend an alternative theory of hallucination that does not suffer from these problems. In presenting this theory, I focus on the case of pure hallucinations that take place in the absence of any background experience of the world. Pure hallucinations will therefore not have an acquaintance-based phenomenal character. What is more, if we are to steer clear of the screening off concerns outlined in section 4.2, we should also reject the claim that pure hallucinations acquire phenomenal character of some different kind from an alternative source. This is why the theory I present here is, as has already been foreshadowed, *eliminativist* about hallucinatory phenomenal character.

Because I am claiming that hallucinations lack phenomenal character, an explanation of hallucinatory indiscriminability in terms of phenomenal character is therefore not available. Instead, my theory is epistemic, as Martin's is, but with important differences. As Martin notes, the requirement that a subject could not come to know that the state he or she is in is not a veridical perception of a certain kind places two important constraints on what must be true of the state of hallucination: it "must not lack any property necessary for veridical perception, the absence of which is recognisable simply through reflection, [nor must it] possess any property incompatible with veridical perception whose presence is recognisable through reflection" (2004: 65). Although such conditions do bear on important and interesting questions concerning the nature of reflection or introspection, these questions do not have to be answered here.[12] Given an understanding of indiscriminability as

12. However, having said this, I should note that Martin argues that the disjunctivist must reject a theory that claims that introspection involves a perception-like introspective mechanism. This is partly because the disjunctivist must resist the view that "one's incapacity to distinguish the two situations of veridical perception and hallucination is... matched by an objectivity tracked through introspection" (2006: 393). The reason for this is to avoid an analogue to the case in which a lemon and an indiscriminable lemon replica share a lemony look. If veridical perception and hallucination could be said to share an introspective look, this would once again raise the screening off problem.

involving not-knowable distinctness, then what is of central importance to the question of whether two states are indiscriminable is a matter not of the mechanisms of introspection themselves, but rather of the knowledge that introspection can yield. Thus, we can interpret the requirements placed on hallucination as insisting (1) that a hallucination must not fail to produce any judgments or beliefs that would have been produced by a veridical perception of the relevant kind and (2) that a hallucination must not produce any beliefs or judgments that would not have been produced by a veridical perception of the relevant kind.[13]

With this in mind, we can see that a hallucination will be indiscriminable from a veridical perception of a certain kind if and only if it produces the same beliefs or judgments that a veridical perception of that kind would have produced. Given this, I can provide a formal definition of the hallucinatory state as follows:

> For all mental events, *e*, in doxastic setting *D* with cognitive effects C (in its subject), *e* is a pure hallucination *of an F*, if and only if
>
> - *e* lacks phenomenal character, and
> - there is some possible veridical visual experience *of an F*, *V*, that has a rational subject who is in *D* and produces *C*, and
> - *C* is nonempty.

Without the restriction "of an F," this definition provides nature-revealing necessary and sufficient conditions for a mental event to be a pure hallucination. In plain English, it states that, for a mental event, *e*, to be a pure hallucination, it must lack phenomenal character yet produce the same cognitive effects that a veridical experience, *V*, would have produced in

13. There are two caveats to note in respect to these claims. First, in some cases, subjects of hallucinations may recognize their hallucination as such. I call such cases *resisted hallucinations*. In resisted hallucinations, the judgments produced by the hallucination will differ from those that would normally be produced by a veridical perception. I discuss resisted hallucinations in section 4.7, after I have provided a full account of the paradigmatic cases of hallucination in which the subject is taken in. Second, considerations familiar from the work of Gareth Evans (1982) would suggest that there are certain kinds of judgments that could be made on the basis of veridical perception—*de re* judgments—that could not be made in the corresponding hallucinatory cases. Martin's claim that indiscriminability entails sameness of judgments must therefore be restricted to exclude judgments of this kind, although, of course, subjects must judge that they have made such judgments. This does not require, of course, an endorsement of some kind of narrow content. The contents of the judgments can still be wide; they just cannot be *de re*. This complication is therefore ignored in what follows.

a rational subject with the same background beliefs, desires, and other mental states (i.e., in the same 'doxastic setting') as the hallucinator. If these conditions are met, then *e* will thereby qualify as indiscriminable from *V*. The restriction to 'pure' hallucination is to allow for the possibility that an experience that does have phenomenal character of its own might, for some reason, come to have the cognitive effects of a veridical experience of a different kind. In such a case, we will have conflicting intuitions as to how that event should be typed. Cases of this kind are discussed further in chapter 6. The two "of an F" clauses are an addition to the definition to provide rough-and-ready necessary and sufficient conditions for a mental state to qualify as a particular type of hallucination/be indiscriminable from a particular type of veridical perception. It adds that, to qualify as a hallucination *of an F, e* must have the same cognitive effects that a veridical perception of an F would have had. The requirement that C be nonempty is then introduced to rule out doxastic settings in which veridical perceptions lack cognitive effects altogether (e.g., coma, perhaps) as relevant for typing hallucinations. Without this restriction in place, the definition would count any mental state that lacks cognitive effects in such a context as indiscriminable from every kind of veridical perception. Issues of hallucinatory typology are discussed further in section 4.9.

There are many other elements of this definition to discuss, but probably the most notable is that, unlike Martin's, it provides an account of what makes a hallucination indiscriminable *on a particular occasion*; it states the conditions that need to be met for a mental event to be indiscriminable from a veridical perception *at a particular time* rather than indiscriminable per se.[14] This is because I suspect the intuition that there could be a hallucination that could not be discriminated from a veridical perception in any possible circumstances itself derives from the intuition that hallucinations share phenomenal character with veridical perceptions—a view that the naive realist is committed to rejecting. But if we can give an account of why a hallucination might be mistaken

14. It would be possible to define a notion of indiscriminability per se by stipulating that the mental event must produce the same cognitive effects as a veridical perception of a certain kind in *all* doxastic settings in which the subject is rational. However, for the reasons given in the text, I am suspicious of the intuition that such hallucinations are possible. More important, in presenting such an account of indiscriminability, this would carry the strong connotation that the hallucination had properties in virtue of which it produced the same effects in all of these settings, which is just the kind of view that I am at pains to reject.

for a veridical perception on a given occasion, we can therein provide a diagnosis of this mistaken intuition. That diagnosis would run as follows: if a mental event was taken to be a veridical perception on a certain occasion, its subject would of course think that his current mental event was *just like* a veridical perception.[15] But if we read "just like" as indicative of similarity not only in actual but also in modal contexts, as it is natural to do, we can see why it would be natural to think that it would therefore be impossible to discriminate from a veridical perception in all circumstances.

The other key elements of this definition that need to be discussed are (1) the notion of a 'cognitive effect,' (2) the disappearance of Martin's 'through reflection' constraint, and (3) the restrictions to rational subjects and same doxastic settings. In explaining the various elements of this account, we will also see how this account of hallucination can explain the fact that hallucinations have what Siegel calls a "felt reality" (2008: 213), how it avoids the dog problem, how it avoids the screening off problem, and how it accounts for the possibility of *resisted hallucination*—the possibility that subjects may hallucinate while being aware that they are so doing.

4.4 Cognitive Effects and the Felt Reality of Hallucination

In arriving at this definition of hallucination, I discussed Martin's insight that a hallucination will be indiscriminable from a veridical perception if it yields the same beliefs and judgments as a perception of that kind would have yielded. My definition of the hallucinatory state captures this insight by requiring a hallucination to produce the same cognitive

15. When considering the evidence that introspection can provide for the nature of hallucination, it is worth noting that Matthew Soteriou has argued that the disjunctivist commitment to the claim that hallucinations and veridical perceptions do not share phenomenal character leads, via the thought that the introspective evidence must be the same in indiscriminable cases of hallucination and veridical perception, to a further commitment—that "*non*-introspective evidence can, in principle, *defeat* the warrant of claims about the phenomenal character of experience that is provided by introspective evidence" (2005: 183). But given this, if claims about phenomenal character can only possibly be warranted by first-person evidence, then in cases in which there is nonintrospective evidence that defeats this warrant (e.g., in cases of hallucination), we will therefore *lack* adequate warrant for the claims we may make about the phenomenal character of hallucination.

effects that a veridical perception would have produced, where such judgments and beliefs are stipulated to be a species of cognitive effect.[16] Yet this feature of the definition enables us not only to account for the indiscriminability of hallucination from perception, but also to account for the 'felt reality' of hallucination despite its eliminativism about hallucinatory phenomenal character.

David Armstrong also emphasizes the fact that the beliefs we form in the hallucinatory case will be the same as those we form (or would have formed) in veridical perception. To use one of his examples, suppose I walk into a room and see that there is a cat on a mat. What would I (normally) come to believe? Well, suggests Armstrong, I would normally come to believe both that there is a cat on the mat, and that I am *seeing* the cat (1961: 83). Now, suppose I come into a room and hallucinate[17] a cat on a mat. In such situations, Armstrong suggests, I would form a pair of beliefs of the very same kind—I would believe that there was a cat there, and I would believe that I *see* that there is a cat there—it is just that in this case, the beliefs would be false.

In highlighting the role of these beliefs, Armstrong's primary concern is to find a way to avoid the conclusion of the base case of the argument from hallucination's positive revision—the claim that, in cases of hallucination, "the immediate object of perception is always a sense-impression or sense-datum" (1961: 80). As we saw in chapter 2, one of the key premises in the argument to this conclusion is the claim that, when we hallucinate, there is some *thing* that we are aware of. But the presence of these false beliefs provides a way of rejecting this premise and thereby of resisting the initial stage of the argument. As long as I believe that I see a cat on the mat before me, I will report that I see a cat on the mat before me. In addition to this, I will also believe, and in some cases report, that I am

16. Some philosophers may balk at the claim that a judgment is an 'effect' of a veridical perception, because use of the term 'effect' may suggest that the explanatory relation that holds between the perception and the judgment is causal when it should be rational. However, I do not here intend for 'effect' to necessarily be read in this strong way. What is important is that the subject's making these judgments is a consequence of the subject's having a certain perception, regardless of whether the explanatory relation underpinning this link is causal or rational. Perhaps, therefore, a better term might be 'outcome' or 'upshot,' because neither of these have the connotation of being a *caused* effect.

17. In his discussions, Armstrong talks more generally of "illusions" and does not strictly distinguish illusions from hallucinations strictly so-called. However, given that I am offering different treatments for illusion and hallucination, I treat Armstrong as though he is talking about hallucination.

having an experience of seeing a cat on the mat before me, and so on.[18] Given that these beliefs can account for our other beliefs/reports about our hallucinatory experience—in particular, our beliefs and claims that, when hallucinating, we take ourselves to be seeing something—Armstrong rejects the need for an *additional* appeal to an actual experience of a sense-datum to account for its seeming to me to be a certain way: "The non-physical object of immediate apprehension is simply a ghost generated by my belief that I am seeing something" (1961: 84).

In this way, Armstrong shows that we can explain everything we need to explain (in other words, everything a hallucinating subject thinks, does, and says) by appeal to the beliefs that the hallucinating subject forms. As long as I sincerely believe that I see that there is a cat on the mat before me, I thereby take myself to be *seeing* a cat on the mat before me—I take myself to be having a veridical perceptual experience of a cat on the mat—even if I am not. These beliefs can therefore be employed to explain *why* hallucinating subjects take themselves to be having an experience with phenomenal character. Even though, on this definition, a hallucination lacks phenomenal character altogether, because it produces the same cognitive effects as a veridical perception, a suitably sophisticated subject would still *believe* that it has phenomenal character, *think* that there is something it is like for him to hallucinate in such a way, and *claim* that he is having an experience of a certain kind, despite being mistaken. To paraphrase Armstrong, the phenomenal character of hallucination is simply a ghost generated by my belief that I am seeing something.[19]

18. When subjects hallucinate, we should always be able to reveal that they hold, or at least held, such a belief. To paraphrase Armstrong, this is shown by the fact that if I am asked why I think the cat is there, I would reply "I can *see* it" (1961: 83). And whenever subjects report the content and nature of their hallucination—report that they see or hear something that is not there—they simultaneously *express* their higher order belief that they hear or see something (see Rosenthal 1990/1997: 747). For example, if I report that "I see that there is a cat in front of me," I thereby express my higher order belief that I see that there is a cat in front of me; any reports that hallucinating subjects provide about what they see, hear, or otherwise experience are at the same time expressions of just the kinds of higher order beliefs Armstrong appeals to.

19. Note also that, given the way I am using the terminology, the claim that a hallucination lacks phenomenal character does *not* entail that there is nothing it is like for the hallucinator. When I introduced this terminology (see chapter 1), I distinguished there being something it is like to be in a mental state, which is a matter of that mental state itself and its properties, from there being something it is like for *the subject* of that mental state, which is a matter of how the range of mental states the subject is in contributes to

The claim that indiscriminability can be grounded, not in the experiences/first-order mental states themselves, but rather in our higher order cognitive states about those experiences can also be found in discussions of higher order theories of consciousness. For instance:

> [A] case in which one has a [higher order thought] along with the mental state it is about might well be subjectively indiscriminable from a case in which the [higher order thought] occurs but not the mental state. (Rosenthal 1990/1997: 744)

> [I]t is possible for a person to be unveridically conscious or aware of a sensation that simply does not exist. You might introspect a sharp, severe pain, when there was in fact no pain at all. (Lycan 1997: 757)

Although these quotes are both framed in the terminology of the two theorists' respective higher order theories, the idea is the same: if subjects believe or judge that a state of a certain kind is present, then it will be for the subjects as though they are in such a state, even in situations in which they are not.[20] This explains how my definition of hallucination is able to account for the fact that hallucinations have a felt reality, even though it also insists that the hallucination itself lacks phenomenal character.[21]

Siegel argues that this approach to accounting for the felt reality of hallucination will not work across the board. She suggests that "a subject might

---

what it is like for the subject. And, given my definition of hallucination, we can be sure that the hallucinating subject will hold a range of beliefs. If there is something it is like to believe (as is argued by, e.g., Strawson 1994; Langsam 1997; Crane 2001; Maund 2003; McCulloch 2003), then there will be something it is like for the subject, so the hallucinator will not be in the same position as a philosophical zombie.

20. This feature of higher order accounts has led to the objection that such theories fail to provide a reductive account of phenomenal consciousness (see, e.g., Byrne 1997: 122). In section 4.8, I show why the present theory does not face an equivalent problem.

21. One might be concerned that the claim that hallucinations are mental events that lack phenomenal character yet are mistaken for veridical perceptions is somehow in tension with Hellie's phenomenological motivation for naive realism that I endorsed in chapter 1. That motivation, recall, made use of the principle that a judgment about an experience to the fact that it is F based on phenomenological study, by experts, under ideal circumstances, will be accurate. Yet because even experts may hallucinate, there will be situations in which experts might judge that their experience is an F (a veridical perception) when it is not. However, we can dispel the apparent tension by appeal to the clause that, to fall under the principle, judgments must be formed "under ideal circumstances." I suggest that the kinds of circumstances in which hallucinations occur—of which some may be internal, e.g., fever, drug intake or mental illness, and some external, e.g., forms of artificial brain stimulation—would be such as to render nonideal the circumstances under which the judgments are formed.

suddenly expire just after veridically perceiving or hallucinating…, in which case the veridical perception or hallucination would not have [the relevant effects]" (2008: 217). And if a hallucination did not have the relevant effects—in particular, if the hallucinating subject did not form the relevant higher order beliefs—this view would then have no resources with which to account for the hallucination's felt reality. In addressing this objection, recall that, on the definition given above, a mental event qualifies as a hallucination only inasmuch as it has the same cognitive effects as a certain kind of veridical perception would have had. If a mental event does not have these effects, then it is not a hallucination. So Siegel misrepresents the claim on the table when she says that a subject might *hallucinate* yet expire before the relevant effects occur. What might occur is that the subject undergoes a mental event that *would have had* the relevant effects—would have *become* a hallucination—had the subject not expired first. So while it is true that the view has no resources to account for the felt reality of the relevant mental state in such a case, it also has no obligation to do so. On the account I present here, a mental event both becomes a hallucination *and* acquires a felt reality as it has its cognitive effects. If the effects do not occur, then the event will not attain a felt reality, but nor will it qualify (perhaps, even, in virtue of this, it will not qualify) as a hallucination.

The same kind of considerations bear on the thought that one might hallucinate yet fail to attend to one's hallucination and hence fail to form any beliefs or make any judgments about what one sees. The suggestion is that one might hallucinate a doorknob, say, but not form any beliefs about either doorknobs or one's experiences because one is so occupied with thinking about pure mathematics.[22] While intuition may suggest that such a situation is possible, my definition of hallucination denies that it is: because the definition requires that the set of cognitive effects be nonempty, if the mental event in question does not yield any cognitive effects at all, it cannot qualify as a hallucination. Yet given the way we account for the felt reality of hallucination, this is as it should be inasmuch as, if the subject does not believe that he sees, then the subject will not take himself to be having an experience. Given this, what grounds do we have for the claim that the subject is hallucinating in the first place?[23] Thus, it is not possible, on this account, to have a hallucination

22. This idea was suggested by Hellie.

23. At this point, let me note that it is not inconceivable that we could discover purely behavioral reasons to attribute a hallucination to a sophisticated subject even though that subject does not claim to experience anything. For example, we could imagine a subject

that completely lacks cognitive effects due to inattention. Moreover, my account enables us to provide a diagnosis of why we might (mistakenly) think that such an unattended hallucination was possible. As before, we mistakenly think that this is a coherent possibility because the very fact of indiscriminability means that a subject will fail to tell his hallucinatory experience apart from a veridical perception. Because of this, the subject will take his hallucination to be just like a veridical perception and, because a feature of veridical perception is that we can see things without paying attention to them, it would therefore be natural to think that, if a hallucination is just like such a case, we could hallucinate something without paying attention to it, too.

4.5 The Dog Problem

In appealing to cognitive states such as higher order beliefs and judgments in order to account for the felt reality of hallucination, my account may seem to run afoul of the dog problem. The concern would be that, in the case of creatures that lack the capacity to introspect, make judgments, or form beliefs, any hallucination would yield the same higher order beliefs as every possible veridical perceptual experience—that is, none. It would therefore qualify as indiscriminable from them all. However, rather than follow Martin and attempt to avoid this objection by reading the indiscriminability claim in an impersonal manner, facing as it does the problem of identifying the relevant state, I stick with the idea that indiscriminability is a matter of the particular subject's capacities.

What enables me to respond to the dog problem without moving to an impersonal conception of indiscriminability is the fact that my definition of hallucination is not specified in terms of sameness of higher order beliefs, but rather sameness in the broader class of cognitive effects, of which higher order beliefs are a species. This therefore leaves room for there to be cognitive effects of other kinds, some of which can apply to creatures lacking in cognitive sophistication. In this way, we can maintain that, when it comes to a dog that lacks the conceptual sophistication required to have higher order beliefs, a veridical perception of, say, a cat

having a certain mental state induced that could be shown to bias his performance on a priming test, even though he denied experiencing anything at all. If so, the account of animal hallucinations that I outline in section 4.5 could easily be extended to cover such cases. I therefore do not discuss this possibility further at this point.

will still have certain kinds of cognitive effects. Of course, because we are assuming that the dog is lacking in higher conceptual capacities, these effects will not include such sophisticated states as higher order beliefs. Instead, they will be primarily behavioral, possibly including barking, straining at the leash, and so on. But then, our evidence for dog hallucinations is essentially a set of behavioral observations, too. If we were to find a dog barking and straining at the leash—in other words, behaving as though it perceived a cat when there was not one there—then we might have good reason to say that, in such a case, the dog is not perceiving a cat but is nevertheless in a mental state that has the same cognitive effects as such a perception, where cognitive effects here include the mental antecedents of the observed behavior. Because such a state has the same cognitive effects as a veridical perception would have had (for a subject in the dog's doxastic setting), my definition of hallucination will count it as indiscriminable from a veridical perception of a cat and will therefore enable us to maintain that the dog is having a hallucination of a cat. Of course, what the dog lacks is a belief that it is actually seeing a cat, but that should be expected because we are explicitly dealing with those creatures that lack the conceptual sophistication required to have such beliefs.

4.6 Rationality and Doxastic Settings

Having spelled out the notion of a cognitive effect and shown how this can account for the felt reality of hallucination while avoiding the dog problem, let me now turn to the question of why we focus only on the cognitive effects a veridical perception has for a rational subject in the same overall doxastic setting. The restriction to rational subjects is in the picture because we can envisage the possibility of bizarre situations—perhaps involving mental breakdown of some kind—in which a veridical perception of a certain kind has radically atypical effects. For instance, Mardi Horowitz reports a case in which dragons and demons were experienced in response to flushing water in a toilet bowl (1964: 515). We might want to describe such a scenario as one in which a veridical perception of flushing water comes to have seriously anomalous effects, including beliefs that one is seeing dragons or demons. But then, if a mental event that lacked phenomenal character came to have effects of this kind, a definition that does not disqualify such a case would therefore threaten to type it as a hallucination of flushing water (because it has the same cognitive effects that a veridical perception of flushing water would have had), rather than, as it intuitively seems it should be classified, as a hallucination of dragons or demons.

The key difference between such a situation and the standard situation—a situation in which a subject takes himself to be seeing flushing water when he veridically perceives flushing water—is that, in some sense, something looks to be going awry when a subject forms beliefs about dragons and demons in response to an experience of flushing water. Such an anomalous belief formation process would seem to indicate some kind of failure in rationality.[24] This is why I have incorporated a clause into my definition of hallucination to rule out aligning hallucinations with veridical perceptions that occur in situations in which rationality fails in this way. I achieve this by requiring that a hallucination be a mental event that lacks phenomenal character but that produces the same cognitive effects as a veridical perception of a certain kind would have produced *in a rational subject*.[25]

The addition of this clause might suggest that we should be able to isolate a standard set of cognitive effects that a particular kind of veridical perception would have in a rational subject. This leads Siegel to suggest that the position is akin to a disjunctive version of analytical functionalism (2008: 216) and, as such, faces some of the same difficulties. In particular, it faces the problem that any effects a mental state has are not effects of that mental state considered in isolation, but are rather effects of that mental state in conjunction with other of the subject's mental states. Even in a rational subject, the particular effects a veridical perception has will differ according to the overall doxastic setting in which the veridical perception occurs. This is why my definition requires not only that the relevant cognitive effects be those in a rational subject, but also that the subject's prevailing doxastic setting be the same.

However, although this definition allows that different cognitive effects may occur in different doxastic settings, we can nonetheless insist that certain effects will be common to many of these settings. In

24. The notion of rationality I employ here should be read in a relatively innocuous sense. As I intend it to be understood, we can say that it is rational for a dog to behave in food-directed ways when it perceives food, yet irrational for the dog to behave in the same way when it perceives, say, a mailbox or an airplane.

25. This is not to say that a subject must be rational in order to hallucinate, but rather that, when we find a hallucinating subject, we determine the content of his hallucination by determining which veridical perception (or perceptions—see section 4.7) would have had those effects had the subject been rational.

particular, we can insist that, if a rational, cognitively sophisticated subject were to veridically perceive an F, then (as long as the prevailing doxastic setting was one in which the subject did not doubt the veracity of his experiences—such cases are discussed shortly) he would at least believe that he sees an F, regardless of the other specifics of the doxastic setting. This has the consequence that, whenever we find a sophisticated subject undergoing a hallucination, we will find a subject who takes himself to be seeing something. In this way, we can ensure that the view has the resources to account for the felt reality of hallucination in all relevant cases.

Siegel challenges this claim. She contends that it "should be possible to have a hallucination that is indiscriminable from a veridical perception of a butterfly, even if the standard effects... don't actually come about" (2008: 217). If this were indeed possible, then the approach would lack the resources to account for the felt reality of such a hallucination. But by our lights, the assumption that such a scenario is possible betrays a failure to grasp the core of the present approach. On the account I have been developing, it is *not* the nature of the hallucinatory state itself that explains why subjects take themselves to be having certain kinds of experiences. Instead, subjects take themselves to be having certain kinds of experiences solely because they undergo a mental event that happens to produce the right kinds of cognitive effects, where the right kinds of cognitive effects include higher order beliefs. It is the presence of the right kinds of cognitive effects that turns an otherwise unexceptional mental event into a hallucination. The hallucination itself has no special features at all that could enable us to identify it as a hallucination in the absence of the right kinds of effects. This means that, if cognitively sophisticated subjects do not believe that they are having an experience of a certain kind, then they are simply not hallucinating. So, *pace* Siegel, it is not possible for a sophisticated subject to have a hallucination that is indiscriminable from a veridical perception of a butterfly in the absence of the right kinds of cognitive effects.[26]

26. What about an animal? Is it possible for an animal to have a hallucination in the absence of the right kinds of effects? Here, things are less clear. Siegel points out that, if a cat "is lethargic from illness and so lacks [the desire to make contact with a butterfly], even if it veridically perceives the butterfly, it won't paw at it or even be disposed to paw at it" (2008: 216). She then takes this possibility to indicate that a cat might hallucinate a butterfly even if it did not strike at imaginary objects in the air. But then, if a cat lay sluggishly in a corner, what evidence would we have for claiming that the creature was nonetheless hallucinating a butterfly? To insist that it

4.7 'Through Reflection' and Resisted Hallucination

It is also the fact that my definition of hallucination relativizes the relevant cognitive effects to the doxastic setting in which the hallucination takes place that explains why we can do without a 'through reflection' clause of the kind Martin advocates. As we saw, this clause was introduced to rule out the possibility that a subject might come to know that his experience was not a veridical perception of an F through testimony, but Sturgeon gave reason to think that this clause would prove problematic to spell out adequately. To see how my definition avoids this difficulty, recall that Martin motivated the inclusion of the 'through reflection' clause with the example of being told that you are going to have a hallucination of an orange artificially induced. There is a sense, Martin suggests, in which we still want to say that this experience could qualify as indiscriminable from a veridical perception of an orange. I agree, but I do not think we need to try to exclude the testimony in order to account for this. Instead, I suggest we need to embrace it. By doing so, we can also account for the felt reality of 'resisted hallucinations': situations in which subjects know that they are hallucinating. The reason that we need an alternative account of the felt reality of such cases is that, because the subjects know they are hallucinating, they will not believe that they are seeing anything. Yet the subjects will nevertheless still claim to have the hallucinatory experience *as of* seeing something. Because we have been accounting for the felt reality of hallucinations by appeal to the subjects' (false) beliefs about what they see, and because resisted hallucinators do not form such beliefs, an adequate account of the felt reality of resisted hallucinations is still lacking.

In order to see how relativizing the relevant cognitive effects to the prevailing doxastic setting enables us to deal with these issues, suppose Martin sets up a psychological experiment in which I (at this point an uninformed naive subject) am placed in a seat with an orange on a table in front of me. When first seeing the orange, in the absence of any reason

---

is possible for the cat to have such a hallucination in the absence of *any* behavioral evidence would seem to take for granted that we can identify a mental state as a hallucination by reference to certain intrinsic features it has. Once again, though, the present account rejects this claim—mental states only qualify as hallucinations inasmuch as they have the right kinds of effects. In the case of animals, however, I do not profess to have any particular intuitions as to what these effects are—I leave answering that question to those who are engaged in these fields of research.

to think that my experience is in some way anomalous, I will of course believe that I see an orange, so in such a case, I have a higher order belief of the following form:

[B1] I believe that [I see that {there is an orange in front of me}].

Now imagine that, as part of the experiment, Martin misleads me by telling me that, as part of a psychological experiment, he will remove the orange but connect me to a visual-cortical stimulator that will induce a hallucination of an orange in me. He then takes away the orange, hooks me up to an impressive-looking machine, and asks me to shut my eyes. I then listen to him flick switches and push buttons and hear the machine hum into action. Martin then tells me to open my eyes. And when I do, lo and behold, I have an experience indiscriminable from the veridical experience of the orange. But unbeknownst to me, Martin is just fooling me, and the machine is just for show—all he has done is put the original orange back in front of me. My experience is indiscriminable from a veridical experience of an orange because it actually *is* a veridical experience of an orange.

The question we need to ask is: What would the cognitive effects of the experience be in such a situation? If I have been taken in by Martin's ruse, his false testimony would lead me to expect that I will be hallucinating when I open my eyes, so when I do, I may be astonished at the apparent reality of the orange in front of me. Then, when asked about my experience, I could imagine saying something like, "It's incredible; I know I am not seeing an orange but it really is just as if I am." In other words, I would declare that I no longer hold a belief of the form [B1], but rather a more cautious belief such as the following:

[B2] I believe that [it is as if I see that {there is an orange in front of me}].

Thus, the cognitive effects of *this* veridical experience would, in this overall doxastic setting, both lack the higher order belief that I see an orange and include the higher order belief that it is *just as if* I do.[27] Although

27. Nothing hangs on the precise nature of the "It is as if I see that" locution. Other locutions might do the job—for example, "I seem to see that" or "It looks as though" could be substituted with no damage to the following arguments. What is important is that, as this example shows, these more cautious attitudes can be acquired from perfectly veridical cases. If this example seems a little far-fetched to explain how we actually acquire these more cautious attitudes from veridical cases, more everyday examples can

none of Martin's story is true, as long as I believe what he is telling me, I will assume that there are countervailing considerations to be taken into account and alter my beliefs accordingly. Now, of course, my *experience* hasn't changed—it is still veridical, just as it was when I was naive—but now I am taking countervailing considerations into account, while I still form a belief, it is a *different* belief from that which I formed in the naive case. Where naive subjects claim/believe that they see, the more cautious subjects merely claim/believe that it is as if they see.

With this in mind, let us now turn to the situation in which Martin's visual-cortical stimulator is not a hoax and a hallucination of an orange really is induced in me. According to my definition of hallucination, what Martin does is induce a mental event that completely lacks phenomenal character, but that has the same cognitive effects as a veridical perception of an orange would have had in the prevailing doxastic setting. In a doxastic setting in which I am *not* aware that I am hooked up to Martin's machine (or perhaps believe the machine to be an elaborate hoax), then, as we have seen, the effects of that mental event will include higher order beliefs of the form [B1]—I will believe that I see an orange. The presence of this belief then enables us to account for everything I, as a hallucinating subject, think, do, and say.

In a doxastic setting in which Martin *has* told me he will induce a hallucination in me and I believe him, I will think that there are countervailing considerations to be taken into account. Given this, the cognitive effects of a *veridical* perception of an orange would, as we have seen, be different: they would not include beliefs of the form [B1], but rather more cautious beliefs of the form [B2]. So, if a mental event that lacked phenomenal character were to have the same kinds of cognitive effects as this veridical perception in the same kind of overall doxastic setting (i.e., when countervailing considerations are being taken into account), it would *also* yield beliefs of the form [B2]—I would *not* believe that I see an orange but *would* believe that it is just as if I do. So this similarity of cognitive effects grounds the indiscriminability of the mental event from the veridical perception, thereby enabling it to qualify as a (resisted) hallucination.

---

be given in which a subject sees something—such as a trompe l'oeil picture, a reflection in a mirror, or a sleight-of-hand trick—and takes himself to see something he does not. Upon being shown that the experience he has just had was misleading in certain ways, in future cases the subject would become more cautious and believe that, when viewing a trompe l'oeil picture, a scene in a mirror, or a magic trick, it is *just as if* he sees a banjo hanging on a door, or people standing over there, or a dove disappear into a handkerchief.

What is more, higher order beliefs of this kind would also enable us to explain everything I, as a *resisted* hallucinator, think, do, and say. If I believe that it is *just as if* I see an orange in front of me, then we can appeal to this belief in order to explain my *claim* that it is just as if I see an orange in front of me, even though I do not believe, and hence do not claim, that I am actually seeing anything at all. In this way, we can explain why subjects who resist their hallucination nevertheless claim to have a certain kind of experience. They claim that it is *as if* they see something because, like the cautious perceiving subject, they *believe* that it is as if they see something.[28]

Sturgeon's crying baby case can also be accommodated along the same lines. After coming to the conclusion that the apparent cries were merely hallucinatory, Sturgeon would thereby end up in a doxastic setting in which, even if the baby *did* cry, he would probably take the experience to be a hallucination and assume that he was merely imagining things again. So, in the doxastic setting Sturgeon found himself in, the cognitive effects of a *veridical* experience of a baby crying would not include the belief that he hears a baby crying, but rather the belief that it is *just as if* he hears a baby crying. But this is precisely the kind of cognitive effect we would expect a hallucination of a crying baby to have *in that doxastic setting*. So, once Sturgeon comes to the conclusion that the apparent cries are merely hallucinatory, any further hallucinations he may undergo would have the same cognitive effects as a veridical perception would have had in the prevailing doxastic setting. This enables us to count Sturgeon's hallucination as indiscriminable from a veridical perception of a baby crying, and account for the felt reality of his experience, even though he has successfully figured out that the cries are merely hallucinatory.

28. This way of thinking about resisted hallucinations gives us a way of constructing the intuitive relations of indiscriminability that seem to hold between veridical perceptions, hallucinations, and resisted hallucinations. Standard deceptive hallucinations have the same kinds of effects a certain kind of veridical perception would have in a doxastic setting in which the subject was trusting and did not take any countervailing considerations into account. This can ground the claim that hallucinations are indiscriminable from that kind of veridical perception. Resisted hallucinations can *also* have the same kinds of effects as a veridical perception of this kind, only in this case the effects are those the perception would have in a doxastic setting in which the subject was more skeptical. So this can ground the claim that resisted hallucinations are also indiscriminable from that kind of veridical perception. This enables us to see how both hallucinations and resisted hallucinations can be indiscriminable from a veridical perception of the same kind. Thanks to Susanna Siegel for pressing me to clarify this.

4.8 Screening Off Revisited

The key to the success of my definition of hallucination turns on the fact that we can explain everything a hallucinating subject thinks, does, and says in a way that is compatible with the hallucination itself lacking a phenomenal character. We achieve this by appealing to erroneous higher order beliefs held by the hallucinating subject, beliefs that are themselves necessary for the mental event to qualify as a hallucination in the first place. But because a hallucinating subject will think, do, and say the same things as a subject who perceives veridically, it may seem that the screening off problem rears its head: could we not therefore explain everything that needs to be explained in the same way, thereby rendering the postulation of a veridical perceptual experience bearing naive realist phenomenal character explanatorily redundant? Indeed, Robinson raises the screening off problem in just this kind of form when he suggests that, "if the experience of seeming to see something red when nothing relevant is red is adequately analysed in terms of acquiring some kind of belief state, then a similar analysis must also be adequate for the experience of seeming to see something red when that experience is veridical" (1994: 51). An alternative way of pressing the same point is as follows. On the account I present here, hallucinations and veridical perceptions do have a property in common, that of yielding certain cognitive effects in a particular doxastic setting. The charge, then, is that it is this property that does all the explanatory work and that this property thereby screens off the naive realist acquaintance properties from playing an explanatory role.

Yet when we consider *how* higher order beliefs suffice to furnish hallucinations with felt reality, we can see that the property of producing certain cognitive effects is an inherited or dependent explanatory property of the sort that was discussed above. A hallucination has a felt reality—*despite* the fact that the hallucination itself lacks a phenomenal character—because the hallucinator falsely believes that he is enjoying a veridical perception. But having such a belief—believing that one's current mental event is a veridical perception of a certain kind—can be sufficient to account for the felt reality of such an event only if there is *already* a felt reality to the event that the subject judges himself to be in.[29] Hallucinations have a felt reality

29. This claim is to be read with wide scope—of something that has phenomenal character, I judge hallucination to be just like it. Thanks to Benj Hellie for pressing me to clarify this. It is worth noting that this is another feature of the situation that distinguishes

because, when we hallucinate, we take ourselves to be perceiving, *and perceptions themselves have a felt reality*. And, of course, the explanation of the felt reality of veridical perception cannot be an explanation of the same kind or we would be locked in a regress. So, if veridical perceptual experiences did not have phenomenal character in the first place—phenomenal character that makes it the case that there is something it is like to be in such states—then the relational property of being indiscriminable from such an experience would not explain why we think that there is something it is like to be in a state that instantiates that relational property. So, the very explanation of the felt reality of hallucination *requires* there to be other states—veridical perceptual experiences according to the theory presented here—that possess phenomenal character. The property of having certain cognitive effects is therefore an inherited or dependent explanatory property and is not subject to the screening off worries.

Interestingly, there is also a further reason for us to resist Robinson's contention that the kind of account I have offered for hallucination must also be adequate for the veridical cases. On my definition of hallucination, a mental event is indiscriminable from a veridical perception if it generates the same higher order beliefs that such a veridical perception would have generated, so a visual hallucination of an F occurs when a subject forms the (false) higher order belief that he sees an F. But, of course, believing that one sees an F requires the subject to possess the concept of an F, so there is a need to leave room in the overall picture for an explanation of how the subject acquires the concepts that go on to appear in the erroneous beliefs we appeal to in the definition of hallucination. Although there is not sufficient room to go into this in detail here, it seems reasonable to suppose that a plausible account will adhere to what Robinson calls the principle of minimal empiricism: the claim that "our grasp on concepts depends on the fact that we experience instances of at least some of them" (1994: 122). If this is the case, then our stock of concepts that are misdeployed in cases of hallucination will be available to be so deployed only inasmuch as they are themselves derived from veridical perception, so there will need to be an alternative explanation of there being something it is like to have a veridical experience—through

the case of a hallucinator from that of a philosophical zombie. If zombies are possible, then neither the hallucinations nor the veridical perceptions of a zombie have phenomenal character. So, for a zombie, judging that one is seeing would not be a matter of believing oneself to be in a state that actually possesses phenomenal character. This account of the felt reality of hallucination would therefore be inapplicable in such a case.

possessing acquaintance-based phenomenal character according to the theory of perception developed in chapter 3—in order to explain how we acquire the concepts that go on to appear in the contents of the erroneous higher order beliefs that occur when we hallucinate.

4.9 Hallucinations and Experiential Kinds

I submit that my definition of hallucination can explain everything that needs to be explained without requiring hallucination to possess phenomenal character. However, the relativity introduced into the definition in order to accommodate some of the problem cases means that the theory will struggle to ground the existence of nice, neat kinds of visual experience where, recall, a mental state is a visual experience of an F if it is a veridical perception of an F, a hallucination of an F, or an illusion of an F. An important theme of Martin's writings on disjunctivism has been an attempt to provide an account of fine-grained visual kinds (e.g., 2004: §9), but his attempts have received some criticism.

One important objection that has been raised for Martin's attempts to provide a fine-grained account of visual kinds turns on the possibility of degraded cognitive contexts (Sturgeon 2006: 204–207; see also Farkas 2006: 215), and a similar problem arises for the view outlined here. For example, one might propose to demarcate fine-grained visual kinds as follows: the class of visual experiences of Fs is the class of veridical perceptions of Fs together with those mental states that are indiscriminable from veridical perceptions of Fs. But given the possibility of degraded cognitive contexts in which two veridical experiences that intuitively differ in phenomenal character (and hence in kind) might nonetheless have the same kinds of cognitive effects, such a proposal will not work. To see why, consider Martin's hasty and inattentive subject John, who treats samples of scarlet and vermillion in the same way (2004: 74). Because of the differences in the shades perceived, we would naturally take veridical perceptions of samples of these two shades to be experiences of different kinds. Yet because John treats the two samples indiscriminately, a nonveridical mental event that has the same effects as *John's* experience of scarlet (or vermillion) in the same overall doxastic setting (i.e., an inattentive setting) would therefore qualify as indiscriminable from *both* of these (putatively distinct) kinds of veridical perception. Cases of degraded cognitive contexts therefore seem to defeat any attempt to group visual experiences into neat kinds.

As Martin points out, there is a problem here only if we take it for granted that we can indeed coherently talk about kinds of visual experience. Therefore, we might take the possibility of John cases and the like to show instead that "there is no well-founded notion of kind of [visual] experience" (2004: 77). Because facts about visual experiences in general are, on the proposal presented here, a matter of facts about veridical perceptions together with facts about nonveridical mental events that have the same effects as veridical perceptions in varying cognitive contexts, we might hold that "this pattern of facts is just not well enough behaved to ground the existence of kinds" (77). So we could simply deny that there are neat fine-grained kinds of visual experience at all.

If we were to accept that we cannot group visual experiences into neat kinds, this would not have the consequence that we could no longer talk about hallucinations *of an F* at all. Suppose, for example, a hallucinating subject forms the higher order belief that he sees a black cat on a mat. There are many veridical perceptions that might yield a higher order belief of this kind—lots of different ways in which the cat might be lying on the mat, eyes open or closed, tail twitching or not, and so on. Yet what all of these veridical perceptions have in common, *ex hypothesi*, is that they yield the higher order belief that a black cat on a mat is seen. This can therefore ground the intuition that the subject is undergoing a hallucination of an F where, in this case, F is {a black cat on a mat}. Indeed, my definition of hallucination enables us to type the hallucination as finely as the subject is able to report—anything that the subject could potentially tell us about the content of the hallucination will thereby express a higher order belief about what is seen. This would therefore enable us to rule out the hallucination's being indiscriminable from any veridical perception that would not have yielded such a belief. The consequence of the denial that there are neat, fine-grained kinds of visual experience is merely that we cannot type the hallucination more finely than the subject can possibly report.[30]

Although both Katalin Farkas (2006) and Siegel (2008) suggest that it is incumbent on the disjunctivist to provide an account of fine-grained

30. Once again, I suspect that any intuitions to the contrary are linked to the erroneous but understandable view that hallucinations and veridical perceptions share phenomenal character. If we take this intuition out of the equation for the time being, we find that there is no obvious reason to suppose that the claim that the subject is hallucinating an F implies that the hallucination is indiscriminable from one, and only one, unique fine-grained veridical experience.

visual kinds, neither explains why the denial of the existence of such kinds is supposed to be problematic. John Hawthorne and Karson Kovakovich, however, do. They argue that "if I am an intrinsic duplicate of another member of my community that is veridically perceiving cream but not white, then I am someone for whom things look cream—whether or not I have the epistemic wherewithal to take this in" (2006: 168).[31] But, of course, this consideration will not move us. For a start, inasmuch as this is supposed to be a case of a hallucination, then the conclusion of the imaginary scenario—that an intrinsic duplicate of an experiencer will have experiences with the same phenomenal character—clearly derives from a tacit acceptance of local supervenience, a thesis that, as explained in chapter 2, the naive realist must reject. Moreover, if I really do lack the epistemic wherewithal to take in the difference between white and cream, then so must the veridical perceiver of whom I am a duplicate. But if such a subject could not become aware of the difference between white and cream, then as noted in chapter 3, it is at least open to question whether such a subject does indeed have the capacity to perceive the difference between the two shades.[32] So while my definition of

31. I should note that Hawthorne and Kovakovich offer another objection to the suggestion that there are no neat kinds of visual experience: that "we should think twice about dismissing large segments of natural language vocabulary as defective" (2006: 168). In reply to this, I can but record my skepticism as to the extent to which "natural language" is indeed committed to the idea of such neat kinds and the associated idea that, for any hallucination, there will be a veridical perception that matches it perfectly. Such a claim cannot be derived from the reports of hallucinators and is not assumed by psychopathologists and clinicians who work with such patients (Bentall 1990: 88; Slade and Bentall 1990: 125; Rankin and O'Carroll 1995: 518).

32. This consideration suggests an alternative response to the threat posed by John cases that would allow for the existence of fine-grained visual kinds. It picks up on the thought that the John case causes a problem only if we do take John's veridical experiences of scarlet and vermillion to be distinct experiences. But as noted in chapter 3, there are reasons to think that there can be situations—often involving such things as inattention—in which facts that we would antecedently expect to feature in the presentational character of an experience may fail to so feature. So it would be open to hold that, if the veridical experiences of the two samples really did have identical effects—if there is nothing in John's speech or behavior that could lead us to say that he treats these samples any differently—then there is therefore no reason to think that John does in fact see the fact of the sample's being scarlet and/or the fact of the sample's being vermillion. Perhaps instead, in both cases, John sees the fact of the sample's being red. In such cases, if we individuate veridical experiences by their phenomenal characters and phenomenal characters by the facts we are acquainted with, then these experiences would be counted as the same kind of veridical experience, and hence a hallucination that had these effects would qualify as the same kind of visual experience.

hallucination will struggle to account for neat kinds of visual experience, this will constitute a problem for the thesis only if we accept that such neat kinds exist. As of yet, I can see no compelling reason why we must do so.

4.10 Conclusion

I submit, then, that a hallucination is a mental event that, while lacking phenomenal character, produces the same cognitive effects in the hallucinator that a veridical perception of a certain kind would have produced in a rational subject in the same overall doxastic setting. However, I imagine that it might be alleged that this account will be incomplete until some account of *why* hallucinations come to have the same kinds of effects as certain kinds of veridical perception has been provided. But given the definition of hallucination presented here, such a demand is misguided. As we have seen, a mental event qualifies as a hallucination only inasmuch as it has the same kinds of cognitive effects that a particular veridical perception would have had, so it would be misguided to demand any further explanation of why hallucinations, considered as a mental kind, have effects like those of veridical perceptions. Because a mental event qualifies as a hallucination only inasmuch as it has the same kinds of effects as a certain kind of veridical perception, asking why *hallucinations* have these kinds of effects would be akin to asking what bachelors have in common in virtue of which none of them are married. Hallucinations *just are* those events that have the same kinds of effects as, and are therefore indiscriminable from, veridical perceptions of a certain kind.

It would be fair to say that the positive story about hallucination embodied in these claims is rather minimal. But this is a consequence of the nature of the dialectic, not a result of quietist tendencies on the disjunctivist's part. Any nonphenomenal mental event, whatever its intrinsic nature, that has the same cognitive effects that a certain kind of veridical perception would have had in the prevailing doxastic setting will thereby qualify (1) as indiscriminable from that veridical perception and (2) as a hallucination. Thus, the essence of hallucination—what distinguishes hallucinations from other mental states—lies in their being indiscriminable from veridical perceptions, not in some antecedently identifiable feature of the event. This is why Martin has it right when he says that, "when it comes to a mental characterisation of the hallucinatory experience, nothing more can be said than the relational and epistemological claim that it is indiscriminable from the perception" (2004: 72).

With my definition of hallucination thus presented and defended, where do we stand with regard to the naive realist response to the argument from hallucination? As we saw in chapter 2, that argument attempts to refute naive realism by showing, first, that naive realism is false in cases of hallucination, and then by generalizing from the hallucinatory case to the veridical perceptual case. Because the base case of the argument is solid, we saw that if we are to defend naive realism, the argument must be blocked at the spreading step. In the version we have been considering here, this phase of the argument appeals to the indiscriminability of hallucination from veridical perception and argues that, given the fact of indiscriminability, if naive realism is false of hallucination, it is false of veridical perception, too. However, adopting a disjunctive approach to visual experiences provides the naive realist with recourse to an alternative tactic: providing *different* philosophical accounts of perception and hallucination, while explaining how the two kinds of experience, so understood, might be indiscriminable from one another.

The account of the veridical perceptual disjunct was then provided in chapter 3, and this chapter has focused on the complementary account of hallucination. Details aside, the claim is that a hallucination of an F is nothing more than a mental event that lacks phenomenal character, but that has the same cognitive effects as those that a veridical perception of an F would have had in those circumstances. Critically, because this definition of hallucination guarantees that suitably sophisticated hallucinators will believe that they are seeing something, it enables us to explain why the subjects claim to see something, or at least that it is as if they are seeing something, even though they do not. So this definition can account for the fact that a hallucination can seem to its subject just like a veridical perception, even though it also insists that the hallucination lacks phenomenal character entirely.

5

Phenomenal Character and the Brain

> No one should underrate the importance of unspoken assumptions. They are often the most powerful because they are part of the scientific culture, and therefore remain unquestioned, though they get perpetuated.
>
> — Semir Zeki, *A Vision of the Brain*

When I introduced the argument from hallucination in chapter 2, we saw how the spreading step of the argument—the step that takes the base case conclusion that naive realism is false in cases of hallucination and attempts to extend it to also cover cases of veridical perception—has often been motivated by the consideration that hallucinations can be indiscriminable from veridical perceptions. In chapter 4, we saw how the fact of indiscriminability can be accommodated in such a way that the spreading step can be resisted, and naive realism protected, by showing how two states that have nothing intrinsically in common could nonetheless be indiscriminable for their subject.

Yet as noted in chapter 2, a number of expositions of the argument from hallucination have augmented the argument with an appeal to the possibility in principle of replicating an experience with the same phenomenal character in the absence of appropriate objects. This claim turns on the acceptance of what I called the 'local supervenience' principle. As we saw, phenomenal character as the naive realist conceives of it—as a property of acquainting the subject with mind-independent existents—could not be created by neural replication alone. Therefore, we should interpret the appeal to the local supervenience principle as a purported refutation of the naive realist view of phenomenal character, thus: given the local supervenience of the phenomenal, we can see that it would be possible to create a hallucination with the same phenomenal character as a veridical perception in the absence of appropriate objects by neural replication. This therefore shows that the naive realist view of phenomenal character must be mistaken. The time has now come, therefore, to assess the strength of the reasons for thinking that the local supervenience principle should be accepted.

5.1 Local Supervenience and the Very Occurrence of Hallucinations

What reasons do we have for thinking that the local supervenience principle is true? One important consideration turns on the very fact that subjects can have hallucinations at all. In chapter 2, we saw Howard Robinson making this kind of appeal, and C. D. Broad, upon wondering whether "it could be shown that, provided a certain area of one's brain were suitably affected, such an experience[1] might occur even though no such object were there occupying the place in question," goes on to suggest that "*the visual...experiences which occur in dreaming and in waking hallucination seem to make this practically certain*" (1951/1965: 39, emphasis added).[2] So why might these thinkers suppose that the very occurrence of states such as waking hallucination make it "practically certain" that local supervenience is true?

1. I read Broad's "such an experience" as, at the very least, an experience with the same phenomenal character.

2. In fact, it is far from clear that the neural activity that occurs during hallucination is of the same kind as that which occurs during veridical perception. James Lance reports a number of cases involving subjects with visual field defects—either homonymous hemianopias (blind in half of the visual field for each eye) or smaller quadrantanopias (blind in a quadrant of the visual field)—who nevertheless experience hallucinations in their blind areas. In discussing these cases, Lance reports that the "calcarine area of the occipital lobe [the location of the primary visual cortex or V1]...was infarcted in many of the cases reported" (1976: 729), which suggests, in accordance with other experimental evidence, that localized damage to the primary visual cortex impairs a subject's ability to enjoy normal conscious perceptual experience in certain parts of the visual field. Yet the fact that these subjects *were* able to experience hallucinations in these areas implies that, in such cases, the neural apparatus that underpins such a subject's ability to experience hallucinations in the relevant area of his or her visual field remains intact. This suggests that the neural mechanisms that underpin a subject's capacity to have a hallucination in a certain area of the visual field are not in fact identical to the neural mechanisms that underpin a subject's capacity to have veridical experiences in that area.

As I understand it, the rationale is simply that hallucinating subjects take themselves to be having veridical perceptual experiences, and this needs explaining. A prima facie plausible explanation would then be as follows. First, the fact that hallucinating subjects take themselves to be having perceptual experiences suggests that hallucinations are mental events that have a phenomenal character that is the same as, or at least similar to, the phenomenal character of veridical perception. Yet given what we know about the etiology of hallucinations, the only thing that seems to be necessary for a hallucination to occur is brain activity of the right kind. A plausible inference to the best explanation would conclude that this neural activity suffices for the existence of the hallucination, together with its phenomenal character. If so, then the hallucinatory phenomenal character is a property whose instantiation is assured by the neural activity alone or, in the terminology of the present chapter, is a locally supervenient property.

As of yet, this is not flatly inconsistent with naive realism. Of course, if the phenomenal character of hallucination is locally supervenient, then it cannot involve a relation to mind-independent reality as the naive realist claims is the case for veridical perception. But we are quite comfortable with the idea that hallucinations are not naive realist—the interest in the thesis is confined solely to the veridical cases. The real force of the appeal to the very existence of hallucinations and the consequent claim about the local supervenience of their phenomenal character turns on the plausible thought that, if neural activity alone suffices for a hallucination to instantiate a phenomenal character of a certain kind, then if that neural activity also occurred in a case of veridical perception, it would likewise suffice for the instantiation of a phenomenal character of the same kind. If the local supervenience principle is true, then, there is a clear case for the conclusion that naive realism is therefore false for both veridical and hallucinatory phenomenal character.

Perhaps the naive realist could avoid this conclusion by claiming that, unlike hallucinations, veridical perceptions have *two* kinds of phenomenal character—a locally supervenient property that they share with hallucinations, together with a naive realist acquaintance property—or that the phenomenal character of a veridical perception is a combination of the contributions from these two sources. While such positions do not seem incoherent, they would seem to run headlong into the screening off problem that we met in chapter 4. The problem is, if the phenomenal character that derived from local supervenience alone did not make the hallucination indiscriminable from the veridical perception, then it could not, by itself, account for the indiscriminability of the two states, so some other explanation of their indiscriminability would be required. Yet if the locally supervenient phenomenal character *was* indiscriminable from the full perceptual phenomenal character, then the screening off problem once again rears its head—it would seem to be the locally supervenient property, rather than the naive realist acquaintance property, that shapes the contours of the subject's conscious experience.

If the very occurrence of hallucinations did indeed prove that neural activity alone suffices for the existence of an experience with phenomenal character, then the naive realist would be in trouble. But as we saw in chapter 4, we can explain everything that needs to be explained about hallucination without making such a claim. There, a definition of hallucination was offered in which hallucinations were defined, in part, as mental events that lack phenomenal character altogether. Given this, the very occurrence of hallucination does not require us to form any hypotheses about what accounts for their phenomenal character because, on the account defended here, they are no longer alleged to have any. Of course, to make this response plausible, the naive realist needs to defend the claim that a mental event that lacks phenomenal character can be indiscriminable from a mental event that possesses it, but this is precisely what was defended in chapter 4.

This response may be argued to miss the point. It might be insisted that hallucinations simply must have phenomenal character.[3] Indeed, in chapter 4 we saw that the nature of hallucination is such that it would incline people to think that hallucinations have phenomenal character. But—and this is absolutely critical—*if* this intuition is going to be used in defense of local supervenience, then the naive realist will insist that the intuition be defended: he or she will want *proof* that at least some of the hallucinations that occur do possess phenomenal character, especially now that there is a theory of hallucination available to the naive realist that explains all the data without making this assumption, as outlined in chapter 4. If an appeal to intuition is not going to be enough here, what other arguments could be provided? We have already seen that an appeal to how the hallucination

3. As we have seen, A. D. Smith comes close to this when he defines hallucinations as states that are sensory or, in our terms, have phenomenal character. Yet Smith does not assume that the kinds of hallucination that actually occur are instances of this kind of 'philosophical' hallucination. Indeed, Smith accepts that actual hallucinations could well be nonsensory states that "seem sensory to the subject" (2008: 185), as the analysis here suggests, so a diagnosis of why Smith thinks that there could be such things as hallucinations in his sense is still lacking (see n7 below).

strikes the subject will be unable to resolve the issues, and it is difficult to see what else could be available to defend the intuition that hallucinations have phenomenal character other than an appeal to similarities in neural activity across veridical and nonveridical cases. But, of course, any attempt to convince the naive realist in this way is going to take the local supervenience of *perceptual* phenomenal character for granted unless an independent argument for this claim is provided. Yet while it would be possible to develop such an argument—we shall consider one in section 5.5—it would in effect be a way of arguing directly for local supervenience and bypassing the need to appeal to the very occurrence of hallucinations. So, given the finely balanced state of the dialectic, an appeal to the very occurrence of hallucinations does not, by itself, give us anything other than question-begging reasons to accept local supervenience.[4]

5.2 Imaginary Cases

As the very occurrence of hallucination does not require us to endorse the local supervenience principle, what other reasons have been given for thinking that phenomenal character supervenes solely on neural activity? In his discussions of local supervenience, Michael Tye suggests that a range of "imaginary cases...play a large role in many philosophers' thinking" on this subject (1995: 152). As an example of such an imaginary case, he develops a version of Hilary Putnam's infamous brain in a vat. In its original form, the key idea is this:

> The person's brain (your brain) has been removed from the body and placed in a vat of nutrients which keeps the brain alive. The nerve

4. Broad appealed to dreams as well as to hallucinations—might dreams provide a better case with which to support local supervenience? I don't think so. While there is not sufficient space to discuss dreams in detail here, it seems to me that if the account outlined in chapter 4 works for hallucinations, it would be plausible to suppose that an account along the same kind of lines might also be presented for dreams. As with hallucinations, the fact that you may, in a dream, think that you are perceiving does not entail that there are no experiential differences between dreams and hallucinations. Indeed, just as with hallucinations, there are reasons to think that dreams are experientially different. For example, Alva Noë argues that "dream sequences tend to be poor in detail, and what detail there is tends to vary unstably between scenes" (2004: 214), and he claims empirical backing for this claim, referencing psychophysiologist Stephen LaBerge. This would suggest that there is ample scope for an alternative explanation of why dreams can sometimes be confused for veridical perceptions along the lines of chapter 4 (for similar claims concerning dreams, see Malcolm 1959; Dennett 1981; Smith 2008).

> endings have been connected to a super-scientific computer which causes the person whose brain it is to have the illusion that everything is perfectly normal. There seem to be people, objects, the sky etc; but really all the person (you) is experiencing is the result of electronic impulses travelling from the computer to the nerve endings. (1981: 6)

Essentially, what Putnam offers us here is a thought experiment. And Tye is right: thought experiments such as this do seem to play an important role in explaining why many philosophers take local supervenience to be true. The question we need to ask, then, is this: Can thought experiments be used to establish the local supervenience principle?

I think the answer to this question is no. To see why, consider Putnam's brain in a vat scenario in more detail. Reading somewhat beyond what Putnam actually says, we can usefully break the situation he presents down into three stages. First, there is a claim that a certain science-fiction scenario—that we might remove your brain from your body, keep it alive in a vat of nutrients, and connect all its nerve endings up to a computer that feeds it the very same electrical impulses your brain is receiving from your senses—is conceivable. Then there is the thought-experiment move: conceivability entails possibility.[5] Thus, it is at least *possible* that such a scenario could be actualized. Then there is the denouement: if such a possible situation were to be actual, then as far as the subject of experience is concerned, there would be no experiential difference—the subject would have the illusion that everything was perfectly normal.

What is interesting about this is that the thought-experiment component of the argument operates by establishing the conceivability, and hence possibility, of the vat-brain scenario and, in particular, of perfect neural replication. To get from neural replication to sameness of experience, however, local supervenience is just assumed. So, as it stands, such a thought experiment does not underwrite local supervenience, but rather takes it for granted. Moreover, we cannot employ the thought-experiment move to directly establish the possibility in principle of phenomenally identical hallucinations, either, at least not in a sense relevant to the present debate. One might think that it would be possible to regard the neural replication to perfect illusion stage of the argument above as a further thought experiment and that, rather than simply claiming that neural replication would result in experiential replication, and thereby

5. This is a much-disputed premise (Hill 1997; Hill and McLaughlin 1999; Chalmers 2002), but I will let it pass. As we will see, even if conceivability does entail possibility, it does so in a sense that is irrelevant given the nature of the current debate.

assuming local supervenience, we make the more cautious claim that it is *conceivable* that neural replication would result in experiential replication. From this, the thought would go, we can reapply the thought-experiment move to conclude that it is therefore possible that neural replication would result in experiential replication, and hence that phenomenally identical hallucinations are at least possible.

Inasmuch as we are interested in the question of whether phenomenally identical hallucinations are possible, we are interested in a quite specific *kind* of possibility. The account we have been developing of perceptual experience is intended to be an account of what perception is *actually* like—about what *our* perceptual access to the world in which we live consists in—as opposed to a claim about any possible form of perception. So, in order for the possibility of phenomenally identical hallucinations to be relevant to these claims, it will not be enough to simply show that phenomenally identical pairs of veridical perception and hallucination are *logically* or *metaphysically* possible—that there could possibly be beings for which their perceptual access to their world was such that neural replication would produce identical experiences.[6] What needs to be shown here is that phenomenally identical hallucinations are *physically* possible—that if *in this world* you were to replicate the neural activity that takes place in my brain when I have a perceptual experience, you would thereby cause me to have a phenomenally identical hallucination. But, of course, conceivability is no guide to this kind of possibility at all: while "there is at least some plausibility in the idea that conceivability can act as a guide to metaphysical possibility…it is very implausible that conceivability entails physical or natural possibility" (Chalmers 2002: 145).

Inasmuch as thought experiments might be thought to support local supervenience, I suggest they will function either by assuming local supervenience or by showing, irrelevantly, that what it is like to have an experience might supervene locally in some logically possible world. Of course, if this were the case, it would follow from the possibility in principle of neural replication that a mental state with a certain kind of phenomenal character (thus understood) might be produced in circumstances that would qualify as nonveridical. But this will not help the defender of local supervenience because we are interested in the

6. I can see no reason to deny this. It does not seem incoherent to suppose that there could possibly be a world, like ours in many ways, in which local supervenience was true. All I claim is that *our* world is not such a world: local supervenience *could have been true*, but it is not.

question of whether the phenomenal characters of *our* veridical perceptual experiences are locally supervenient. Thought experiments give us no additional reasons to think that this must be the case.

5.3 Local Supervenience and Brain Stimulation

Given that thought experiments cannot be used to establish the truth of the local supervenience principle and, indeed, often take it for granted, we need to look elsewhere for the explanation of why philosophers tend to think it so obviously true. One source of this conviction may be that the local supervenience principle is taken to be an empirical hypothesis that has been borne out by the results of brain stimulation experiments.[7] The name most associated with direct brain stimulation experiments is that of Wilder Penfield, who, together with a number of associates, operated on the brains of well over a thousand epileptic subjects and, while these patients' brains were exposed, applied electrical stimulation to various parts of the cortex. His collection of patient transcripts (collated in Penfield and Perot 1963) provides what is still the largest collection of first-person data concerning the effects of brain stimulation.[8] In brief, what Penfield found was that, when stimulation was applied to the visual cortex, patients would sometimes report experiences of "lights, stars, or coloured flashes moving about" (690), but occasionally, when the part of the cortex that lay between the auditory sensory and visual sensory areas was stimulated, subjects would report detailed and even multimodal experiences. Altogether, Penfield stimulated this area of the brain in 520 patients. This kind of detailed experience—what Penfield called an "experiential response"—was reported by 40 of these patients (7.7%), and visual experiential responses were reported in 19 cases (3.7%).[9]

By directly stimulating the brains of these 19 patients, Penfield induced them to enter mental states that were reported as visually experiential, so his results show that, in these subjects, brain activity alone

7. I suspect that this kind of consideration is the source of Smith's conviction that there is a special class of phenomenally identical hallucination. He says that such a hallucination is "the sort of state that could in principle be induced in a subject by stimulating a sense-organ in precisely the way it is stimulated when the subject actually perceives something" (2008: 184; see also 2002: 203).

8. At least, the largest collection that I could discover.

9. Similar experiences have also been reported in stimulation of the limbic system (Halgren 1982) and deep-brain stimulation of the subthalamic nucleus (Diederich et al. 2000).

is sufficient for the occurrence of a visual experience. But this is not to accept (yet) that brain stimulation results support the claim that brain activity is sufficient for experiences *with phenomenal character*, because we have seen how hallucinations might be a special class of visual experiences that lack phenomenal character.

The fact that Penfield produced visual experiences in his patients as a result of direct brain stimulation has, however, been taken by philosophers to support local supervenience. For example, we find E. J. Lowe stating that, although visual experiences "are normally caused by light impinging on the retina of the eye,... they can also apparently be caused by direct stimulation of certain parts of the cortex, as the well-known findings of Wilder Penfield suggest" (1992: 80). Here, Lowe clearly assumes that the visual experiences produced by Penfield are visual experiences of the same kind as occur in veridical cases—that is, experiences with phenomenal character. In order to assess how compelling we should find this motivation, we need to carefully consider to just what extent Penfield's findings do support the claims of local supervenience.

Alva Noë suggests there are two reasons to doubt that Penfield's results could prove that "consciousness is a matter of what is going on in the head alone" (2004: 210). The first reason is that even if it were "possible to produce *some* experiences [by directly stimulating the brain], it [would] not follow that it is possible to produce *all* experiences" (211). The second reason is that, even if it were the case that any experience could be produced by directly stimulating a human subject's brain, this would not suffice to establish the claim of sufficiency. Noë explains this with an example:

> Consider a comparison: The states of a car's engine are necessary conditions of its driving activity... But it is absurd to think that the states of the engine alone are sufficient for driving! The engine needs to be properly embodied in a vehicle, and the car itself must be situated in an appropriate environment. A car suspended from a hook, or up to its windows in mud, won't drive, no matter what the state of the engine. (2004: 211)

These considerations suggest that it may be useful to distinguish between two dimensions of the supervenience claim. The first concerns its *extent*. In order for the truth of local supervenience to bolster the argument from hallucination, it is important that the local supervenience be *total* where, by a total local supervenience, I mean one that claims that *every aspect* of the phenomenal character of a veridical perceptual experience is locally supervenient. In contrast to this, we can envisage a *partial* local supervenience that claims that, say, the phenomenal character of a simple phosphene experience (a small, circumscribed sensation of light) supervenes locally, but not generalize this to the claim that the phenomenal character of a rich perceptual experience is also locally supervenient.

The second dimension concerns the local supervenience claim's *scope*. Suppose someone were to claim that the states of an engine sufficed for driving activity. Such a claim might, implausibly, be taken to range over all possible replica engines (what I will call a 'brute supervenience' thesis) or it may be taken, far more realistically, to range over only some of them, say, those properly embedded in a car that itself is appropriately situated in an environment. Because the scope of the sufficiency claim is qualified in this way, we can call this a 'qualified supervenience' thesis. In the case of phenomenal character, a brute local supervenience thesis would hold that any replica of a brain currently enjoying a veridical experience, *no matter how it came into being or what kind of environment it was in*, would, if it were to undergo the same kind of neural activity, have an experience with the same phenomenal character. A qualified local supervenience thesis would incorporate a restriction on this claim, holding instead that a replica of such a brain would have an experience with the same phenomenal character when supporting neural activity of the same kind, *as long as it was like the original brain in certain other relevant ways*.

Given the limitations imposed by Penfield's sample of patients, it is far more plausible to see his results as supporting a suitably qualified local supervenience thesis, because there simply is no way that his results could be plausibly generalized to show that duplication of brain state *alone* is sufficient for duplication of visual experience. After all, all of the brains that he stimulated were the brains of patients who were, prior to the operation, *already* perceivers, so every brain Penfield stimulated was (1) in a body, which (2) was in an environment and (3) had already supported perceptual experiences. Given that Penfield himself points out the risks involved in generalizing the results from brain stimulation of embodied, environmentally situated, epileptic perceivers to conclusions concerning embodied, environmentally situated, nonepileptic perceivers, he himself would not have thought his results supported such a brute local supervenience thesis. Given this limitation on Penfield's subjects, all that his results could possibly prove would be some kind of qualified claim: that neural activity is sufficient for an experience with phenomenal character in that limited collection of cases where some other conditions—in this case, (1), (2), and (3)—are met.

We will consider to what extent the brain stimulation results support such a qualified version of local supervenience in due course. Before we do, it may be instructive to see just how far away we actually are from any kind of empirical proof of a brute local supervenience claim. To get such a proof, we would need to first get hold of a brain that did not satisfy these extra conditions, and then see if experiences with phenomenal character could be induced in such a brain by direct electrical stimulation. Now, as far as brains that satisfy this constraint (never mind their being physical replicas of our brains) are concerned, we are strictly within the realm of philosophical fantasy. No such brains exist, we have little idea how to create them, and even if we did, given that we cannot ascertain the presence of experience simply by looking at the brain, we would have no idea how to judge whether stimulation of that brain did or did not yield experiences of any kind. Even if we were to somehow hook the brain up to a computer or a loudspeaker that turned activity in the speech areas of the brain into speechlike sounds, we still could not possibly interpret the "assertions" such a brain might "make" without begging the question (McCulloch 2003: 130).

Having said this, a remark by Lowe does suggest a way in which support for a brute local supervenience thesis might at least be strengthened. Immediately after citing Penfield's work, he goes on to suggest that it is conceivable that "a congenitally blind person (one whose eyes or optic nerves were damaged beyond repair) should be capable of enjoying [visual] experiences and have sight conferred artificially by being fitted with a prosthetic device" (1992: 80). This reference to the blind being induced to have visual experiences is suggestive because, while we do not have, and will probably never have, access to brains that do not meet any of conditions (1), (2), and (3), we do have access to brains that fail to meet condition (3): the brains of those who are blind. What is more, we can be far more confident—although there are still serious difficulties about interpretation—that we could get into a position to make non-question-begging judgments as to whether such a brain could be made to have visual experiences (by simply asking the person whose brain it is). If we could establish that visual experiences could be induced in a blind subject, this would at least strengthen the support for a brute sufficiency thesis. Of course, it would still not be demonstrative—for one, the brains of blind subjects still meet conditions (1) and (2)—but it would nevertheless be evidence in favor of such a thesis because it would be evidence that visual experiences could be induced in all the brains we have access to.

When considering this possibility, we need to tread carefully. Often the word "blind" can be used to refer to those who have no *useful* vision. Such a use would class subjects who have sight, but where the sight they have is practically useless, as blind. But, "as anyone can verify by practising 'seeing' with the eyes closed, under some conditions—particularly bright sunlight—quite a lot of visual experience is possible under conditions similar to the worst lens cataract or corneal opacity" (Gregory and Wallace 1963: 7). In addition to this, people can go blind. So a subject who now has no functional vision whatsoever may still have had vision at some point in the past. In order to test whether experiences could be induced in a brain that did not meet condition (3), however, we would need to test subjects who were both completely blind and had been so since birth.

Given this caveat, those famous cases of people who have had their sight restored after years of blindness do not provide the kind of evidence we are looking for. These subjects all had *some* visual experience—albeit not useful visual experience—prior to the operation. But as Richard Gregory and Jean Wallace point out, "where blindness is literally complete surgery is always out of the question.... This point cannot be overstressed.... In this sense there are *no cases of recovery from blindness*" (1963: 7). So, as philosophically intriguing as such cases are, cases of recovery from "blindness" do not provide any extra evidence for a brute local supervenience thesis. There are subjects, however, who *have* been completely blind since birth and have therefore never had any kind of visual experience whatsoever. If we could establish that such a subject could be induced to have visual experiences, this could be argued to support a brute local supervenience thesis.

One way in which completely blind subjects might have visual experiences is in their dreams. Donald Kirtley, in *The Psychology of Blindness* (1975), collated almost two centuries' worth of questionnaire and interview studies on the dreams of the blind and, on the basis of this, concluded that "there are no visual images in the dreams of those born without any ability to experience visual imagery in waking life" (quoted in Hurovitz et al. 1999: 183). This negative result has been corroborated by more recent studies under controlled conditions (Kerr et al. 1982; Hurovitz et al. 1999). Another possibility is that blind subjects might have visual experiences induced by brain stimulation. And while I have been unable to find any studies of *direct* electrical stimulation of the brains of the blind, there have been studies that make use of transcranial magnetic stimulation (TMS) (Gothe et al. 2002). TMS works by using a pulsed magnetic field to excite or inhibit the activity of specific areas of the brain (Hallett 2000: 147), and this technique has resulted in a number of reports by nonblind subjects of simple visual phosphenes. In the study by Janna Gothe and colleagues, however, the ability of TMS to produce visual phosphenes in the blind declined as the severity of the blindness and the length of time blind increased. In sighted subjects and those subjects who qualified as blind yet had some residual visual function (<20/400), TMS produced phosphenes in every subject. In those blind subjects who had residual perception of movement or light, phosphenes were produced in 60% of cases. For subjects who had no residual vision whatsoever, only 2 out of 10 subjects experienced phosphenes under TMS. Most important, however, no experiences of any kind were induced in the two subjects from the last group who had been blind from birth.

Let me be clear precisely what the relevance of this is. First, two subjects is a very small sample, so we should not attempt to conclude from this that TMS *cannot* induce phosphenes in the totally, congenitally blind. Second, the defender of local supervenience can provide explanations as to *why* these results should be expected. There is evidence that the plasticity of the human brain is such that, if a subject does not receive input from the eyes, the areas of the brain normally assigned to visual processing do not lie dormant, but rather are reassigned to take part in the processing underlying other sensory modalities (Sadato et al. 1996; Pons 1996). Because these areas of the visual cortex are no longer assigned to visual processing, the defender of local supervenience might argue, we should not *expect* activation of them to lead to visual experiential responses.[10]

This is all entirely correct. I do not intend to claim that any of the data cited here in any way show that a brute local supervenience thesis is false. All I contend is that they do not show that a brute local supervenience thesis is *true*, either. The sum total of the evidence so far is that some visual experiences can be produced in subjects who are, or were, perceivers. But while this could still, in a very loose sense, be classed as evidence *for* brute local supervenience, it is thoroughly unpersuasive. What we have is evidence that visual experiences can be induced in brains that are (1) in a body that (2) is in an environment and (3) already

10. Although this would, in turn, suggest that even if phenomenal character did supervene locally, it would supervene on some level of functional organization, rather than on neural activity per se.

supports a perceiver. Inasmuch as we have any evidence whatsoever for brains that do not meet (1), (2), or (3)—and we do not have much at all—it is negative. Yet brute local supervenience claims that *any brain* that is identical to the brain of a perceiving subject, whether or not it is embodied, whether or not it is in an environment, and whether or not it has previously supported experiences, would support the same kind of experiences if the right kinds of neural conditions were induced. As far as this thesis is concerned, the evidence we have does not support it at all—our evidence base is far too restricted to make drawing such a general conclusion remotely plausible.

5.4 Brain Stimulation and Total Local Supervenience

It does remain the case that, the more we qualify our local supervenience thesis—restricting it to only brains that are embodied, to only brains that are embodied in an environment, and so on—the more strongly this kind of evidence will seem to support the claim that neural replication is sufficient for experiential replication. And most important, for the purposes of the argument from hallucination, we only need it to be true that you or I—embodied perceivers—could be induced to have a hallucination that had the same phenomenal character as a veridical experience. Therefore, it would be enough if this evidence supported a qualified local supervenience thesis that claims that neural replication will suffice for replication of phenomenal character *when limited to a brain that meets (1), (2), and (3).*

While the argument from hallucination does not require a brute local supervenience thesis, it is nevertheless crucial that the local supervenience thesis be total. What needs to be shown is that you or I could be induced to have a hallucination with the same phenomenal character as a given perceptual experience. As Noë points out, it would not be enough to show that the phenomenal characters of some simple experiences such as phosphenes (or, indeed, some *aspects* of the phenomenal character of a more complex experience) were locally supervenient, if it turned out that the phenomenal characters of complex experiences (or other aspects of complex experiences) did not supervene locally. Therefore, let us acknowledge that brain stimulation results do support the claim that neural activity suffices (in a suitably qualified sense) for a certain kind of visual experience. The question we now need to ask, to determine whether a total local supervenience thesis is supported, is whether the visual experiences that can be elicited by direct stimulation of the brain are states with phenomenal character.

Of course, given the theory of hallucination presented in chapter 4, it would always be possible for us to hold firm and deny that the visual experiences induced by brain stimulation do not have phenomenal character, *no matter what*. However, because my intention in this chapter is to try to preach to the unconverted, such an approach would not get me very far. Instead, I will attempt to show that a close examination of Penfield's extensive findings provides no more support for the claim that phenomenal character is locally supervenient than was provided by the very occurrence of hallucinations. In doing this, my approach will be to show that there is no good reason to think that the visual experiences that Penfield induced were anything other than artificially induced variants of the kind of hallucination discussed in chapter 4.

This interpretation of Penfield's findings looks to conflict with the kinds of claims Penfield himself makes about the nature of these visual experiences, which can seem to support the notion that these states *did have* perception-like phenomenal character after all. For example, he claims that the patient "seems to re-live some previous period of time, and is aware of those things of which he was conscious in that previous period. It is as though the stream of consciousness were flowing again as it did once in the past" (Penfield and Roberts 1959: 45). Such a claim implies, or at least can seem to imply, that as far as the stream of consciousness is concerned, it is *just the same as* having the original experience. This sort of implication is also present in other quotes. Elsewhere, Penfield claims that direct brain stimulation "is capable of bringing back a strip of past experience in complete detail without any of the fanciful elaborations that occur in a man's dreaming" (1975: 34). From claims such as these, it can seem as though Penfield has, through direct electrical stimulation of the brain, induced the subject to undergo experiences *of the very same kind* as the original perceptual experiences. And such an interpretation is backed up by some of the things that appear in the records of patient reports. For example, patient N.C. says that his experience under stimulation is a "true experience" (Penfield and Perot 1963: 643), a sentiment echoed by patient J.T., who calls his induced experiential response "a real experience" (653). Another patient, E.Wh., said she felt as though "she were re-living the experience" (612), and patient T.S., when asked by the experimenter whether he was remembering the event or whether he actually seemed to be there, replied that he "seemed to be there" (652).

A close reading of the transcripts of the patient reports, however, suggests that things are not quite as clear-cut as Penfield's claims can sometimes suggest. Consider his claim that "it was evident at once that these [experiences] were not dreams. They were electrical activations of the sequential record of consciousness, a record that had been laid down during the patient's earlier experience" (1975: 21). Despite it supposedly being "evident at once" that the experiential responses he induced were not dreams, 10 out of the 40 patients *explicitly* use the word "dream" in their reports.[11] As for their being "[re-]activations of the sequential record of consciousness," three patients explicitly claimed they had no recall of having had the original experience (M.Wh. [Penfield and Perot 1963: 632], M.Ri. [638], M.M. [650]), and others report experiences that simply could not have been reruns of veridical experiences they actually had. For example, patient E.Wh. described experiencing a scene that "consisted of herself as she appeared in childbirth... she suddenly saw herself in childbirth" (612) and patient T.S. described an experience in which "he seemed to be looking at himself at a younger age" (652).

Anomalies such as these prompted George Mahl and colleagues to revisit Penfield's transcripts of his patients' responses. When they did, they claimed that they could see no good reason to conclude that the induced visual experiences were replays of past experiences rather than "essentially new creations based on memories, analogous to dreams" (1964: 357). In fact, prompted by some notable correlations between "the interview content prior to stimulation and the content of the [induced] experiences themselves," Mahl et al. offered the alternative hypothesis that "the patient's 'mental content' at the time of stimulation is a determinant of the content of the resulting hallucinatory experiences" (358).

This hypothesis was then put to the test by Mardi Horowitz and colleagues, who carefully monitored both the content of patients' thought processes prior to stimulation, and the contents of the experiences they induced in those patients. They concluded that Penfield's original memory-rerun model was too simple, and they listed four reasons for this (1968: 484): (1) their findings showed that no two stimulations at the same site produced the same experience; (2) the contents of some experiences included events that had probably never actually

11. For mention of dreams, see descriptions by patients R.B. (Penfield and Perot 1963: 614), M.G. (621), C.Ft. (634), G.Le. (635), H.P. (637), S.Be. (640), N.C. (643), G.E. (644), and H.N. (653). Other patients used similar nonperceptual terms, such as imagining (J.V. [630]) and memory (M.M. [651]).

been experienced by the subject; (3) on some occasions, the experience seemed to be elaborated from a more simple hallucination of light, color, or shape; and (4) many of the experiences had contents that were related to "recent perceptions, active ideas or current motives," as Mahl et al. had suggested. Indeed, according to Horowitz et al., the "relationship between the prestimulation mental content and the sensory experience resemble[s] the process of dream construction" (471). Similar findings are also reported by Eric Halgren, who concludes that the "particular [experiential] response evoked [by stimulation of the limbic system] is... related... to the patient's psychological traits and concerns" (1982: 251).

These findings provide reasons to be skeptical of Penfield's conclusion that the visual experiences he induced were cases in which a strip of past experience was brought back in complete detail. The results above give us cause to doubt the claim that the visual experiences were replays of past events, and there are very good reasons to think that the claim that they were experienced in "complete detail" is a significant overstatement. Far and away the most damning evidence from the point of view of the claim that Penfield's experiments produced experiences with the same phenomenal character as a veridical perception, however, is his own admission that "none of the patients has ever confused the hallucination with reality except for a moment. All have retained awareness of the operating room and the events occurring in it, even during the time of an experiential response" (Penfield and Perot 1963: 679). This "dual awareness" comes through in a few of the patient interviews. For example, patient G.Le. states, "I see the people in this world and in that world too, at the same time" (635), and patient S.Be. was "asked if the person [he saw] was there [and answered], 'Yes, sir, about where the nurse with the eyeglasses is sitting over there'" (640).

The problem is not that the patients do not take their experiences to be real, but that they all retain an awareness of the operating room. With this in mind, what sense can we possibly make of the claim that what it is like to have such an electrically induced experience is the same as what it is like to have a waking perceptual experience? For Penfield's evidence to support a total local supervenience thesis, we would need to be able to make sense of the claim that one could have a perceptual experience of an operating theater, with all its operating-theater-esque presentational character, while having another experience, with a completely different presentational character, at the same time. But what would it be to experience two different presentational characters simultaneously? Given that a perceptual experience fills the visual field, it could not be that one experience appeared in one half of the visual field, and the other appeared in the other half—in this case, *neither* would be like a waking experience. Yet if both the perceptual experience of the operating theater and the induced experience were, in some sense, superimposed on one another over the whole visual field—as though one were looking at the operating theater through glass on which something else was reflected—then at least one of the two experiences would not be like a waking experience because such experiences are not translucent. But how could two opaque experiences be experienced at the same time? If we can't make sense of this, then we can't make sense of the claim that the visual experiences Penfield succeeded in inducing have the same phenomenal character as veridical perceptions.

Taken together, then, what support does the empirical evidence from brain stimulation offer for versions of local supervenience? As far as brute versions of local supervenience are concerned, I think the answer is very little. We have succeeded only in inducing visual experiences in those brains that are already embodied, in an environment, and support perceivers. Inasmuch as we have tried to induce visual experiences of any sort in brains that do not match this description, we have failed. As for a total version of local supervenience, while we can undoubtedly induce visual experiences in some subjects, I suggest the evidence actually points to the conclusion that these visual experiences are not experiences that have phenomenal character that is identical to that a veridical perception would have, as a total local supervenience would require. For one, such a claim is difficult, if not impossible, to assimilate with Penfield's own admission that all the patients remain aware of the operating theater while undergoing these experiences. Second, as some of his own patient reports suggest, and as is borne out in later work, Penfield was overly hasty in assuming that these patients "'re-lived' all that [they] had been aware of in [an] earlier period of time" (1975: 21).

Instead, the visual experiences that have been induced by direct stimulation of the brain look much more like the kinds of hallucinations considered in chapter 4 than they do fully detailed reruns of perceptual experiences. Admittedly, some of these hallucinations have been reported as being unusual, perhaps more vivid than normal, but these hallucinations *are* unusual—the patient's brain is being artificially stimulated by an electric probe. Yet despite them being different in these ways, I see nothing in the evidence that should force us to conclude that the hallucinations created by direct stimulation of the brain are an importantly different *kind* of hallucination—a hallucination with phenomenal character—to the cases discussed in chapter 4. And as we have seen, the occurrence of such hallucinations can be explained without appeal to local supervenience.[12]

5.5 Phenomenal Character and Visual Processing

A further empirically based motivation for local supervenience can be found in Barry Maund's book *Perception*. There he claims that "there are good theoretical reasons for claiming that [a total local supervenience thesis is true]. These theoretical reasons depend on what is known of the brain and what is known of its role in pure acquiring and exercising perceptual capacities that we possess" (2003: 119). While it is not completely clear what defense Maund is offering here, a plausible interpretation—and whether or not this is what Maund is actually getting at, it is a suggestion worth considering—is that he is drawing our attention to the parallels that exist between the kinds of visual processing that take place in the brain and the different aspects of the phenomenal characters of veridical visual experiences.[13]

Let me clarify how such an appeal might work. First, such an approach cannot try to establish local supervenience as directly as before. The appeal to the brain stimulation findings was direct inasmuch as it focused on nonveridical experiences in the first instance. The argument was that, first, brain stimulation results show that hallucinations can be produced by neural stimulation, and second, that the hallucinations thus produced had the same phenomenal character as veridical perceptions. An attempt to establish local supervenience by appeal to the nature of visual processing, however, does not focus on hallucination in the first instance, but on veridical perception. It starts

12. Although allowing that the simple phosphene experiences were locally supervenient would not threaten the version of naive realism I have been developing (because it would be compatible with this to insist that the phenomenal characters of veridical perceptions were not locally supervenient), I see no reason why even phosphene experiences, afterimage experiences and the like, should not submit to the same kind of explanation. The claim would be that, in such cases, subjects think that they see/seem to see a flash of light, a red patch (or perhaps, a patch that is redder than the background), and so on.

13. A similar suggestion was made by Ned Block in conversation.

from the empirical evidence that, in order to have *veridical perceptual experiences* involving certain kinds of phenomenal property (e.g., those pertaining to color or motion), there must be activity in certain areas of the brain.

The first clues that certain kinds of activity in particular areas of the brain are a necessary condition of our having experiences with certain kinds of phenomenal property come from clinical evidence concerning the kinds of experiential deficits that attend patients with certain neurological disorders or damage. For example, Zeki (1990) reports that patients who have lesions on the ventral surface of the occipital and temporal lobes will lose the ability to perceive the world in color despite the fact that other visual abilities, such as the ability to perceive form, remain intact. This condition is known as achromatopsia. Similarly, patients who have damage to the middle temporal (MT) area of the brain suffer from akinetopsia: they lose the ability to perceive motion (Zeki 1991). These results on experiential deficits, stretching back many years, give us our first clue that our ability to have experiences that instantiate certain kinds of phenomenal property depends on the operation of certain fairly well-defined areas of the brain. These findings have engendered a mission to find the "neural correlates of consciousness," a search that is being advanced by the development of better and more precise means of studying the intact brain. In a book recounting his search, with Francis Crick, for the neural correlates of certain forms of conscious experience, Christof Koch backs up Zeki's findings and reports that "cells in [brain area] V4 and neighboring regions of the human fusiform gyrus are tuned to color" and that "functional brain imaging reveals that human [brain area] MT is strongly active when subjects perceive…motion" (2004: 151).

Now, whether or not the kinds of relationships described by Zeki and Koch will ultimately be strong enough to support the claim that a certain type of activity in a certain area of the brain reliably correlates with the instantiation by experiences of a certain kind of phenomenal property, it nevertheless remains the case that, the more we learn about the brain, the more evidence we acquire that there are certain functionally defined areas that underpin our ability to experience certain features. So, for example, I can have an experience of a certain color only inasmuch as there is a part of my brain that detects that color; likewise, I can experience motion only if there is a part of the brain that is dedicated to the detection of movement. This suggests that, in order for me to be conscious of a certain feature, I have to (1) have some kind of neural mechanism in my brain that is attuned to register the presence of that feature, and (2) have activity in that neural mechanism.

How might these findings constitute an argument for local supervenience? Imagine that the search for the neural correlates of consciousness succeeded in providing us with a detailed list of accepted correlations between certain kinds of neural processing and the kinds of phenomenal property that can be instantiated by perceptual experiences. This list would constitute a set of *necessary* conditions (necessary, at least, when limited to the case of biological creatures such as ourselves): they would show that neural activity of a certain kind is necessary for a subject to enjoy an experience with a certain kind of phenomenal property. Because local supervenience itself is a claim about *sufficiency*, these findings would not directly support the thesis, but it would be possible to argue for the truth of a sufficiency claim from the truth of a necessity claim via an inference to the best explanation. In this case, the claim would be that the best explanation of why a certain kind of neural activity is necessary for an experience to instantiate a certain kind of phenomenal property is that the neural activity produces, or constitutes the supervenience base for, a phenomenal property of that kind. In particular cases, the inference to the best explanation would work as follows. Why is it that I have a conscious experience of redness when, and only when, an area of V4 is active? Because that activity in V4 causes, or is the supervenience base for, an experience with a reddish phenomenal property. Why can I be conscious of motion only when a particular collection of neurons in MT are firing? Because the phenomenal character of the experience of motion is either caused by or supervenes upon those neurons firing in the right kind of way. Therefore, the claim would be that the best explanation of the existence of the empirically established correlations is that the phenomenal properties of the relevant experiences supervene upon the activity in certain areas of the brain in just the kind of way envisaged by the local supervenience thesis.

Because the form of this argument is an inference to the best explanation from accepted necessary conditions to putative sufficient conditions, we can counter the argument by offering a *different* "best" explanation: an alternative way of conceiving of the relationship between neural processing and the phenomenal aspects of perceptual consciousness. There is an obvious alternative available. As C. W. K. Mundle points out, "The processes in the sense-organs and [central nervous system] on which perception depends must, presumably, function in one or other of two ways—revealing what is there or creating sense-data which represent what is there" (1971: 130). Robinson describes this as a distinction between *selective* and *generative* accounts of the role of causal processes in perception. According to the generative account, the relevant neural processing generates a phenomenal character for the mental state; according to the selective account, "the process does not generate a content but puts one in touch with the stimulus that is already out there" (1994: 70).

In this way, we can see the outlines of a plausible explanation of why certain neural activity should be a necessary condition for an experience with a certain phenomenal property that does not assume that the neural activity is also sufficient. The broad form of this explanation would begin by treating the neural processes as selective rather than generative. If I, as a subject, am to be able to discriminate red things from blue things, then my brain—my discriminating organ—has to be able to differentiate between the *effects* that red things and blue things have on me. And if brain area V4 is the area where much of the decisive processing that underlies hue discrimination takes place, then we would expect to find activity in V4 when I pick up on the fact of an object's being red, and we would expect to find that localized damage to V4 will disrupt my ability to see and discriminate colors. But none of this requires that the redness is, in some sense, a *product* of this brain activity. Instead, this brain activity is an *enabling condition* of my awareness of the instance of redness in the world—the right kinds of brain activity are required for me to become consciously acquainted with the worldly fact of an object's being red. As John Campbell says, in endorsing just such a view of the relationship between experience and brain activity, "[W]e have to think of cognitive processing as 'revealing' the world to the subject; that is, as making it possible for the subject to experience particular external objects. Without the cognitive processing, there would be no experience of the objects.... But without the objects, there would be no experience of objects either" (2002: 118).

This conception of the role of the brain in experience sees it not as the organ that somehow generates conscious experiences, but rather as the organ that enables us to detect different features of the world in which we live. J. J. Gibson is a notable example of a psychologist who sees the brain in this kind of way. He holds that "the brain can be treated as the highest of several centers of the nervous system governing the perceptual systems. Instead of postulating that the brain constructs information from the input of a sensory nerve, we can suppose that the centers of the nervous system, including the brain, resonate to information" (1966: 267).

On this view, the brain is merely one component of our perceptual systems, albeit a crucial one. It is that component of our perceptual systems that performs the processing that enables us, in Gibson's terms, to "resonate to information" that is out there in the world. Neurobiologist Semir Zeki makes a similar sounding claim. He describes the cerebral cortex as a "categorizer" and says that "the function of the sensory parts of the cortex is to act as categorizers of the stimuli in our environment" (1993: 241). Moreover, Mohan Matthen has argued at length for the claim that "sensory systems classify and categorize; they sort and assign distal stimuli (i.e., external sensed objects) to classes" (2005: 13). In the terminology I have been using, the suggestion is that in order to have the capacity to see a certain kind of fact, we have to have the ability to classify or categorize things as being facts of that kind, and that, because the brain is the organ that underpins such abilities and capacities, the right kinds of brain function and activity will be required for the relevant processes of categorization to take place. In this kind of way, we can explain any correlations the neuroscientists find *without* assuming that brain function generates phenomenal character. On this alternative way of interpreting the quest for the neural correlates of consciousness, instead of seeing it as a search for the particular kinds of activity that cause experiences with a certain kind of phenomenal property, I suggest we should see it as a search for the particular types of neural activity that underpin our capacity to become acquainted with certain aspects of the world in experience.

This ties in with the account of veridical perception outlined in chapter 3, where I suggested that, for a subject to become acquainted with a particular worldly fact in experience, the subject of experience must have the capacity to see facts of that kind. In this light, we can see the search for the neural correlates of consciousness as providing further details of what is required for a subject to have the capacity to see facts of certain kinds. If activity in V4 is necessary for the subject to have experiences of color, then a functional V4 is required for a subject to have the capacity to see color facts, and so on. But because we need only claim that this is *part of* what is involved in having the capacity to see certain facts, such a claim can be made compatible with the kind of undemanding conceptualist stance that was tentatively favored in that chapter. In addition to requiring that the brain areas function correctly, we could also hold that, for the activity in areas of the brain devoted to color discrimination to enable *me* to be aware of different colors, this activity would have to be suitably integrated into the system as a whole.[14]

It is also important to note that the selective account can explain the clinical evidence of experiential deficits just as straightforwardly as the generative account. Take achromatopsia as an example. The generative account would explain achromatopsia by holding that the damage to V4 disrupts the brain's ability to generate color experiences, but leaves the brain's ability to generate experiences of form intact. The selective account would hold instead that the damage to V4 means that the subject's discriminating organ—the brain—loses the ability to adequately process information about color, which in turn deprives the subject of the capacity to become aware of color facts. However, because other areas of the brain remain intact, the subject is still picking up on other facts, such as facts about shape, position, and motion. In discussing a particular achromatopsic patient, Zeki offers an explanation of the subject's particular disorder that could have sprung straight out of this mold. He says that it "is not that such a patient sees colours but is not conscious of them...or that he sees colours but does not understand them. It is just that he sees and understands what the limited capacities of his V1 cells enable him to see and therefore to understand" (1993: 312).

The alternative explanations of achromatopsia offered by the selective and generative accounts also suggest that the generative account will carry an explanatory burden that the selective account does not. According to the generative account, the occurrence of achromatopsia is explained by allowing that the ability to generate phenomenal experiences of color can come apart from the ability to generate phenomenal experiences of form, motion, and so on. This potential for disconnection

14. Of course, given the complexity of the brain, it will be far more difficult to isolate where the critical stages of discrimination occur. This would explain why the search for the neural correlates of consciousness is proving to be so complex. Consider the processing that occurs when I see something red. From the moment my retina is stimulated, information will be processed by my brain that is apt for the discrimination of red. But it may be very difficult indeed to isolate at which point the information goes from merely being "available to the system" to the system actually having made a discrimination *on the basis* of this information.

raises the question of how, in a normal perceiver, these different facets of an experience are brought together. This is a phenomenal version of what is known as the 'binding problem': the problem of explaining how, given the functional specialization of the brain, "the information processed by different sensory systems [is] brought together to provide a unified representation of the world" (Garson 2001: 381). Once we assume that the function of the brain is to generate experiences with phenomenal character, we face the problem of explaining how, if the phenomenal experience of motion is caused by/supervenes upon activity in MT and the phenomenal experience of color is caused by/supervenes upon activity in V4, this is brought back together to generate the homogeneous phenomenal experience of a single object. If we endorse the selective account, however, this problem disappears. On this account, activity in MT enables us to perceive facts about an object's motion; activity in V3/V3a, facts about its orientation; and activity in V4, facts about its color. So the color, motion, orientation, and so on, are all initially bound together in the external object. Processing in the brain then enables the subject to become acquainted with each of these different facts in which that object features. Because the selective account does not claim that the brain, having completed this processing, has to somehow generate a phenomenal experience, there is no need to have a theory of how these different processing streams come to be bound together once again.

To recap, inasmuch as the correlations between the nature of our visual processing and the different aspects of the phenomenal characters of our perceptual experiences provide an argument for local supervenience, that argument must be that local supervenience is the *best explanation* of why there are these correlations. I suggested that, to counter this argument, we need an *alternative* vision of why certain kinds of brain processing are necessary for certain kinds of phenomenal property to be instantiated by the subject's perceptual experiences. That account is a selective account on which the brain is the organ that enables a subject to engage in tasks involving discrimination, differentiation, and classification. So, if there's no brain, there's no discrimination, differentiation, or classification. Likewise, if a subject's brain is unable to work in a particular kind of way, then the subject will be unable to make a particular kind of discrimination. By contraposition, if the subject is able to make, or is indeed making, a particular kind of discrimination, then the brain will need to be able to work, or will indeed be working, in the right kinds of way. Nevertheless, the features that the subject is enabled to discriminate by this neural activity are features of the external world.

5.6 Hallucination and Neural Replication

We have seen that neither of the two empirically based motivations for local supervenience gives us particularly compelling reasons to endorse the principle. This does raise the question of why it is so often taken for granted that the phenomenal character of our experiences supervenes directly upon the states of our brains. Noë suspects that this is because local supervenience "is not so much a working hypothesis as it is an assumed starting point" (2004: 210). Yet as Zeki points out in the epigraph that began this chapter, we should be wary of assumptions that are perpetuated yet remain unquestioned, and this circumspection should be even more characteristic of philosophers. So why does Robinson claim that local supervenience is "clearly true" (1994: 151) and A. D. Smith insist that it is "surely not open to serious question" (2002: 203)? Why is it so widely assumed that, by replicating the neural activity that occurs when a subject perceives something, we would thereby produce an experience with identical phenomenal character to that perception?

As we saw at the outset, the very existence of hallucinatory states may be a key motivator. Because it can be difficult to see an alternative to concluding that hallucinations are states with phenomenal character, and because hallucinations seem to require only neural activity to occur, this can quite naturally lead to the assumption that local supervenience is true. In the absence of any other theories of hallucination, local supervenience has attained the status of the only game in town. In a sense, then, my suggestion is that the prima facie plausibility of local supervenience derives, in no small part, from a lack of alternatives. Local supervenience seems so reasonable to us, not because we have some deep intuitive insight into the relationship between experience and the brain, but rather because we *lack* any such insight. So, when offered local supervenience as a putative explanation, it will of course seem reasonable: any explanation is better than no explanation. And then *once this assumption is in place,* the empirical results can look to provide *further* confirmation of the thesis. If we already think that neural activity suffices for an experience with phenomenal character, then of course the brain stimulation findings and the discovery of neural correlates of consciousness are going to seem to support that.

Yet if we set aside the intuition that local supervenience is already true, and then look again at whether the empirical results support local supervenience over the alternative account I have been outlining, we can see that they do no such thing. For one, it seems to be perfectly compatible with the overall body of brain stimulation evidence to treat the visual experiences obtained by brain stimulation as artificially induced variants of the kinds of hallucinations described in chapter 4. There is nothing in the brain stimulation results, over and above the very fact that nonveridical mental states were induced, that could be seen to favor a conception of these experiences as states with phenomenal character over this hypothesis. In addition to this, we can explain *why* certain neural activity should reliably correlate with certain aspects of phenomenal character *without* assuming that the neural activity causes, or provides the supervenience base for, a mental state with that phenomenal character. So I suggest that it is thoroughly justifiable for the naive realist to refuse to endorse local supervenience.

If we do reject local supervenience, however, we thereby forgo the comfortable and, it seems, intuitive account it offers of what would occur if we were to succeed in precisely replicating the neural conditions that occur during a veridical perceptual episode. If the kind of vat-brain scenario envisaged by Putnam is indeed possible in principle, and there are no reasons to suppose that it is anything other than fiendishly difficult in practice, then something ought to be said about what would be the mental upshot for the subject if such a situation were to become a reality. Now local supervenience claims, apparently in accord with intuition, that in such a situation the subject would have an utterly convincing hallucination. This is because the computer that feeds signals to the brain ensures that the neural conditions in the brain are as they would be for a veridical perceiver, and this, together with local supervenience, ensures that the brain supports mental states with the same phenomenal character that it would have supported had the subject in fact been enjoying veridical experiences.

If local supervenience is rejected, then even in the heavily qualified cases of (recently) embodied brains that had supported environmentally situated perceivers, experiences with phenomenal character will not be produced by neural replication. So, to provide the discussion with a little more focus, let us ask what, according to the thesis presented here, would be the mental outcome of the kind of neural replication Putnam envisages. Brain stimulation findings clearly give us reason to be confident that some kind of mental state would be produced, even if a hazard is involved in generalizing from the brains of epileptics to the general population. As to whether the mental state produced would be a completely convincing hallucination, I'm not sure. What I can say, however, is that it is *compatible* with the definition of hallucination I have defended to claim that the kind of externally driven neural replication envisaged by the brain-in-a-vat scenario would yield not only a visual experience, but also an utterly convincing hallucination.

Let me explain how this might work. It is possible that psychologists could discover that there are significant similarities between the kinds of physical processing that underlie hallucination and veridical perception. Given that we have rejected local supervenience, we would not simply assume that, by replicating physical processes of the same kind, we would thereby produce an experience with the same phenomenal character. Yet it is *possible* that whatever information-processing story there is to tell would have the consequence that perfect replication of the neural underpinnings of a certain kind of perceptual experience would produce the same kinds of higher cognitive effects as would be produced by a perceptual experience of that kind. Because these effects would include the same introspective beliefs about their experiences, subjects would make all the right kinds of claims about the perception-like nature of their experiences. What is more, this could even hold if the subjects are willing participants in a neural replication experiment. As we saw in chapter 4, even if a subject *knew* that we were going to induce an utterly convincing hallucination of an orange in front of him, and if, as it happened, we did nothing to his brain but instead cunningly installed a suitably located orange without him noticing, our subject would not come to believe that he saw an orange, but merely that it was *exactly as if* he saw an orange. And it is consistent with the story I have been telling that, if neural replication took place against a similar set of background beliefs and expectations, it might indeed have cognitive effects of just these kinds.

Therefore, it is compatible with naive realism (although not entailed by it) that in certain heavily qualified cases, *something* is locally supervenient. Of course, on the naive realist account, what is locally supervenient is not an experience with phenomenal character. However, it could be that the kinds of cognitive effects that I appealed to in chapter 4 to account for the felt reality of hallucination might be locally supervenient (in a suitably qualified sense). If that were the case, then whenever we have perfect replication of the kind of neural activity that occurs during a veridical perception of an F, we would *take ourselves* to be having just such an experience. Thus, this approach can even explain our intuitions that neural replication could yield an utterly convincing hallucination without endorsing local supervenience about phenomenal character.

5.7 Conclusion

As to whether the story I have just told is actually *true*, I simply don't know. But the very fact that it is there to be told suggests that the ability of local supervenience to account for this intuition should not constitute a reason to prefer the theory of hallucination it provides over the account presented in chapter 4. Indeed, the reasons for endorsing local supervenience seem either to be directly accommodated by the alternative I have developed, or to provide very little in the way of compulsion. Just like local supervenience, the alternative can explain why hallucinations are indiscriminable from veridical perceptions; it can even allow (although, unlike local supervenience, it does not entail) that in cases of neural replication, a subject may undergo perfectly indiscriminable hallucinations. It can also accommodate the brain stimulation findings and allow us to understand why the right kinds of brain activity are necessary conditions of having perceptual experiences that instantiate certain phenomenal properties. All in all, then, I suggest that the naive realist's refusal to accept the local supervenience principle is entirely justifiable. If, despite this, it is insisted, along with Smith (2008), that the kind of hallucinations that philosophy should be concerned with have phenomenal character *by definition*, my response is simply that, because we have seen how nonsensory states could be mistaken as sensory, we have been given no good reason to think that such hallucinations are possible. Unless further considerations are adduced, then, appeals to a special class of 'philosophical' hallucinations, like appeals to the local supervenience principle itself, are examples of just the kind of unspoken, unquestioned, and, ultimately, unsupported assumptions that Zeki warns us against.

6

Illusion

The naive realist response to the argument from hallucination is now complete. That argument operates by claiming, first, that naive realism is not true of hallucination (base case) and, second, that we must give the same account of veridical perception as we gave of hallucination (spreading step). Because the base case of this argument is undoubtedly correct, the only way to defend naive realism for the core case of veridical perception is by resisting the spreading step in the way recommended by the disjunctivist. In taking this option, however, the naive realist shoulders the responsibility of providing an explanation of how two mental events can be indiscriminable from one another without sharing a common mental component. Chapters 3 and 4 developed theories of veridical perception and hallucination in order to discharge this responsibility. Chapter 5 then considered the merits of a more recent variation of the argument from hallucination's spreading step, which appeals to the possibility in principle of neural replication in support of the claim that the phenomenal character present in cases of veridical perception could also occur in nonveridical cases. However, on investigating the key principle on which this contention is based—the local supervenience principle—we found that the reasons commonly given in support of the principle were persuasive only against the background of a tacit acceptance of the principle itself.

This gives us the two poles of our disjunctive theory of visual experience: veridical perception and hallucination. The question we now face is what the naive realist should say about cases of *illusion*. One possible course of action would be to simply lump all cases of illusion with hallucination in the nonveridical disjunct. However, given the definition of hallucination provided in chapter 4, such an approach would leave us squarely facing the kinds of implausible consequences highlighted in chapter 2. As noted there, our experience of properties such as shape seem to depend on our experience of color—we see, at least in many cases, the shape of an object *by* seeing its color—and this also appears to hold true even in cases of color illusions. If we were to treat such illusions like hallucinations—as states that lack phenomenal character—then it becomes difficult to see how we might veridically perceive an object's shape by merely believing that we see its color. Moreover, if cases of illusion are as prevalent as suggested by the cases in which there is experiential continuity from veridical perception to illusion, such an approach to illusion would have the consequence that we only occasionally enjoy experiences with phenomenal character; the rest of the time we just think we do.

If we do not try to accommodate illusions alongside hallucinations, then the argument from illusion is still fully in force. According to the version of naive realism I have been presenting, the phenomenal character of a particular veridical perceptual experience is its property of acquainting the subject with certain worldly facts. Because illusions are cases in which a particular can *appear* to us to exemplify a property that it objectively lacks, then unless we are willing to endorse a realm of objective nonfacts, there appear to be no suitable facts with which the subject could be acquainted in illusory experience. So while we are unwilling to give illusions the same treatment as hallucinations, we are unable to give them the same treatment as veridical perceptions. Illusions therefore remain unexplained, the argument from illusion remains in force, and the defense of naive realism is as yet incomplete.

In this chapter, I complete the defense of naive realism by offering a theory of illusion that combines the theories of veridical perception and hallucination. This is possible because the common thread that binds different cases of illusion together is that illusions occur when something is *seen*, but seen in a way that it is not. In such cases, then, there is usually some particular feature of an object that is misperceived while at the same time other features of the same object are perceived accurately. The fact that illusions all involve some features of an object being seen correctly and other features being seen wrongly, however, should not blind us to the fact that there are significant differences between the sorts of scenarios that fall under the broad banner of illusion. Section 6.1 clarifies some of the different kinds of visual illusion. Sections 6.2–6.5 then offer accounts of these different types of illusion. Section 6.6 concludes both the chapter and the book by bringing together the different threads of this defense of naive realism.

6.1 Types of Illusion

To enable us to focus more easily on the individual features that are seen/misperceived, in presenting these theories of illusion I will sometimes talk about specific *aspects* of the phenomenal character of an experience, what I called *phenomenal properties* in chapter 1. While we have been talking about a veridical experience possessing *one* property involving *one* acquaintance relation to *many* facts (that property's being the experience's phenomenal character), we may instead talk about that experience as possessing *many* properties, each involving *one* acquaintance relation to *one* fact, where each of these acquaintance properties is a distinct phenomenal property of the experience. Recalling David Chalmers's claim that "two perceptual experiences share their phenomenal character if... [they] instantiate the same phenomenal properties" (2006: 50), we can talk of a pure case of veridical experience as possessing either *a* phenomenal character or *an array of* phenomenal properties—as many phenomenal properties as there are facts that the subject is presented with in the experience—each of which involves a single thread of acquaintance to a worldly fact.

When considering the different types of illusion, we should note that many "illusions" are in fact situations with which we are familiar from everyday life. For example, simple objects such as tables and coins can look to be different shapes and colors when viewed from different angles and in different lighting conditions, and a straight stick placed in water will appear bent. These cases are all intersubjective—by which I mean that many people might be subject to the same illusion at the same time—and highly predictable. Indeed, as noted in chapter 2, such cases may be so mundane and well understood that one might balk at describing them as illusory at all. When we reflect on these everyday cases and consider what explanation to give of the illusion that we are subject to, we find that the explanation of *why* things look as they do is a matter of how things are in the external world. For example, to explain why the stick in water appears bent, we need only appeal to the natural physical phenomenon of light being refracted as it passes through materials of different refractive indices. In a sense, then, the explanation of the illusion—or at least, that part of the explanation that is peculiar to the illusory scenario—is complete by the time we get to the subject. Even if our perceptual processing of this visual information is unimpeachable, as it often is, we will still suffer from an "illusion" because of the particular way that things out there in the world affect the patterns of light incident upon our retina. A similar, purely physical explanation can be given of the other cases cited above (although, as we shall see, color experience will prove to be somewhat less straightforward). For this reason, I call such cases *physical* illusions.

The reason that there is an illusory appearance in the case of physical illusions, then, is purely a matter of what is going on in the world and how that affects the patterns of light that impinge upon the subject. This is why physical illusions all have the interesting property of being able to be photographed. Another class of illusions have a number of similarities to physical illusions as well as important differences. Within this group we find many of those cases that are constructed by artists or visual scientists and often go under the title of *optical* illusions;[1] examples include perspective illusions such as the hallway illusion, the Ponzo illusion, the Ebbinghouse illusion, and the moon illusion, as well as illusions of shape such as the Hering figure, and other illusions such as the Poggendorf illusion, the Kanizsa triangle, and the famous Müller-Lyer illusion.

Like physical illusions, optical illusions are similarly predictable and intersubjective—if they were not, there would not be much of a market for books of the illusions. And, like physical illusions, they also require the world to be a certain way in order for us to be subject to the illusion. So, for example, for the Hering figure illusion to occur (in which two parallel bars seem to bow outward), the parallel bars have to be presented against a background of lines that radiate out from a central

1. Calling this class of illusions "optical illusions" is just to give them a convenient and familiar name. It is not to imply that illusions that fall into other classes do not have features related to the study of optics. Indeed, in many ways, physical illusions are a more optical class of illusion than are optical illusions.

point between the bars. The key difference between physical and optical illusions, however, is that the occurrence of optical illusions cannot be *completely* accounted for by appeal to the way things in the world affect the patterns of light incident on the retina.

In the most part, optical illusions are arrived at by a combination of luck and design in which a particular figure is created in order to somehow trick or mislead our perceptual processing mechanisms. So while the particular setup of the physical world—the figure—is important (because it contains the cues that lead our perceptual processing astray), what sets these illusions apart from physical illusions is that this is not the whole story. Some kind of appeal to the way in which the subject's perceptual processes are misled by the figure has to be made if we are to explain why we are subject to an illusion in such cases. The precise nature of this appeal is something we will discuss in due course, but for now simply note that it is the need to make such an appeal that is the key point of difference between optical illusions and physical illusions.

While both physical illusions and optical illusions have the features of being both intersubjective and predictable, there are other cases of illusion that lack these features. Yet this new class of illusion is similar to optical illusions inasmuch as an explanation of the illusion must appeal to the particular contribution made by the *subject*. The kinds of illusion that fall under this heading are those in which we see something—for example, a coil of rope or a horse—but take it to be something it is not, such as a snake or a cow. Because of the importance of the way the subject misinterprets the object, I call such cases *cognitive* illusions. Now, the boundaries between cognitive illusions and optical illusions may not be clearly defined. For example, on some occasions—particularly if contrived—cognitive illusions may be quite intersubjective. The most paradigmatically *non*intersubjective cases, however, would be those occasions in which a subject's suffering from such an illusion is drug induced or due to some kind of idiosyncratic mental breakdown.

In considering different types of illusion, then, we can see that these two key dimensions need to be taken into account: first, that the way things are in the world is important when it comes to a perceiver's susceptibility to illusion and second, that the way in which a perceiver responds to the information from the world can lead to an illusion. In some cases, these can (to a greater or lesser extent) be disentangled, but in others, these aspects work together inasmuch as things in the world need to be a certain way in order for our perceptual systems to be systematically misled. What is more, the precise nature of the contribution of either the world or our perceptual mechanisms may differ between different cases of illusion. These issues are explained in more detail as we proceed.

Before we move on to theorizing about these different kinds of illusion, let me make it clear that, by bracketing illusions into these three classes, I do not intend to imply that there are clear boundaries between the different kinds of illusion any more than there will be clear boundaries between veridical perceptions and illusions, on the one hand, and illusions and hallucinations, on the other. There will be cases in which it is unclear into which category a particular case of illusion fits or, indeed, whether a particular case qualifies as an illusion *at all*, instead of a hallucination or a veridical perception. Having provided this crude map of the territory we find ourselves in, the remainder of the chapter begins by concentrating on those cases in which the explanation of our susceptibility to illusion is purely a matter of how things are in the world. I then progress to consider cases of cognitive illusion in which the contribution of the subject is critical, before moving on to the cases of optical illusions, in which both the world and the subject play a role.

6.2 Physical Illusions I: Color Illusions

The central examples of physical illusions are those in which an object looks to be a shape and/or color other than the shape or color that it really is. For example, if I view a round penny from an oblique angle, it looks elliptical; if I view a red car under a street lamp, it looks orange. With the terminology of phenomenal properties, we can focus on the specific phenomenal property that corresponds to the illusory aspect of the experience. So, according to the theory of veridical perception outlined in chapter 3, a veridical experience of the car as red would have, as one of its phenomenal properties, the property of acquainting the subject with the fact of the car's being red. Yet because the experience of the car under streetlights differs from this experience—the car now looks orange—what it is like to have this experience differs from what it is like to have the veridical experience. To capture this difference between the veridical and illusory experiences, then, the phenomenal property of the illusory experience that corresponds to the color of the car should differ from that of the veridical perception. But nothing about the car has changed—it is still red—so it looks as though the only available color fact for the subject to be acquainted with remains the fact of the car's being red. So either the illusory experience acquaints the subject with the fact of the car's being red—in which case, the phenomenal property is the same after all—or it does not, in which case there is no obvious alternative fact that the subject is acquainted with. Either way, then, there looks to be no way of supplying the illusory experience with an alternative phenomenal property with which to account for the difference in what it is like to have the illusory experience of the relevant feature. As things stand, then, naive realism looks to be false for physical illusions.

It would be possible to wheel in our account of hallucination at this point and say that the illusory experience *lacks* a phenomenal property that corresponds to the car's color. This would be to claim that we do not actually *see* the car's color at all; we just falsely *believe* that the car is orange. Yet as I have already noted, there are good reasons to resist such a treatment of physical illusion. The first is that we see the shape of the car under streetlights in part by seeing the color it merely appears to be. But if such illusions were akin to hallucinations, this would be to claim that, in such a case, we do not see the car's color at all but merely believe that we do. This leaves us without a plausible explanation of how it is we can nevertheless veridically see the car's shape given that we fail to see its color. The second reason not to treat the illusory aspects of physical illusion along the lines of hallucination is that it is physical illusions (and, interestingly, *only* physical illusions) that we find appearing in presentations of the continuity cases that are used to generalize the conclusion of the base case of the argument from illusion to the case of all visual experiences. By explaining the illusory aspects of physical illusions along the lines of our account of hallucination, we would be left with the kind of picture of our experiential interaction with the world ridiculed by A. D. Smith.[2] For these reasons, I focus on developing an alternative account of physical illusion that ultimately treats physical illusion as a special case of veridical perception.

To say that a physical illusion is a special case of veridical perception is not, of course, to deny that it is an illusion. As Smith says, "[C]ommon sense embraces two theses: that we are directly aware of the physical world (realistically construed), and that illusion is possible" (2002: 22). Physical illusions are just the kind of illusion that common sense

2. Wherein the "picture of our daily commerce with the world through perception that therefore emerges is one of a usually indirect awareness of physical objects occasionally interrupted by direct visions of them glimpsed in favoured positions" (Smith 2002: 28).

acknowledges. Against the background of these two commonsense theses, Smith suggests that the argument from illusion consists in, first, showing that these two theses are incompatible and hence that one must be given up and, second, showing that we should give up the first, naive realist thesis. To say that illusion is possible is to say that there are "perceptual situation[s] in which a physical object is actually perceived, but in which that object appears other than it really is" (23). In the case of illusions of color, this requires us to be robustly realist about color properties—to assume that there really is a color that these objects objectively are (Smith suggests that this is a presupposition of naive realism [23])—and to accept that objects can nevertheless look to be colors other than this color. As we saw in the case of the car, these two claims alone are incompatible with offering a naive realist account of physical illusion and would therefore take us to the culmination of the negative revision of the base case of the argument from illusion. But the proponent of the argument from illusion is after bigger game: naive realist accounts of all visual experiences. This requires a spreading step that Smith presents using a continuity case: "[C]onsider the way in which our awareness of the colors of objects changes as dawn gives way to the full light of morning, or as dusk descends" (2002: 27). The assumption here is that, over the course of the day, we switch from seeing the objects to have the colors they objectively do (veridical perception) to seeing them to have colors they objectively do not (physical illusion). So, to support the claim that the possibility of such physical illusions is incompatible with naive realism per se, the smooth experiential continuity between these physical illusions and veridical perceptions is then exploited as a way of showing that it is implausible to suppose that we can give different accounts of the two situations.

What options are available to the naive realist here? One possibility would be for the defender of naive realism to bite the bullet and insist that we can offer distinct accounts of veridical perception and physical illusion despite this experiential continuity. This option is problematic for the reasons just outlined. A second possibility—the possibility the proponent of the argument from illusion urges—is to offer the same theory of veridical perception as we do of physical illusion, where this theory is not naive realism. This alternative is clearly not available to the naive realist. Two other options suggest themselves: either we could accept the incompatibility and reject the second thesis—effectively, deny that physical illusions occur—or we could accept both theses and attempt to show how they are, contrary to first appearances, compatible.

David Armstrong seems to take the first of these options and deny that physical illusions occur: "It seems to me that we must admit that a real change in quality occurs at surfaces that, as we *say*, 'appear to change' when conditions of illumination are changed. I can see no ground for saying that such changes are in any way illusory or merely apparent" (1968: 284). If the quality in question here is the object's color, then Armstrong claims that objects really do change their color under changes of illumination. On such a picture, the specific color an object exhibits on a given occasion is not a matter simply of the object's intrinsic reflectance properties, but also of the brightness and spectral distribution of the illuminant. What is more, simultaneous contrast illusions show that *even under fixed illumination conditions*, the precise color a particular exhibits is also dependent upon the nature of its surrounds. So we might bring the threads of this kind of response together in the claim that the specific color a particular exhibits on any given occasion depends not only upon its intrinsic surface properties, but also on facts about its 'setting'—facts about the illuminant and the object's surround.

Although these color-determining aspects are not intrinsic aspects of the particular itself, they are still aspects of the objective physical world. This means that a realist about color—which, of course, the naive realist must be—might conceivably attempt to accommodate these factors in a theory of color. And indeed, when considering ways in which color realists might account for the fact that objects can look different in different conditions, color realist Michael Tye assays *two* options he considers to be "consistent with color realism of a commonsense sort" (2000: 152)—not only the claim that an object's color is an intrinsic, nonrelational (physical) property, but also the possibility that an object's color is a *relational* physical property. Which physical property? Well, this is an issue I cannot address in detail here, but if we are to try to account for simultaneous contrast effects as well as the effects of differences in illumination, we might begin by looking not simply at the light of different wavelengths reflected by the surface (the color signal), but rather at the *ratio* of the different elements of this color signal to the corresponding elements of the color signal reflected from the surround.

This relational property is not gerrymandered, nor is its postulation ad hoc. As it turns out, there are in fact good empirical reasons to employ this kind of relational property in a theory of color vision. For example, Christof Koch tells us that "a V4 cell responds to the middle wavelength region of the spectrum within its receptive field *relative to* the spectral distribution of stimuli in an extended region of the entire visual field" (2004: 138). So, in the area of the brain that seems, on current evidence, to be the area that supports our ability to experience color, we find cells that respond to just this kind of relational property. Indeed, Semir Zeki goes so far as to say that there is a "simple and obvious relationship between the physical characteristics of the object being viewed and the colour that the brain assigns to it.... It lies in a *comparison* of the wavelength composition of the light reflected from a surface and the wavelength composition of the light reflected from surrounding surfaces" (1993: 232). These relational properties are not ad hoc substitutes for intrinsic surface properties either. On the contrary, they approximate "as much as possible" to the actual intrinsic reflectance properties of objects (236). So there is good reason to think that these are the properties that we really do see—because picking up on these properties is the next best thing to actually picking up on the invariant intrinsic surface properties of objects.

If we adopt some kind of *relational* view of color along these lines, we can then deny that, in any given situation, the color that a particular possesses is an intrinsic property and hence the same in all situations. Instead, as Armstrong suggests, the color a particular has will *differ* according to its surroundings. And this is just what the naive realist requires. On such a conception of color, as the lighting conditions and the reflectance properties of an object's surround changes, so would the color that the particular possesses. As the color changes, then so does the color *fact* that has the particular and that color property as constituents. Thus, the fact that the subject is acquainted with in experiencing the object will indeed change as the relevant viewing conditions change, and the relevant phenomenal property of the experience—the property of acquainting the subject with the relevant color fact—will likewise change.[3]

3. What of the claim that the same Munsell color chip may nonetheless still be seen as different colors by different subjects, even under controlled conditions (see Hardin 1988: 79–80)? There are two possible claims that the naive realist could make here. The first would be to accept that the subjects' color experiences differ and hold that the particular color signal ratio each picks up on is, due to physical differences between the two subjects, slightly different. The second possibility is to note that, strictly speaking, these studies report only that subjects make different *judgments* about the colors they see. To assume without further argument that these studies prove different color *experiences* is therefore an unwarranted leap of faith. Given this, the naive realist might offer an alternative interpretation of these studies along the lines of Daniel Dennett's claim that qualia are our "idiosyncratic complex[es] of dispositions" to respond to sensory input (1992: 389). Because we will each have different learning histories for color words,

With such an understanding of the situation in hand, we can explain how our experiences of shape can continue to remain dependent on our experiences of color, even in cases of color illusion. On the view just presented, an illusory color experience is in fact a special case of veridical perception, so we can in fact be said to see the shape of the object by seeing the color it appears to be. And Smith's continuity case ceases to be problematic for the same reason. As the sun rises and sets, an object's color changes, so it turns out that such a continuity case is not one in which we switch from illusory experiences to veridical experiences and back again—all the color experiences the subject has throughout the day would qualify as equally veridical.

I can foresee two major objections to this proposal, which are related in an important way. The first of these objections is that relationalism about color is implausible. David Lewis, in a list of things that it just "won't do to say" about the colors, includes the claim that colors "change with every change in the illumination" (1997: 325). And as Tye points out, although we know that an object's *shape* can be made to appear different by altering its surroundings (as in many well-known optical illusions), we do *not* therefore conclude that the shape of a particular is a relational property. We simply say that the square (the particular) *looks* or *appears* nonsquare (2000: 153–154). In the color case, our linguistic practices are similar. We do not say that the blue square against a red background is greenish, only that in these circumstances the blue square looks or appears greenish. Linguistically, there seems to be a tacit commitment to the square's remaining the *same* color. The second objection is that, in offering this kind of treatment of color illusions, we are effectively denying the very possibility of illusion. As Mohan Matthen complains, "[T]here is no question of... error here—what you see is what you get when you get it" (2005: 254).

I will deal with these objections in turn, as my response to the first is taken up in my response to the second. The first problem revolves around Lewis's claim that it won't do to say that colors change with every change in illumination. Yet, rather than undermining an appeal

---

and hence slight idiosyncrasies in our individual mappings of how color words apply to the colors themselves, if two subjects were to have their color judgments tested under highly controlled conditions—say, if two subjects were asked to judge whether a particular Munsell tile was at all greenish—it is possible that these idiosyncrasies would show up in subjects' making different *claims* about the tile. Yet this is entirely consistent with the subjects *experiencing* the color of the tile in the same way.

to relational color properties, this objection actually points to a revision of the proposal that enhances its credibility. To see how this revision might proceed, consider John McDowell's suggestive characterization of Gareth Evans's contention that color experience outstrips our conceptual capacities: "[Whereas] color expressions like 'red,' 'green,' or 'burnt sienna'... express concepts of bands on the spectrum... Evans's thought is that color experience can present properties that correspond to something more like lines on the spectrum, with no discernible width" (1994: 56). Evans's thought is that our everyday concepts of colors—*and hence our everyday talk about color*—do not carve things as finely as our experience of color. But then, even if it is true that our linguistic practices include a tacit adherence to nonrelationalism about color—inasmuch as we say that a particular *is* red or green or burnt sienna—we are not thereby tacitly committed to the claim that a particular really is a highly determinate color, what we might call a 'fine-grained shade.'

Should we nevertheless concede that when we say a particular is or has a specific color, we mean that it is or has a specific fine-grained shade? If we did, this would raise a couple of knotty problems. First is the problem of saying which, of the many shades an object might exhibit, is the object's "real" shade. Even under a range of observation conditions that would qualify as normal, an object may well exhibit many different shades of color. We might stipulate that of these shades, its "real" shade is the shade that it appears under certain, narrowly prescribed observation conditions. But if it exhibits shades other than this shade in other unexceptional conditions, what justification is there for claiming that particulars reveal their true colors only in those precise conditions? In addition to the seemingly ad hoc nature of this stipulation, there is also the worry that, if we interpret the claim that a particular has a specific color in the fine-grained shade sense, it would seem to have the consequence that a great deal of our everyday experiences of particulars get their color wrong.

It is also interesting to note that Tye, in a paper with Peter Bradley, *defines* the *color* (pure) red as follows: "[A] surface is (pure) red if and only if it has a surface reflectance that disposes it, under normal viewing conditions, to reflect... significantly less" middle wavelength light than long wavelength light, and "approximately the same" short wavelength light as the total middle and long wavelength light combined (2001: 481). What I want to draw attention to in this definition is the vague terminology that Bradley and Tye employ. They talk about long, middle, and short wavelength light, rather than light of specific wavelengths, and they require the amount of light of a particular wavelength to be "approximately the same as" or "significantly less than" the amount of light of other wavelengths. Given the vagueness of these criteria, it would seem likely that two surfaces might both meet these criteria while appearing different shades to a given observer under normal viewing conditions. All this suggests that, in defining redness in such terms, Bradley and Tye are *not* attempting to define something quite as fine-grained as a shade.

Although these considerations are not conclusive, they do at least suggest that when we *say* a particular is a specific color, we are not explicitly committing ourselves to the claim that it really is a specific shade of that color. Given this, I suggest that there is scope within our everyday thinking about color for a position on which we are nonrelational about the *color* (understood as a spectral band) that a particular is or has, while endorsing relationalism about the specific (fine-grained spectral line) *shade* that a particular exhibits on any given occasion. On this account, a particular would be or have one unique color, regardless of the situation it was in, as long as its surface has the right kind of surface reflectance property—perhaps along the lines suggested by Bradley and Tye above. This would satisfy the constraints of our intuitions and linguistic practices. In addition to this, however, we could hold that the particular exhibits different shades in different situations, where the shade a particular exhibits is a relational property—a property that depends not only on the object's nonrelational surface property (its color on this account) but also, in a way yet to be spelled out in detail, on the spectral distribution of the illuminant and the reflectance properties of the surround.

This claim may be clarified with an analogy.[4] Any physical object has a mass, and the mass it has is an intrinsic, nonrelational physical property of the object—its having that mass does not require it to stand in any particular relations. While in a gravitational field, any object with a mass will also have a weight. But the weight it has is a matter not only of its mass, but also of the strength of the gravitational field it finds itself in. Something that is heavy in one setting (say, here on Earth) might be light in another—on the moon for example. So the weight an object has in a particular situation is a relational property, which depends both upon

4. This analogy was prompted by various passages in Tye (2000: 152) where he considers whether colors are like mass *or* weight—he never explicitly considers that they might be like *both*, however.

the object's nonrelational mass and facts about its setting. According to the suggestion outlined above, color and shade are usefully analogous to mass and weight, respectively. On this view, an object's color is an intrinsic, nonrelational property of its surface, and it has this color regardless of what setting it finds itself in. However, in any particular situation a colored particular will exhibit a specific fine-grained shade. The shade it exhibits is determined in part by its surface properties (its color) but also by things outside itself—the spectral distribution of the illuminant and the reflectance properties of the surround. So the shade a particular exhibits, while determined in part by its intrinsic color, is nonetheless a relational property of the particular. With this account in hand, the naive realist can hold that the fact that the subject is acquainted with in a fine-grained color experience is not the fact of an object's being a particular color, but rather the fact of an object's exhibiting a particular (relational) shade.[5]

Drawing a distinction between colors and shades in this way also enables us to block Matthen's objection that a relationalist approach to color precludes the very possibility of color illusion. Consider the following suggestion about color perception and misperception: If a particular is a certain color, then in those situations where the shade it exhibits falls within the spectral band that corresponds to that color, we say that we veridically see the object's color. If, as in cases of unusual illumination or simultaneous contrast, the shade it exhibits falls outside that spectral band, then we say that we misperceive it. But inasmuch as this is a form of misperception, it is a peculiar one. Indeed, it is a kind of veridical misperception inasmuch as the "false" shade we see it to have in those circumstances is entirely predictable as well as intersubjectively verifiable. So while this theory of physical illusion does indeed treat such occurrences as special cases of veridical perception, we can nonetheless still make a case for treating such experiences as illusory.[6]

With this explanation of color illusion in hand, the following explanation of Smith's continuity case can be derived. Because this is a case where

5. Recall the point made in chapter 3 that, although facts like these can feature in the presentational characters of our experiences, they do not have to. It is possible that, because we are not attending to those aspects of a situation, we do not see the fact of an object's exhibiting a particular shade, and see only the fact of its being a particular color. This could help to explain why often we do not notice that objects seldom "look" the color they "are."

6. In a defense of color relationalism published after this chapter was written, Jonathan Cohen makes a similar suggestion about the compatibility of color relationalism and color error (2004: 473–474).

there is continuity between veridical perception and physical illusion, we have a series of cases in which the shades that objects are (veridically) perceived to exhibit slowly change, and in which this slow change in facts that the subject is acquainted with corresponds with the changes in the relevant phenomenal properties of the subject's experiences. And if the shade an object exhibits moves gradually from being a shade that falls within the spectral band that corresponds to the object's (real) color, to being outside that spectral band, we can conclude that we have gone from a case of veridical perception to a case of illusion in experientially small degrees. At either end of this process—at sunrise and midday, perhaps—there will be cases that qualify as clearly veridical and clearly illusory. But there will also be intermediate stages as the shade exhibited gets to the edge of the spectral band and beyond where it is unclear whether we want to say that the case is illusory or not. The critical claim from the point of view of naive realism is that at no point does such a continuity case require us to claim that the subject has suddenly lost perceptual touch with reality. In this way, we can see that this response to Smith's continuity case does not, in fact, proceed by denying the very possibility of illusions. Instead, it takes the remaining option: it offers a way of understanding color illusions that allows naive realism to be true of them.

A further objection might be that, whatever the merits of this proposal for physical illusions of color, it will not work for physical illusions of shape. Consider A. J. Ayer's penny again. When viewed from an oblique angle, a round penny will look elliptical. Likewise, when viewed from the pavement, a rectangular window on the fourth floor will look square. But as Christopher Peacocke reminds us, "a way in which a shape property may be perceived is to be sharply distinguished from a way of being shaped. A way of being shaped has to do with shapes themselves—it is a way of occupying space—and does not have to do with the way in which shapes are perceived" (2001: 248). So the property of being square is not, as may be the case with color properties, a matter of the way a particular looks in the right conditions. On the contrary, being square is a matter of how the particular fills out space. While this is true, we can nevertheless extend the suggestion just outlined so that it works in the shape case, too. Just as in the case of colors, there are different aspects that can alter the way in which a particular shape is perceived. The most familiar factor is the angle from which a shape is perceived—to a perceiver looking at a building from the pavement, a rectangular first floor window that is taller than it is wide will look rectangular, while the same shaped window on the fourth floor will look square.

In the color case, I distinguished the intrinsic color that the particular is from the relational shade that it exhibits and held that these relational shade properties are the constituents of the facts that the subject is acquainted with in fine-grained color experiences. The similarities above suggest that we might also distinguish between the intrinsic shape that a particular is (a way of filling out space) and the relational shape that it exhibits to a perceiver looking at the particular from a specific point. J. J. Gibson calls each possible vantage point a "station-point." He asks us to consider "one object and many surrounding station-points. The faces... of the object will be 'projected' to all of these station-points in accordance with the laws of projective geometry. An 'aspect' of each face is obtainable anywhere in the medium" (1966: 15). These "aspects" of objects are the relational shape properties I am suggesting are constituents of the facts that feature in fine-grained shape experiences. Alva Noë calls such properties "perspectival properties (or P-properties)" (2004: 83). He goes on to point out that while P-properties are perfectly "real" or "objective," they are, like the shade properties discussed in the case of color, relational. "In particular," he notes, "P-properties depend on relations between the perceiver's body and the perceived object.... P-properties are, in effect, relations between objects and their environment. That a plate has a given P-shape is a fact..., one determined by the plate's relation to the location of a perceiver" (83).

Noë's explicit reference to a perceiver may seem to make P-properties a little too mind dependent to be of use to the naive realist, but his assertion that P-properties are relations between objects and their environment may suggest a reading more in line with Gibson's. According to this reading, an object presents a different P-shape to each different station-point in surrounding space, where the P-shape it presents to each point is determined by the laws of projective geometry. And while such a station-point would be a *possible* location of an observer, an observer need not actually be situated at that point in order to talk about the P-shape the object presents to that point. With this clarified, it would seem that P-shapes are perfectly suited to feature in a parallel naive realist explanation of physical shape illusions. The rectangular P-shape that a first-floor window exhibits to a subject looking from a station-point about six feet above the pavement is just as predictable and intersubjectively verifiable as the shade it exhibits, and therefore seems to be in just as good a standing to be a constituent of perceptible facts as the shades we have thus far considered. If we are willing to include such relational shades and P-shapes in our ontology, we can thereby ensure that we can always locate a suitable property to feature in the facts with which the subject is acquainted in physical illusions. Because a phenomenal property of an experience is a property of acquainting the subject with a particular fact, differences in these facts will correspond with differences in the phenomenal properties that the experiences of these facts possess. This, then, can account for the differences in what it is like to see the same object across different observation conditions.

6.3 Physical Illusions II: Lenses

The account offered in section 6.2 shows how the naive realist can account for certain kinds of physical illusions, in particular, physical illusions of color and shape. However, John Foster's presentation of the argument from illusion—the argument, note, that he thinks finally refutes naive realism—contains an importantly different continuity case that makes use of distorting lenses:

> Suppose we have ten lenses, which can be arranged in a series, the first being simply a piece of plain, flat glass, of the sort one would find in an ordinary window, and the others being curved in a way which, for someone looking through them, distorts the sensible appearance of shape in a systematic fashion, the amount of distortion being very slight initially, but steadily increasing as we move through the series.... Now, given this set-up, suppose we have a circular object O, and we have a subject who views O through each lens in turn in reverse order.... Throughout the first nine viewings, the object is seen, non-veridically, as elliptical, the shape of the ellipse beginning as something which is paradigmatically oval, but becoming steadily less elongated (more squat) as the series progresses, until, at the ninth (the penultimate) viewing, it is scarcely discriminable from the circular shape which characterizes the appearance of the final [veridical] perception. (2000: 67–68)

It is clear how the continuity case is intended to work in this example. We have nine nonveridical experiences that become progressively more experientially similar to the final, veridical, experience. So our options, once again, are these: to offer distinct accounts of the veridical and illusory cases despite this experiential continuity, to offer an account of all ten experiences that is not naive realist, or to try to show how these cases can occur in a way that is compatible with naive realism. As before, the first option seems desperate, and the second option is to give up naive realism. That leaves us with the third.

As with the color and shape cases discussed in section 6.2, this case is clearly a physical illusion. If we were to take photographs of object O through the ten lenses, the first photograph would show a paradigmatically oval shape, the next eight would show progressively more squat ovals, and the tenth and final photograph would show a circle. Therefore, an explanation of why the illusion occurs does not require us to go beyond an explanation of how the different lenses refract the light reflected from object O. Yet lenses offer a unique set of difficulties for the naive realist. The fact that the images cast by lenses can be photographed might suggest that what is seen, when one looks at an object through a distorting lens, is not the object but rather the image on the lens (compare Brewer 2008: 173). The problem is that an attempt to claim that what is seen is the image on the lens becomes implausible in light of Foster's continuity case. At the end of his series we find a flat glass; in light of the experiential continuity between the mildly distorting lens and the flat glass, such a response would suggest that, even in the flat glass case, we see an image on the lens rather than the object behind the lens. But this would conflict with many of our commonsense intuitions: it would require us to say that we do not really see through windows, but see the images they cast; it would require us to say that a subject wearing eyeglasses does not really see the world, but only the images on his spectacles. So the naive realist should be very wary indeed of developing a position that holds that we do not see through lenses. This serves to illustrate the problem that faces us. We want to allow that we see *through* lenses—that we see through the lens to the object behind. But the object behind the lens in Foster's continuity case is not elliptical, yet the action of the lens makes it look elliptical.

To see how this problem can be resolved, we need to note an important feature about lenses. Consider microscopes: we use microscopes because the action of a microscope's lens enables us to become aware of additional facts—facts that we were unable to become aware of without using the microscope. If we look at blood through a microscope, the action of the lens enables us to become aware of facts concerning the shapes and colors of the different components of blood that we were not aware of before. Not all lenses do this, of course—a perfectly flat glass will not enable you to become aware of any new facts—but as long as the microscope contains a lens of the right kind, we can use it to gain access to an array of facts that we did not have access to before. Note, however, that the action of a lens that permits the awareness of new facts does so at the expense of preventing the awareness of other facts that we would have been able to see without the lens. When we view blood through a microscope, the action of the lens blocks us from seeing, among other things, facts about the color of blood itself.

With this in mind, let us look back at a slight variant of Foster's continuity case. The only difference between the case I will present here and Foster's original scenario lies in the fact that we do not see just one circular object—O—through the lens, but a series of five such objects with O lying in the middle. This is represented in figure 6.1a. This alteration is not significant from the point of view of Foster's argument; it merely serves to make my explanation of the illusions easier to grasp. Now suppose that a flat, circular lens, marginally larger than O and bordered by a mask, is placed over the scene (figure 6.1b). What we see when we look through the lens is illustrated on the left of this diagram. The portion of the scene that is seen *through* the lens is shown by the dashed line on the right. Now suppose we replace the flat glass with a mildly distorting lens (figure 6.1c). Again, what we see is illustrated on the left;

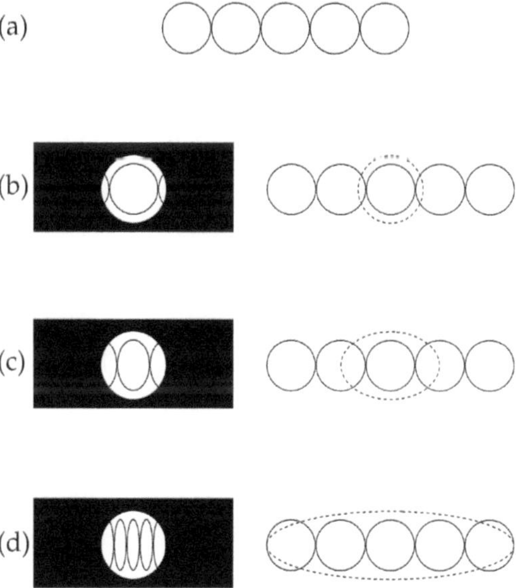

Figure 6.1. A series of circular objects (a) seen through a clear lens (b), a mildly distorting lens (c), and a strongly distorting lens (d). In diagrams b–d, the view of the lens, with the objects seen through it, is shown on the left; the portion of the scene viewed through the lens (indicated by the dashed line) is shown on the right.

the portion seen, on the right. Finally, we replace the mildly distorting lens with a strongly distorting lens (figure 6.1d).

In chapter 3, we saw that any difference in what it is like to have two perceptual experiences demands that there be a difference in the facts that the subject is acquainted with in having those experiences. Because what it is like to have these three experiences seems to be clearly different, the phenomenal characters of the three experiences would perforce be distinct, and we should therefore expect to find differences in the facts with which the subject is acquainted. And we do. Consider the differences in area of the regions bounded by the dashed line in figure 6.1b–d: as each lens is replaced by a more distorting lens, the area of this region increases as we become able to see more of the scene that lies behind the lens.

This suggests that we may be able to account for the differences in the phenomenal characters of the three experiences by appealing to differences in the facts that the subject is acquainted with in having those experiences. In the initial, flat glass setup (figure 6.1b), we are aware of an array of facts, including facts about O's shape and the color of its outline, as well as relational facts about its being flanked by other shapes. By the time we get to the strongly distorting lens (figure 6.1d), we are picking up on facts about all five objects. The kinds of facts we are picking up on include the fact that each object is a bounded figure, facts about the colors of their outlines, facts about their positions relative to one another, facts about their size relative to one another, and so on. The distorting lens functions, to this extent, in the same way as a microscope lens. It permits subjects to be aware of more facts than they were previously aware of, but like the microscope lens, in permitting the awareness of additional facts, the action of the distorting lens also serves to prevent the awareness of other facts. In this case, it prevents the subject being acquainted with facts concerning the shapes of objects seen through the lens.

We can therefore account for the differing phenomenal characters of these experiences by appeal to the differences in the facts that the subject is acquainted with in having these experiences. In the case of the strongly distorting lens, we are picking up on facts about an elliptical tract of the environment by looking through a circular aperture. This can account for what it is like to have the experience of looking through the strongly distorting lens without requiring us to appeal to the subject's being acquainted with any facts about the image on the lens, which in turn enables us to give sense to the intuitive idea that we see *through* the lens. When we look through the distorting lens, we see the area of the environment demarcated by the dashed line.

The explanation of our old friend the bent stick in water will also proceed in this way, but with the water acting as the lens. As before, the distorting action of the water alters the array of facts we can see by precluding us from seeing some facts and enabling us to see others. Because the particular way this occurs will be highly dependent on the particular situation, it will not be possible to give the kind of neat graphic account given above of just how this happens. However, merely by attempting to view something through a regular tumbler full of water, you can see for yourself how, for example, you are precluded from seeing the elements of the scene immediately behind the edges of the glass. The suggestion here is that it is action of this kind that also accounts for the phenomenon known as the bent stick in water by precluding us from seeing the fact of the stick's being straight and altering the way in which we are aware of the various facts pertaining to the part of the stick that lies beneath the surface of the water. Of course, it remains the case that subjects looking at the stick in water might come to *think* that they were seeing the fact of its being bent, or that subjects who did not know they were looking through a distorting lens might come to *think* that they were seeing the facts of the objects' being elliptical, but to explain what is going on in cases in which subjects take themselves to be seeing something they do not, we will need the resources afforded us by the account of cognitive illusions. So let us now turn to those cases.

6.4 Cognitive Illusions

The central cases of cognitive illusion occur when we see something—a horse, a shadow, or a coil of rope, for example—and take it to be something it is not, such as a cow, a person, or a snake. In order to ground our discussion, let us begin with a concrete example. Suppose that we have a subject who is afraid of snakes and must enter an enclosure in which he is told, by someone he trusts, that a snake is lurking. He enters the enclosure and catches a glimpse of a coil of rope nestled under a log. Because of the subject's heightened state of anxiety, he has the illusion of seeing the rope to be a snake and, on the basis of this, turns and runs. Here we have an example of a cognitive illusion; we have a subject who perceives one thing—a coil of rope—but sees it as something else: a snake. For the sake of highlighting the issues, let us suppose as well that because the subject immediately flees, he never comes to veridically perceive the rope as rope. So upon questioning, we find that our subject honestly takes himself to have seen a snake, rejects suggestions that he might have been mistaken, and so on. Cases such as this cause problems for naive realism because they involve situations in which we appear to have an experience as of a snake under a log, but where there is no fact of a snake's being under a log for the subject to be acquainted with in the illusory experience. So what explanation can we give of an illusion of this kind?

The first thing to note is that this case is not quite *hallucinatory*; whatever error it is that the subject is making, there nevertheless does seem to be some kind of perceptual awareness of the particular (the rope) occurring. To see this, imagine a somewhat bolder ophidiophobe who, rather than immediately fleeing the enclosure, braces herself and takes a moment to attend to what she is seeing. In doing this, she may well quickly come to realize that the object she is seeing is not a snake after all, but a coil of rope. But in so doing, it would seem implausible to suggest that this subject suddenly comes to see the particular in the world where she did not before. So there is good reason to suppose that, like physical illusions but unlike many cases of hallucination, cognitive illusions do involve some kind of perceptual relation to the object in the world—that the subject sees the coil of rope yet mistakes it for a snake.

Although cognitive illusions do seem to involve some kind of perceptual experience of the relevant particular, it would be implausible to try to give them precisely the same treatment that was given to physical illusions. Essentially, physical illusions involve the veridical perception of an unusual fact, but to motivate the claim that the constituents of such facts are suitably mind independent, we appealed in part to the intersubjectivity and predictability of these illusions. The subjective and capricious nature of cognitive illusions means that such an approach would be far less credible in such cases; it would be implausible to suppose that, for any possible illusion of this kind, there must be a fact that the subject is seeing. But then, if there are no snake-involving facts available for the subject to be acquainted with in such experiences, a cognitive illusion of misperceiving a rope as a snake *cannot* be a matter of the subject's being acquainted with an unusual fact, as we have argued is the case for physical illusion.

Now that we are clear about the problem, let us start on the solution. To do this, we begin by asking two questions: First, if cognitive illusions do involve some kind of veridical experience, what facts is the subject acquainted with in having these experiences? Second, given this, what is the explanation of the illusion? In answer to the first of these questions, note that a cognitive illusion may well acquaint the subject with many of the facts that he or she would have been acquainted with had the experience been wholly veridical. To see this, think of the courageous counterpart of our cowardly subject who, despite initially seeing the rope as a snake, overcomes her fear long enough to realize that it is really a rope she is looking at. A natural description of such an episode of realization would be that the subject comes to realize that the coiled, brown thing she is looking at under the log is not a snake after all, but a rope. This suggests that, even when under the illusion, the subject still veridically perceives many facts about the particular (the rope), facts that she continues to perceive after realization dawns. Even while mistaken, she still perceives the object's being brown, its being coiled, its being under a log, and so on—the experience in a case of cognitive illusion still has phenomenal properties corresponding to these seen features. What is important is that, because the subject *fails* to perceive the fact of the object's *being rope*, the experience initially lacks a phenomenal property acquainting the subject with that fact. Then, when the subject realizes what she is really looking at, she comes to perceive that fact as well, and her experience acquires a further phenomenal property.

To see how this kind of illusion can occur, think back to the idea, discussed in chapter 3, that in order for a subject to see a fact, the subject must have the *capacity* to see that fact. There I tentatively endorsed a theory according to which such capacities are *conceptual-recognitional* capacities—capacities that require the subject to possess a particular concept. The same thing is true of cases of cognitive illusion. In order for a subject to have the capacity to *mistake* a coil of rope for a snake, that subject would need to possess the concept of a snake. We can then start to see the outlines of an explanation of cognitive illusion developing when we consider how these conceptual-recognitional capacities are deployed in experience. As we saw, our conceptual-recognitional capacities are not actively exercised in experience; rather, they are passively deployed or exploited. And as to what determines which conceptual-recognitional capacities are deployed if not the determination or choice of the subject, I suggested that the conceptual-recognitional capacities that are deployed will be determined by two things: the nature and layout of the environment the subject is facing, on the one hand, and facets of the subject's mental makeup/learning history, on the other.

One of the reasons we need to appeal to idiosyncratic features of the subject's mental makeup is that psychological findings suggest that certain conceptual-recognitional capacities can be *primed* in such a way that they become more likely to be deployed in experience. In the experimental context, such priming effects are usually induced by presenting the subject with particular stimuli prior to the critical test stimulus, but it is possible that such conceptual-recognitional capacities may also be primed to be deployed for far more idiosyncratic reasons. For example, it is plausible to suppose that an ophidiophobic subject in a heightened state of anxiety may well be primed to deploy his snake conceptual-recognitional capacity in a way in which a nonphobic subject is not. If this were so, then in a normal (nonphobic) case when a subject sees a coil of rope under a log, we would expect the layout of the environment together with the subject's normal mental makeup to lead that subject's rope conceptual-recognitional capacity to be passively deployed, and the deployment of this conceptual-recognitional capacity would enable the subject to become aware of the fact of the object's being rope. In the case of the cowardly ophidiophobe, however, when the subject enters the enclosure to find a coil of rope nestled beneath a log, although he has a veridical experience of the object's being brown and the object's being coiled, the priming effects just discussed lead the subject to passively, but erroneously, deploy his snake conceptual-recognitional capacity in place of his rope conceptual-recognitional capacity. That the subject fails to deploy his rope conceptual-recognitional capacity explains why he fails to latch on to the fact of the object's being rope.

This gives us an explanation of the negative difference between the veridical and the illusory cases—that the veridical, but not the illusory, experience possesses a phenomenal property acquainting the subject with the fact of the object's being rope. This, in turn, yields a difference in what it is like to have the two experiences. However, there still appears to be a critical difference that has not yet been accounted for. To see this, imagine that we have a third, unsophisticated, subject who lacks the capacity to see things as either ropes or snakes. As with the ophidiophobic subject, such a subject would fail to pick up on the fact of the object's being rope (although, in this case, the failure is due to his lack of conceptual sophistication) yet would pick up on all the rest of the facts concerning the rope that the ophidiophobe successfully sees. So it would appear that both the ophidiophobic subject and the unsophisticated subject could be acquainted with exactly the same set of facts and would thereby enjoy experiences with the same phenomenal character. Yet there does seem to be a crucial difference between the two cases—the ophidiophobic subject, unlike the unsophisticated subject, is under the illusion that the object under the log is a snake. We do not yet have an adequate account of this important difference.

To get this, what we need is an explanation not only of why the deluded subject fails to see the fact of the object's being rope, but also why that subject additionally takes himself to see a snake. In chapter 4 we discussed cases in which subjects take themselves to see something when they do not: cases of hallucination. And there I appealed to the false beliefs that hallucinating subjects form about what they see in order to account for this kind of error. A similar explanation can be employed here—subjects under the illusion take themselves to see a snake because they mistakenly believe that they see a snake. Why? Well, as we have seen, when our cowardly ophidiophobe is faced with an environment containing a brown, coiled object under a log, the priming effects of his cognitive disturbance—his phobia together with his heightened state of anxiety—result in his passively deploying his snake conceptual-recognitional capacity. The suggestion is that this misdeployment will not only explain why the subject fails to see the fact of the object's being rope, but also explain why he comes to (falsely) *believe* that there is a snake under a log, that he saw a snake, and so on. Of course, I am not claiming that, in misdeploying this conceptual-recognitional capacity, the subject sees the fact of the object's being a snake; there is no such fact for the subject to see. All I am suggesting is that, having exploited that conceptual-recognitional capacity in error, the subject *takes himself* to have seen such a fact. So while the successful perception of facts in which the rope itself is a constituent (despite its not being seen as such) allows us to explain the intuition that, even while under the illusion, the subject nevertheless sees the rope, the subject's forming false beliefs about this experience could account for his having the illusion of seeing the rope to be a snake.[7]

As was the case with hallucination, these erroneous beliefs would enable us to account for everything the subject does and says. His false belief that there is a snake under a log would, in conjunction with his other cognitive states (e.g., the desire to avoid snakes), explain why he flees. Likewise, his false belief that he saw a snake could be appealed to in explaining his verbal behavior: the subject claims to have seen a snake under the log

7. A similar kind of explanation could be provided for the lens case in which subjects come to believe that they are seeing something elliptical. The array of facts that subjects see through the circular aperture of the lens, in the absence of any knowledge that the lens in question is a distorting lens, might explain why they deploy their ellipse concept. Of course, because there is no fact of the object's being an ellipse to pick up on, deployment of this recognitional capacity fails to enable the subjects to become aware of a fact, but it could nonetheless explain why they wrongly take themselves to have seen such a fact. Likewise for the bent stick in water.

because he believes he saw a snake under a log; he claims to have had a thoroughly snakelike experience (and not a ropelike experience) because he believes he had a perceptual experience of a snake, and so on.

Of course, the apparent snakeishness of the experience would usually evaporate as soon as the subject realizes what is really going on. It is an important aspect of this imaginary scenario that our cowardly ophidiophobe immediately flees because this allows us to stipulate that he remains committed to his initial snap judgment, and in turn to emphasize his claims about the nature of his experiences. Normally, however, as the courageous counterpart to our original subject suggests, further perceptual investigation will often result in false judgments of this kind—and hence illusions of this kind—being swiftly overcome. Having said this, there may well be situations—taking drugs and mental illness come immediately to mind—in which the cognitive disorder that leads to this kind of breakdown in judgment-forming processes is somewhat more significant and long term, and this could well lead to cognitive illusions that are far more persistent than normal.

Although this account of the illusory aspects of cognitive illusions borrows heavily from the account of hallucination outlined in chapter 4, there are nevertheless two important differences between the two types of state. The first difference concerns the relationships that exist between the successful aspects of the subject's overall experience and the erroneous judgments. What makes the case an illusion rather than a hallucination of a snake is that, while the false higher order judgment that the subject sees a snake would be made in both cases, in this case, the subject does successfully see the brownness, the coiledness, and the under-a-log-ness of the rope. This is what enables us to give sense to the claim that the subject sees the rope but gets it wrong.

In some situations, however, we may be inclined to classify an experience as one of hallucination rather than illusion, even though something in the world is seen. Such a case will, of course, not be a pure hallucination of the kind discussed in chapter 4, but it may have enough similarities to justify the title. We will be more inclined to classify a particular situation as hallucination rather than illusion in those cases in which the subject's cognitive disorders are more important than the layout of the world when it comes to explaining why the false beliefs occur. So, in paradigmatic cases of illusion, although we do need to appeal to the subject's phobia and heightened state of anxiety to explain why the snake conceptual-recognitional capacity is deployed in error, this is far from the whole story. It is also critical that the environment the subject is facing contains something brown, coiled, and under a log—something suitably snakelike to fool the subject. So, in cases of illusion, the explanation of the perceptual error will require both an appeal to idiosyncratic features of the subject's mental makeup and an appeal to features of the nature and layout of the environment the subject is facing.

In other cases, the nature of the error will be such that appeals to the layout of the environment the subject is looking at will tend to have little or no explanatory role to play in accounting for the occurrence of the particular anomalous beliefs. Take, for example, the subject mentioned in chapter 4 who took himself to be seeing dragons and demons in response to flushing water in a toilet bowl. In such a case, the particular patterns produced by the water are of only minimal relevance when it comes to explaining why the subject took himself to be seeing dragons and demons—an adequate explanation of why the water is seen *in that particular way* must appeal primarily to the subject's cognitive disturbance. In such a borderline case, the bulk of the explanation of why the erroneous beliefs occur will involve an appeal to the subject's cognitive disturbances. This is what inclines us to say that the subject is no longer suffering from an illusion, but rather a hallucination. As we become more inclined to classify situations as cases of hallucination, the influence of the layout of the environment will disappear altogether and the explanation of *why* the false beliefs occur will have only a correlate of the cognitive disorder component. At the end of this continuum, we find pure hallucinations of the kind discussed in chapter 4: mental states that have the effects they do solely because of disturbances in the subject's overall doxastic state. In such cases, there is no *additional* component of the explanation that appeals to the subject's experience of the world.

Again, we might initially think that a subject could be under the illusion that the object under the log was a snake, even if the subject does not come to *believe* that the object under the log is a snake. Yet once again, this fails to grasp the core idea of this approach. On the account I have presented, the snakeish aspect of the illusion is not a feature of the experience itself. If we could investigate the phenomenal character of the experience in isolation, we would find nothing there that would indicate to us that the subject was suffering from the illusion that the object is a snake rather than just failing to pick up on the fact of the object's being rope. In both cases, the subject is acquainted with the same set of facts, and the phenomenal characters of the two experiences would therefore be the same. Yet in the former case, the subject takes himself to see a snake and therefore takes himself to be having an experience with an additional phenomenal property. The subject's being under an illusion is purely a matter of him having formed this false belief—if there is no false belief, then there is no illusion.[8]

6.5 Optical Illusions

In section 6.1, I outlined three broad classes of illusion. We have now discussed two. According to the account I have been developing, the first of these, physical illusion, is in fact a special case of veridical perception that involves the successful perception of somewhat unusual facts. The account of the second of these, cognitive illusion, draws from the accounts presented of both of the primary disjuncts: veridical perception and hallucination. A particular cognitive illusion is based upon a veridical perception of an array of facts from the subject's environment, and it is this facet of a cognitive illusion that accounts for our intuitions that, in such illusions, objects are seen. However, due to the way the environment interacts with idiosyncratic disturbances in the subject's doxastic state at the time of the experience, inappropriate conceptual-recognitional capacities are deployed that lead these perceptual states to have anomalous cognitive effects. In sophisticated subjects, the cognitive effects they have involve, like the effects of a pure hallucination, false higher order beliefs that something is seen. As was the case with pure hallucination, these effects then ground the unusual actions and pronouncements of the subject of illusion.

Our final broad class of illusions, optical illusions, has similarities with both kinds of illusion discussed so far. The similarities with physical illusions are, first, that optical illusions are intersubjective and predictable and, second, that in order for optical illusions to occur, the world has to be a specific way. However, unlike physical illusions, the particular way the world needs to be for a certain kind of optical illusion to occur cannot completely account for the illusory appearance.[9]

8. This may not be true in certain cases, in particular, cases of optical illusions where we know that things are not as they appear. These special cases are discussed in section 6.5.

9. At least, not on the face of it. When discussing the Müller-Lyer illusion, Charles Travis remarks that, "in the Müller-Lyer, two lines are contrived (by means of accompanying wedges) to have a certain look. They do not just *seem* to have that look; that is actually the way they look" (2004: 68). This claim—that the lines really do have this look—could, if defensible, clear the way for a view claiming that, when we see the Müller-Lyer lines, we veridically perceive the look that they really do have.

Take the Müller-Lyer illusion, for example. Although the presence of the different arrowheads makes the lines seem to be different lengths, the size of the retinal images produced by the horizontal components of the two lines are the same. We cannot explain our susceptibility to the illusion purely by appeal to how things in the world affect the light impinging upon our retinas. So while things in the world do have to be a certain way for the illusion to occur—the lines need to have the different arrowheads or they will not seem to be different lengths—the arrowheads do not have this effect by somehow expanding or contracting the pattern of light leaving the figures. Instead, the arrowheads are required to produce an illusion because of the effects they have on our perceptual processes.

The reason optical illusions lead to a nonveridical experience is that the relevant features of the perceived scene function so as to trick or mislead our perceptual mechanisms. For instance, Richard Gregory (1970: 91) suggests the Müller-Lyer illusion may work as follows. We interpret the arrowheads on the ends of the horizontal lines as angles formed by two intersecting planes. The horizontal line is thus taken to be the corner formed by the joining planes. Now, if the arrowheads point inward, the planes would be seen as receding from the corner at which they join, whereas if they point outward, the planes would be seen as projecting toward the perceiver. According to Gregory, the arrowheads therefore provide perspective cues that make the receding corner (arrows out) seem to be farther away than the projecting corner (arrows in). But if the receding corner were indeed farther away than the projecting corner, it would have to be larger in order to cast a horizontal image of the same size on to the retina. This leads us to interpret the receding corner to be larger than the projecting corner, which accounts for the illusory appearance of the arrows-out line as longer.

The similarity optical illusions have to physical illusions is that the world has to be a certain way for the illusion to occur. The similarity with *cognitive* illusions is that a full explanation of optical illusions will also have to appeal to what goes on *in the subject*. This suggests that we might be able to account for the illusory *aspects* of optical illusions along essentially the same lines as the explanation of cognitive illusions. The perceptual experience of the Müller-Lyer lines has a number of phenomenal properties corresponding to various facts about the lines: their shapes, colors, relative locations, and so on. However, because of the way the lines have been contrived to produce misleading perspective cues, we cannot but passively deploy an inappropriate conceptual-recognitional capacity—our capacity for recognizing things to be different in length—in our experience of these lines. Because of this, the subject fails to become acquainted with the relational fact of the two lines' being the same length, and instead erroneously believes that the two lines are of different lengths. As with cognitive illusions, these false beliefs can then be appealed to in order to explain why the subject claims that one line is longer than the other and why the subject claims that they see two different length lines.

There is a critical difference between optical illusions and cognitive illusions that means that this approach will not work across the board. According to the approach just suggested, we account for the illusion that one Müller-Lyer line is longer than the other by appealing to the subject's erroneous belief that she sees two different-length lines. Now in the case of cognitive illusions, we would expect that if a subject knew, say, that the object under the log was not a snake but a rope, he would neither judge that the object under the log was a snake, nor have the illusion that it was. In the case of optical illusions, however, those who are familiar with the illusion *know* that the Müller-Lyer lines are the same length and therefore no longer form the belief that they see two different-length lines. Despite this, however, one's knowledge that the lines are the same length does not stop the illusion from occurring—the two lines continue to seem different lengths.

The unique problem that optical illusions pose for us is as follows. Here we have a situation in which the subject has the illusory experience of two lines being of different lengths when the lines themselves are the same length. This means that there are no objective properties of the situation that could be constituents of the right kinds of relational facts: the only relevant fact is that of the two lines' being the same length. Given this, the approach taken in the case of physical illusion—to ground the occurrence of the illusion in unusual facts that the subject is acquainted with in experience—will not work. Yet if subjects know that the lines are the same length, they will not form the belief that they see two different-length lines, so the approach taken in the case of cognitive illusion—to ground the illusion in subjects' erroneous beliefs about their experiences—will not work either. We still lack an adequate explanation of optical illusions.

Once again, our prior discussions have provided us with the means to supply such an explanation. In chapter 4, we discussed the particular problems posed by resisted hallucinations. These, recall, are cases of hallucination in which, because the subject is aware that there are reasons to doubt that things are as they seem, the subject does not believe that she actually *sees* anything at all, but the anomalous experience nevertheless persists. There are clear similarities between resisted hallucinations and optical illusions. To see this, imagine we have a naive subject coming across the Müller-Lyer illusion for the first time and we ask him about the relative lengths of the two lines. Such a subject would be likely to claim (and thereby express his belief) that the arrows-out line is longer than the arrows-in line. Then suppose that we explain the nature of the illusion, and convince the subject by measuring the lines that they are in fact the same length before asking him once again about the relative lengths of the lines. Armed with this new knowledge, the subject no longer makes the naive judgment that the arrows-out line is longer than the arrows-in line, but claims instead that they are the same length. But suppose we ask the subject whether the lines *look to be* the same length. Because the subject would still be, *ex hypothesi*, subject to the illusion, the subject would claim (and thereby express his belief) that it looks as though the arrows-out line is longer than the arrows-in line.

Just as we found in cases of resisted hallucination, while the well-informed subject of the Müller-Lyer illusion no longer entertains the judgment that the arrows-out line is longer than the arrows-in line, he does yet entertain the judgment that it seems to be longer. The belief that it looks as though one line is longer than the other could then be appealed to in order to explain why the subject claims that the lengths of the two lines still look different: because that is precisely what the subject judges to be the case. So the contents of these beliefs can be appealed to in order to explain the illusory aspects of the experience, just as with cognitive illusions and the optical illusions of naive subjects.

There is still a question of why optical illusions, unlike cognitive illusions, are persistent in this way. If I were to learn that the coiled object under the log is really a rope and not a snake at all, not only would I not believe that I see a snake, but I would also not believe that it looks as though I do, either. However, on discovering that the Müller-Lyer lines are really the same length, while I no longer judge that the lines are the same length, I supposedly judge that they seem to be. But why is there this difference between the two cases? To answer this question, recall that the explanation of the appearance of false judgments in cases of cognitive illusion had two elements: one that appealed to the nature of the disturbances in the subject's overall doxastic state, and another that appealed to the particular layout of the environment. Where optical illusions are concerned, I suggest a two-component explanation also applies, but the nature of each explanatory component will be somewhat different than in the case of cognitive illusion.

In the case of cognitive illusion, the first component of the explanation—the aspect of the explanation that appeals to the subject's doxastic state—might mention some evanescent disturbance such as the subject's tiredness, state of anxiety, or perceptual priming. Then, the second component—the aspect of the explanation that appeals to features of the environment the subject is looking at—would appeal to something that was sufficiently snakelike (relative to the significance of the cognitive disturbance) to trigger the deployment of an inappropriate conceptual-recognitional capacity. The evanescent nature of the kinds of cognitive disorders appealed to by the first component would then go some way toward explaining why cognitive illusions are relatively subjective and unpredictable. What is more, the kind of similarities that would qualify as sufficient by the second component may well alter as the disturbance in the subject's doxastic state gets more or less unstable to the point at which we take ourselves to be no longer dealing with illusions but rather with something that is more accurately described as a hallucination.

Where optical illusions are concerned, the explanation corresponding to the second component—the component that appeals to the layout of the environment—will be quite different. This will involve a standard appeal, dependent upon the particular optical illusion in question, to the relevant illusion-inducing features of the perceived scene. For example, it might appeal to the arrowheads of the Müller-Lyer illusion, the converging lines of the Ponzo illusion, or the radiating lines of the Hering figure. Then the first component—the aspect of the explanation that appeals to the subject's doxastic state—will appeal not to the unpredictable way these features happen to affect us given a transient disturbance of our doxastic state, but rather to the robust and predictable way those particular illusion-inducing features lead us to passively deploy inappropriate conceptual-recognitional capacities.

The fact that optical illusions are so intersubjective and predictable suggests that the illusion-inducing features of the figures act at a fairly low level. And while there are reasons to think that some of the responses may be learned rather than innate,[10] the widespread susceptibility to these illusions suggests that this process of acquisition does not require a very specific learning history at all, and that the responses

10. See, e.g., Gregory and Wallace's findings that a subject who had never had any useful visual experience was not susceptible (1963).

quickly become firmly established to the point at which they function as though they are innate. Now, exactly why these illusion-inducing features have the effects they do is an interesting question, albeit one for visual scientists to answer. I suspect it is likely that illusions such as these take advantage of what we might loosely call "shortcuts" that the visual system has devised in order to underpin the quick and accurate deployment of conceptual-recognitional capacities.

For instance, consider the well-known Kanizsa triangle, which consists of three colored circles, positioned in a triangle shape, each of which is missing a pie-shaped wedge. The illusion is that, rather than seeing incomplete circles, we "see" a triangle of the same color as the background partially occluding completed circles. What it is like to have an experience of this figure is, I suggest, a matter of the subject's having an experience with an array of phenomenal properties corresponding to the range of facts concerning the incomplete circles. However, because we are primed to see the world in terms of bounded objects, these features of the figure have the consequence that the subject's triangle conceptual-recognitional capacity is erroneously deployed, which in turn explains why the subject falsely judges that there is, or at least that it looks as though there is, a white triangle occluding the rest of the scene. And because the misleading aspects of the figure operate at such a low level, their contribution cannot be offset by higher cognitive factors. This is also why our knowledge that the Müller-Lyer lines are really the same length only serves to modulate the judgments that are made, rather than to stop us making such judgments altogether.

6.6 Conclusion

Over the course of this chapter, we have seen how the naive realist might address the argument from illusion. This builds on the naive realist's disjunctive response to the argument from hallucination but, physical illusion aside, it does not operate by treating the entire illusory experience as falling under either of the two primary disjuncts. Instead, adequate accounts of the other cases of illusion all involve aspects of *both* theories: the account of veridical perception is called upon to explain those respects in which the illusion involves seeing something, and we appealed to the theory of hallucination in order to explain those respects in which the illusion involves getting it wrong. To this extent, we do not treat illusions per se in the same way as either veridical perceptions or hallucinations. Rather, we break an illusory experience down into its constituent elements and then claim that some of those elements—the seen components—correspond to acquaintance-based phenomenal properties that the experience possesses. The illusory components, however, are not correlated with any phenomenal properties of the experience itself, but are merely "hallucinated": the subjects take themselves to be seeing certain things/take their experience to have certain additional phenomenal properties, when in fact it does not.

In many ways, this approach follows McDowell's formulation of disjunctivism, but at the level of individual facts that the subject is acquainted with in experience, rather than at the level of whole experiences. McDowell, recall, characterized the key disjunction thus: "[A]n appearance that such-and-such is the case can be *either* a mere appearance *or* the fact that such-and-such is the case making itself perceptually manifest to someone" (1982/1998: 386–387). According to the position presented here, one's seeming to see a particular worldly fact is a matter *either* of one's being acquainted with that fact *or* one's mistakenly taking it to be the case that one is acquainted with such a fact. Therefore, at the level of individual phenomenal properties, there is no class of illusion; there are only two ways of seeming to see a particular feature: either veridically or nonveridically. The key to the picture, however, comes with the recognition that any normal visual experience will seem to the subject to present not just one, but an array of worldly facts. At the level of whole experiences, illusions occur when some features are seen veridically and others nonveridically.

When it comes to the level of whole experiences, then, this theory can usefully be viewed as claiming that all visual experiences fall between two poles or disjuncts: the pole of perfect veridical perception, on the one hand, and the pole of pure hallucination, on the other. Yet on this theory, it is not an either/or case in which only one of the two accounts applies to any given situation. Instead, there can be cases in which each account applies to a greater or lesser extent. In a case of perfect veridical perception, every fact that the subject takes himself or herself to see would indeed be a fact with which the subject of experience is acquainted—there would be a phenomenal property of acquainting the subject with each of these facts. Because the subject is only able to be acquainted with these facts in virtue of his or her possessing the right kinds of conceptual-recognitional capacities, if the subject's deployment of these capacities becomes less reliable, some of these worldly facts may cease to be veridically perceived, and some of the experience's phenomenal properties would drop out of the picture. However, at the same time, the misdeployment of certain capacities may in turn lead the subject to form erroneous beliefs about the world and his or her experiences. In the case closest to perfect veridical perception, just one of the many facts that we take ourselves to see is not seen veridically, but is merely apparently seen. To explain this aspect of the experience, we need to appeal to the theory of hallucination. Yet the mistake might be so insignificant that we are nonetheless willing to concede that the experience as a whole remains veridical. Then, as the influence of the veridical perception mode of explanation drops away, and the influence of the subject's idiosyncratic response to the world increases, we would move away from experiences we are prepared to call veridical perceptions of the environment, to those we think involve some kind of illusion. Often, as with the sort of cognitive illusion discussed in section 6.4, these will be quickly overcome, and the subject will return to perceiving veridically, but in other cases, as with optical illusions, the illusion will persist.

Inasmuch as such an experience does indeed involve seeing something, the particular seen is still seen in a thoroughly naive realist way: the subject is still acquainted with *some* of the worldly facts involving that particular. Insofar as the subject gets something *wrong*, the mistake comes in only at the level of the cognitive effects *of* that experience. The layout of the tract of the environment that the subjects are open to, for some reason or another, leads them to deploy inappropriate conceptual-recognitional capacities and thereby form erroneous beliefs and judgments about their experiences of that particular. The subjects will therefore take themselves to be seeing the particular to be a way it is not. Such beliefs can explain the occurrence of the illusion in a way consistent with naive realism—the "illusion" is just a ghost generated by the subject's belief or judgment that they are seeing something.

As we move farther away from veridical perception and increase the influence of the hallucinatory mode of explanation, we will find cases in which the subject still perceives some aspects of the environment, and where the cognitive effects of this experience still include erroneous beliefs, but where we find it more and more difficult to explain *why* the subject forms these beliefs by looking at the nature and layout of the environment experienced. For example, a subject may be seeing aspects of the room in which he or she is sitting, but come to judge that there is a person in the room, even though there is nothing in that part of the room that is being seen and erroneously taken to be a person.

By this point, we may be more inclined to classify this case as a hallucination. To explain the hallucinatory aspects of such an experience, there is no longer anything to be gained by pointing to the particular layout of the environment—it does not help to explain why the subject forms the beliefs that he or she does—all we can do is point to whatever cognitive breakdown it is that saddles the subject with those particular beliefs. Finally, at the far end of the scale, when the perceptual mode of explanation has dropped out altogether, we reach cases of pure hallucination in which *every* fact that we take ourselves to see would be merely apparently seen.

This concludes the defense of naive realism against the arguments from hallucination and illusion. By going disjunctivist, the naive realist purchases the means to retain a naive realist account of veridical perception for the price of an alternative account of hallucination and an explanation of how two different kinds of state might come to be indiscriminable for a subject. To meet this debt, I argued that pure hallucinations are mental states that lack phenomenal character but that have the same cognitive effects as veridical perceptions of certain kinds would have had in the same overall doxastic setting, had the subject been rational. Because these cognitive effects include higher order beliefs and judgments about one's own experiences, this in turn accounts for their indiscriminability from perceptual experiences of those kinds.

This account of how radically different mental states can nevertheless be indiscriminable from one another defeats the argument from hallucination as an argument against naive realist accounts of veridical perception. But as long as it is inadequate to simply class illusory experiences together with hallucinatory experiences, as I have accepted it is, the argument from illusion remains in force. To counter *this* argument, then, we also need an account of illusion. In the case of illusion, I suggest, *both* theories are in force. Inasmuch as illusion involves seeing something, the account of veridical perception is invoked to explain how the thing seen is indeed seen. Inasmuch as illusion involves getting it wrong, the account of hallucination is summoned to explain why the subject takes that thing to be a certain way when it is not. But this way of understanding illusion is consistent with a naive realist theory of veridical perception (and, indeed, with a naive realist theory of *some* aspects of illusory experience). So, as an argument against naive realist accounts of veridical perception, the argument from illusion is also put out of play.

To sum up, then, according to the theory presented here, in cases of veridical experience, the phenomenal character of an experience is a matter of the subject's being acquainted with facts: elements of the mind-independent environment. In this way, the theory legitimates the claim that, in those cases in which we are not misled, the layout of reality shapes the contours of our conscious experiences. This is not to claim, of course, that we cannot be misled; we can be and often are. But when we are misled, this is not because we enter a state that has phenomenal character of a different kind—say, involving the subject's being acquainted with a fact proxy or merely representing that certain facts are present when they are not—but rather that we simply take ourselves to be acquainted with a certain fact, and hence to be in a state with a certain kind of phenomenal character, when in reality we are not. In this way, we can see how the possibility of hallucination and illusion can be made compatible with an acquaintance-based conception of vision.

References

Armstrong, D. M. (1961) *Perception and the Physical World* (London: Routledge and Kegan Paul).

——. (1968) *A Materialist Theory of the Mind* (London: Routledge and Kegan Paul).

——. (1997) *A World of States of Affairs* (Cambridge: Cambridge University Press).

Austin, J. L. (1962) *Sense and Sensibilia* (Oxford: Clarendon Press).

Ayer, A. J. (1940) *The Foundations of Empirical Knowledge* (London: Macmillan).

——. (1956) *The Problem of Knowledge* (Middlesex: Penguin).

Bar, M., and I. Biederman (1998) "Subliminal Visual Priming." *Psychological Science* 9, 464–469.

Bentall, R. P. (1990) "The Illusion of Reality: A Review and Integration of Psychological Research on Hallucinations." *Psychological Bulletin* 107, 82–95.

Blaser, E., Z. W. Pylyshyn, and A. O. Holcombe (2000) "Tracking an Object through Feature Space." *Nature* 408, 196–199.

Block, N. (1980) "Are Absent Qualia Impossible?" *Philosophical Review* 89, 257–275.

——. (1990) "Inverted Earth." In J. E. Tomberlin (ed.), *Philosophical Perspectives*, Vol. 4: *Action Theory and Philosophy of Mind* (Atascadero, CA: Ridgeview), 53–79.

Block, N. (1995) "On a Confusion about a Function of Consciousness." *Behavioral and Brain Sciences* 18, 227–287.

Brewer, B. (2008) "How to Account for Illusion." In A. Haddock and F. Macpherson (eds.), *Disjunctivism: Perception, Action, and Knowledge* (Oxford: Oxford University Press), 168–180.

Broad, C. D. (1951/1965) "Some Elementary Reflexions on Sense-Perception." In R. J. Swartz (ed.), *Perceiving, Sensing and Knowing* (Berkeley: University of California Press), 29–48.

Byrne, A. (1997) "Some Like It HOT: Consciousness and Higher-Order Thoughts." *Philosophical Studies* 86, 103–129.

——. (2001) "Intentionalism Defended." *Philosophical Review* 110, 199–240.

——. (2002) "DON'T PANIC: Tye's Intentionalist Theory of Consciousness." In *A Field Guide to the Philosophy of Mind* symposium on Tye's *Consciousness, Color, and Content* <http://host.uniroma3.it/progetti/kant/field/tyesymp_byrne.htm>.

——. (2004) "What Phenomenal Consciousness Is Like." In R. Gennaro (ed.), *Higher-Order Theories of Consciousness* (Amsterdam: John Benjamins), 203–225.

Byrne, A., and H. Logue (2008) "Either/Or." In A. Haddock and F. Macpherson (eds.), *Disjunctivism: Perception, Action, and Knowledge* (Oxford: Oxford University Press), 57–94.

Campbell, J. (2002) *Reference and Consciousness* (Oxford: Clarendon Press).

Chalmers, D. J. (1995/1997) "Facing Up to the Problem of Consciousness." In J. Shear (ed.), *Explaining Consciousness: The Hard Problem* (Cambridge, MA: MIT Press), 9–32.

——. (1996) *The Conscious Mind* (New York: Oxford University Press).

——. (1997) "Moving Forward on the Problem of Consciousness." In J. Shear (ed.), *Explaining Consciousness: The Hard Problem* (Cambridge, MA: MIT Press), 379–422.

——. (2002) "Does Conceivability Entail Possibility?" In T. S. Gendler and J. Hawthorne (eds.), *Conceivability and Possibility* (Oxford: Oxford University Press), 145–200.

——. (2004) "The Representational Character of Experience." In B. Leiter (ed.), *The Future of Philosophy* (Oxford: Oxford University Press), 153–181.

——. (2006) "Perception and the Fall from Eden." In T. S. Gendler and J. Hawthorne (eds.), *Perceptual Experience* (Oxford: Clarendon Press), 49–125.

Child, B. (1994) *Causality, Interpretation, and the Mind* (Oxford: Clarendon Press).

Clark A. (2000) "A Case Where Access Implies Qualia?" *Analysis* 60, 30–37.

——. (2002) "Is Seeing All It Seems? Action, Reason and the Grand Illusion." In A. Noë (ed.), *Is the Visual World a Grand Illusion*? (Thorverton, UK: Imprint Academic), 181–202.

Cohen, J. (2004) "Color Properties and Color Ascriptions: A Relationalist Manifesto." *Philosophical Review* 113, 451–506.

Corne, S. J., and R. W. Pickering (1967) "A Possible Correlation between Drug Induced Hallucinations in Man and a Behavioural Response in Mice." *Psychopharmacologia* 11, 65–78.

Cornman, J. W. (1975) *Perception, Common Sense, and Science* (New Haven: Yale University Press).

Crane, T. (1992) "The Nonconceptual Content of Experience." In T. Crane (ed.), *The Contents of Experience: Essays on Perception* (Cambridge: Cambridge University Press), 136–157.

——. (2001) *Elements of Mind: An Introduction to the Philosophy of Mind* (Oxford: Oxford University Press).

Dancy, J. (1985) *Introduction to Contemporary Epistemology* (Oxford: Blackwell).

——. (1995) "Arguments from Illusion." *Philosophical Quarterly* 45, 421–438.

Davies, M., and G. W. Humphries (1993) *Consciousness: Psychological and Philosophical Essays* (London: Blackwell).

Dennett, D. C. (1981) "Are Dreams Experiences?" In Dennett, *Brainstorms: Philosophical Essays on Mind and Psychology* (Brighton: Harvester Press), 129–148.

——. (1992) *Consciousness Explained* (London: Penguin).

——. (1996) "Seeing Is Believing: Or Is It?" In K. Akins (ed.), *Perception* (Oxford: Oxford University Press), 158–172.

Diederich, N. J., A. Alesch, and C. G. Goetz (2000) "Visual Hallucinations Induced by Deep Brain Stimulation in Parkinson's Disease." *Clinical Neuropharmacology* 23, 287–289.

Dodd, J. (1995) "McDowell and Identity Theories of Truth." *Analysis* 55, 160–165.

Dretske, F. (1969) *Seeing and Knowing* (London: Routledge and Kegan Paul).

——. (1990) "Seeing, Believing and Knowing." In D. N. Osherson, S. M. Kosslyn, and J. M. Hollerbach (eds.), *Visual Cognition and Action*, Vol. 2 (Cambridge, MA: MIT Press), 129–148.

——. (1993) "Conscious Experience." *Mind* 102, 263–283.

——. (1995) *Naturalizing the Mind* (Cambridge, MA: MIT Press).

——. (2003) "Experience as Representation." In E. Villanueva (ed.), *Philosophical Issues*, Vol. 13: *Philosophy of Mind* (Atascadero, CA: Ridgeview), 67–82.

Evans, G. (1982) *The Varieties of Reference* (Oxford: Oxford University Press).

Farkas, K. (2006) "Indiscriminability and the Sameness of Appearance." *Proceedings of the Aristotelian Society* 106, 205–225.

Firth, R. (1949/1965) "Sense-Data and the Percept Theory." In R. J. Swartz, (ed.), *Perceiving, Sensing and Knowing* (Berkeley: University of California Press), 204–270.

Fish, W., and C. Macdonald (2007) "On McDowell's Identity Conception of Truth." *Analysis* 67, 36–41.

Florio, V., J. A. Fuentes, H. Ziegler, and V. G. Longon (1972) "EEG and Behavioural Effects in Animals of Some Amphetamine Derivatives with Hallucinogenic Properties." *Behavioural Biology* 7, 401–414.

Fodor, J. A., and Z. W. Pylyshyn (1981) "How Direct Is Visual Perception? Some Reflections on Gibson's 'Ecological Approach.'" *Cognition* 9, 139–196.

Foster, J. (1985) *Ayer* (London: Routledge and Kegan Paul).

——. (2000) *The Nature of Perception* (Oxford: Oxford University Press).

Garson, J. W. (2001) "(Dis)Solving the Binding Problem." *Philosophical Psychology* 14, 381–392.

Gibson, J. J. (1966) *The Senses Considered as Perceptual Systems* (Boston: Houghton Mifflin).

Gothe, J., S. A. Brandt, K. Irlbacher, S. Röricht, B. A. Sabel, and B.-U. Meyer (2002) "Changes in Visual Cortex Excitability in Blind Subjects as Demonstrated by Transcranial Magnetic Stimulation." *Brain* 125, 479–490.

Greenwald, A. G., S. C. Draine, and R. L. Abrams (1996) "Three Cognitive Markers of Unconscious Semantic Activation." *Science* 275, 1699–1702.

Gregory, R. L. (1970) *The Intelligent Eye* (London: Weidenfeld and Nicholson).

Gregory, R. L., and J. Wallace (1963) "Recovery from Early Blindness: A Case Study." *Experimental Psychology Society Monographs* No. 2 (London: Heffer).

Grimes, J. (1996) "On the Failure to Detect Changes in Scenes across Saccades." In K. Akins (ed.), *Vancouver Studies in Cognitive Sciences*, Vol. 5: *Perception* (Oxford: Oxford University Press), 89–110.

Halgren, E. (1982) "Mental Phenomena Induced by Stimulation in the Limbic System." *Human Neurobiology* 1, 251–260.

Hallett, M. (2000) "Transcranial Magnetic Stimulation and the Human Brain." *Nature* 406, 147–150.

Hardin, C. L. (1988) *Color for Philosophers: Unweaving the Rainbow* (Indianapolis: Hackett).

Hawthorne, J., and K. Kovakovich (2006) "Disjunctivism." *Proceedings of the Aristotelian Society* 80 (supplement), 145–183.

Hellie, B. (2007a) "Factive Phenomenal Characters." *Philosophical Perspectives* 21, 259–306.

——. (2007b) "'There's Something It's Like' and the Structure of Consciousness." *Philosophical Review* 116, 441–463.

Hill, C. S. (1997) "Imaginability, Conceivability, Possibility, and the Mind-Body Problem." *Philosophical Studies* 87, 61–85.

Hill, C. S., and B. P. McLaughlin (1999) "There Are Fewer Things in Reality Than Are Dreamt of in Chalmers's Philosophy." *Philosophy and Phenomenological Research* 59, 446–454.

Hinton, J. M. (1967) "Visual Experiences." *Mind* 76, 217–227.

——. (1973) *Experiences: An Inquiry into Some Ambiguities* (Oxford: Clarendon Press).

Horowitz, M. J. (1964) "The Imagery of Visual Hallucinations." *Journal of Nervous and Mental Disease* 138, 513–523.

Horowitz, M. J., J. E. Adams, and B. B. Rutkin (1968) "Visual Imagery on Brain Stimulation." *Archives of General Psychiatry* 19, 469–486.

Hurovitz, C. S., S. Dunn, G. W. Domhoff, and H. Fiss (1999) "The Dreams of Blind Men and Women: A Replication and Extension of Previous Findings." *Dreaming* 9, 183–193.

Johnston, M. (2006) "Better than Mere Knowledge? The Function of Sensory Awareness." In T. S. Gendler and J. Hawthorne (eds.), *Perceptual Experience* (Oxford: Clarendon Press), 260–290.

Kanai, R., and F. A. J. Verstraten (2006) "Attentional Modulation of Perceptual Stabilization." *Proceedings of the Royal Society of Biological Sciences* 273, 1217–1222.

Kerr, N., D. Foulkes, and M. Schmidt (1982) "The Structure of Laboratory Dream Reports in Blind and Sighted Subjects." *Journal of Nervous and Mental Disease* 170, 286–294.

Kirk, R. (2005) *Zombies and Consciousness* (Oxford: Oxford University Press).

Kirkham, R. L. (1992) *Theories of Truth: A Critical Introduction* (Cambridge, MA: MIT Press).

Koch, C. (2004) *The Quest for Consciousness: A Neurobiological Approach* (Englewood, CO: Roberts).

Kriegel, U. (2002) "PANIC Theory and the Prospects for a Representational Theory of Phenomenal Consciousness." *Philosophical Psychology* 15, 55–64.

Lance, J. W. (1976) "Simple Formed Hallucinations Confined to the Area of a Specific Visual Field Defect." *Brain* 99, 719–734.

Langsam, H. (1997) "The Theory of Appearing Defended." *Philosophical Studies* 87, 33–59.

Levine, J. (1983) "Materialism and Qualia: The Explanatory Gap." *Pacific Philosophical Quarterly* 64, 354–361.

——. (2001) *Purple Haze: The Puzzle of Consciousness* (New York: Oxford University Press).

——. (2003) "Experience and Representation." In Q. Smith and A. Jokic (eds.), *Consciousness: New Philosophical Perspectives* (Oxford: Clarendon Press), 57–76.

——. (2006) "Conscious Awareness and (Self-)Representation." In U. Kriegel and K. Williford (eds.), *Self-Representational Approaches to Consciousness* (Cambridge, MA: MIT Press), 173–198.

Lewis, D. (1997) "Naming the Colours." *Australasian Journal of Philosophy* 75, 325–342.

Lormand, E. (2004) "The Explanatory Stopgap." *Philosophical Review* 113, 303–357.

Loux, M. (2002) *Metaphysics: A Contemporary Introduction* (London: Routledge).

Lowe, E. J. (1992) "Experience and Its Objects." In T. Crane (ed.), *The Contents of Experience: Essays on Perception* (Cambridge: Cambridge University Press), 79–104.

Lycan, W. G. (1996) *Consciousness and Experience* (Cambridge, MA: MIT Press).

Lycan, W. G. (1997) "Consciousness as Internal Monitoring." In N. Block, O. Flanagan, and G. Güzeldere (eds.), *The Nature of Consciousness* (Cambridge, MA: MIT Press), 755–771.

——. (1999) "Dretske on the Mind's Awareness of Itself." *Philosophical Studies* 95, 125–133.

——. (2001) "The Case for Phenomenal Externalism." In J. E. Tomberlin (ed.), *Philosophical Perspectives*, Vol. 15: *Metaphysics* (Atascadero, CA: Ridgeview), 17–35.

——. (2004) "The Superiority of HOP to HOT." In R. Gennaro (ed.), *Higher-Order Theories of Consciousness* (Amsterdam: John Benjamins), 93–113.

Mack, A., and I. Rock (1998) *Inattentional Blindness* (Cambridge, MA: MIT Press).

Mahl, G. F., A. Rothenberg, J. M. R. Delgado, and H. Hamlin (1964) "Psychological Responses in the Human to Intracerebral Electrical Stimulation." *Psychosomatic Medicine* 26, 337–368.

Malcolm, N. (1959) *Dreaming* (London: Routledge and Kegan Paul).

Martin, M. G. F. (1994) "Perceptual Content." In S. Guttenplan (ed.), *A Companion to the Philosophy of Mind* (Oxford: Blackwell), 463–471.

——. (1997) "The Reality of Appearances." In M. Sainsbury (ed.), *Thought and Ontology* (Milan: FrancoAngeli), 81–106.

——. (1998) "Setting Things before the Mind." In A. O'Hear (ed.), *Current Issues in Philosophy of Mind* (Cambridge: Cambridge University Press), 157–180.

——. (2002) "The Transparency of Experience." *Mind and Language* 17, 376–425.

——. (2004) "The Limits of Self-Awareness." *Philosophical Studies* 120, 37–89.

——. (2006) "On Being Alienated." In T. S. Gendler and J. Hawthorne (eds.), *Perceptual Experience* (Oxford: Clarendon Press), 354–410.

Matthen, M. (2005) *Seeing, Doing and Knowing: A Philosophical Theory of Sense Perception* (Oxford: Clarendon Press).

Maund, B. (2002) "Tye on Phenomenal Character and Color." In *A Field Guide to the Philosophy of Mind* symposium on Tye's *Consciousness, Color, and Content* <http://host.uniroma3.it/progetti/kant/field/tyesymp_maund.htm>.

——. (2003) *Perception* (Chesham: Acumen).

McConkie, G. W., and D. Zola (1979) "Is Visual Information Integrated across Successive Fixations in Reading?" *Perception and Psychophysics* 25, 221–224.

McCulloch, G. (1995) *The Mind and Its World* (London: Routledge).

——. (2003) *The Life of the Mind: An Essay on Phenomenological Externalism* (London: Routledge).

McDowell, J. (1982/1998) "Criteria, Defeasibility, and Knowledge." In McDowell, *Meaning, Knowledge and Reality* (Cambridge, MA: Harvard University Press), 369–394.

——. (1984/1998) "*De Re* Senses." In McDowell, *Meaning, Knowledge and Reality* (Cambridge, MA: Harvard University Press), 214–227.

——. (1986/1998) "Singular Thought and the Extent of Inner Space." In McDowell, *Meaning, Knowledge and Reality* (Cambridge, MA: Harvard University Press), 228–259.

——. (1994) *Mind and World* (Cambridge, MA: Harvard University Press).

——. (2008) "The Disjunctive Conception of Experience as Material for a Transcendental Argument." In A. Haddock and F. Macpherson (eds.), *Disjunctivism: Perception, Action, and Knowledge* (Oxford: Oxford University Press), 376–389.

Metzinger, T. (1995) *Conscious Experience* (Schöningh: Imprint Academic).

Mulligan, K., P. Simons, and B. Smith (1984) "Truth-Makers." *Philosophy and Phenomenological Research* 44, 287–321.

Mundle, C. W. K. (1971) *Perception: Facts and Theories* (Oxford: Oxford University Press).

Nagel, T. (1974/1979) "What Is It Like to Be a Bat?" In Nagel, *Mortal Questions* (Cambridge: Canto), 165–180.

Noë, A. (2004) *Action in Perception* (Cambridge, MA: MIT Press).

Olson, K. R. (1987) *An Essay on Facts* (Stanford: Center for the Study of Language and Information).

O'Regan, J. K. (1992) "Solving the 'Real' Mysteries of Visual Perception: The World as an Outside Memory." *Canadian Journal of Philosophy* 46, 461–488.

O'Regan, J. K., and A. Noë (2001) "A Sensorimotor Account of Vision and Visual Consciousness." *Behavioral and Brain Sciences* 24, 939–973.

Pani, J. R. (2000) "Cognitive Description and Change Blindness." *Visual Cognition* 7, 107–126.

Peacocke, C. (2001) "Does Perception Have a Nonconceptual Content?" *Journal of Philosophy* 98, 239–264.

Penfield, W. (1975) *The Mystery of the Mind: A Critical Study of Consciousness and the Human Brain* (Princeton: Princeton University Press).

Penfield, W., and P. Perot (1963) "The Brain's Record of Auditory and Visual Experience: A Final Summary and Discussion." *Brain* 86, 595–696.

Penfield, W., and L. Roberts (1959) *Speech and Brain Mechanisms* (Princeton: Princeton University Press).

Plantinga, A. (1976) "Actualism and Possible Worlds." *Theoria* 42, 139–160.

Pons, T. (1996) "Novel Sensations in the Congenitally Blind." *Nature* 380, 479–480.

Putnam, H. (1981) *Reason, Truth and History* (Cambridge: Cambridge University Press).

Rankin, P. M., and P. J. O'Carroll (1995) "Reality Discrimination, Reality Monitoring and Disposition towards Hallucination." *British Journal of Clinical Psychology* 34, 517–528.

Robinson, H. (1994) *Perception* (London: Routledge).

Rosenthal, D. (1990/1997) "A Theory of Consciousness." In N. Block, O. Flanagan, and G. Güzeldere (eds.), *The Nature of Consciousness* (Cambridge, MA: MIT Press), 729–753.

——. (1992) "Thinking That One Thinks." In M. Davies and G. Humphries (eds.), *Consciousness: Psychological and Philosophical Essays* (Oxford: Blackwell), 197–223.

Russell, B. (1912/1967) *The Problems of Philosophy* (Oxford: Oxford University Press).

Sadato, N., P.-L. Alvaro, J. Grafman, V. Ibanez, M.-P. Deiber, G. Dold, and M. Hallett (1996) "Activation of the Primary Visual Cortex by Braille Reading in Blind Subjects." *Nature* 380, 526–528.

Schellenberg, S. (2008) "The Situation-Dependency of Perception." *Journal of Philosophy* 105, 55–84.

Searle, J. R. (2005) "Consciousness: What We Still Don't Know." *New York Review*, 36–39.

Shoemaker, S. (1975) "Functionalism and Qualia." *Philosophical Studies* 27, 291–315.

——. (1981) "Absent Qualia Are Impossible: A Reply to Block." *Philosophical Review* 90, 581–599.

——. (1994) "Phenomenal Character." *Nous* 28, 21–38.

Siegel, R. K., J. M. Brewster, and M. E. Jarvik (1974) "An Observational Study of Hallucinogen-Induced Behaviour in Unrestrained *Macaca mulatta*." *Psychopharmacologia* 40, 211–223.

Siegel, S. (2004) "Indiscriminability and the Phenomenal." *Philosophical Studies* 120, 90–112.

——. (2008) "The Epistemic Conception of Hallucination." In A. Haddock and F. Macpherson (eds.), *Disjunctivism: Perception, Action, and Knowledge* (Oxford: Oxford University Press), 205–224.

Simons, D. J. (2000) "Attentional Capture and Inattentional Blindness." *Trends in Cognitive Sciences* 4, 147–155.

Simons, D. J., and C. F. Chabris (1999) "Gorillas in Our Midst: Sustained Inattentional Blindness for Dynamic Events." *Perception* 28, 1059–1074.

Simons, D. J., and D. T. Levin (1997) "Change Blindness." *Trends in Cognitive Science* 1, 261–267.

——. (1998) "Failure to Detect Changes to People during a Real-World Interaction." *Psychonomic Bulletin and Review* 5, 644–649.

Slade, P. D., and R. P. Bentall (1990) *Sensory Deception: A Scientific Analysis of Hallucination* (London: Croom Helm).

Smith, A. D. (2002) *The Problem of Perception* (Cambridge, MA: Harvard University Press).

——. (2008) "Disjunctivism and Discriminability." In A. Haddock and F. Macpherson (eds.), *Disjunctivism: Perception, Action, and Knowledge* (Oxford: Oxford University Press), 181–204.

Snowdon, P. (1981) "Perception, Vision and Causation." *Proceedings of the Aristotelian Society* 81, 175–92.

——. (1992) "How to Interpret 'Direct Perception.'" In T. Crane (ed.), *The Contents of Experience: Essays on Perception* (Cambridge: Cambridge University Press), 49–78.

——. (2005) "The Formulation of Disjunctivism: A Response to Fish." *Proceedings of the Aristotelian Society* 105, 129–141.

Soteriou, M. (2000) "The Particularity of Visual Perception." *European Journal of Philosophy* 8, 173–189.

——. (2005) "The Subjective View of Experience and Its Objective Commitments." *Proceedings of the Aristotelian Society* 105, 177–190.

Srinivas, J. (1993) "Perceptual Specificity in Nonverbal Priming." *Journal of Experimental Psychology [Learning, Memory and Cognition]* 19, 582–602.

Strawson, G. (1994) *Mental Reality* (Cambridge, MA: MIT Press).

Strawson, P. F. (1979/1988) "Perception and Its Objects." In J. Dancy (ed.), *Perceptual Knowledge* (Oxford: Oxford University Press), 92–112.

Sturgeon, S. (1998) "Visual Experience." *Proceedings of the Aristotelian Society* 98, 179–200.

——. (2006) "Reflective Disjunctivism." *Proceedings of the Aristotelian Society* 80 (supplement), 185–216.

——. (2008) "Disjunctivism about Visual Experience." In A. Haddock and F. Macpherson (eds.), *Disjunctivism: Perception, Action, and Knowledge* (Oxford: Oxford University Press), 112–143.

Thau, M. (2004) "What Is Disjunctivism?" *Philosophical Studies* 120, 193–253.

Thompson, B. (2008) "Representationalism and the Argument from Hallucination." *Pacific Philosophical Quarterly* 89, 384–412.

Travis, C. (2004) "The Silence of the Senses." *Mind* 113, 57–94.

Tye, M. (1992) "Visual Qualia and Visual Content." In T. Crane (ed.), *The Contents of Experience: Essays on Perception* (Cambridge: Cambridge University Press), 158–176.

——. (1995) *Ten Problems of Consciousness: A Representational Theory of the Phenomenal Mind* (Cambridge, MA: MIT Press).

——. (2000) *Consciousness, Color and Content* (Cambridge, MA: MIT Press).

——. (2002) "To PANIC or Not to PANIC: Reply to Byrne." In *A Field Guide to the Philosophy of Mind* symposium on Tye's *Consciousness, Color, and Content* <http://host.uniroma3.it/progetti/kant/field/tyesymp_replytobyrne.htm>.

——. (2003a) "Blurry Images, Double Vision, and Other Oddities: New Problems for Representationalism?" In Q. Smith and A. Jokic (eds.), *Consciousness: New Philosophical Perspectives* (Oxford: Clarendon Press), 7–32.

——. (2003b) *Consciousness and Persons: Unity and Identity* (Cambridge, MA: MIT Press).

Tye, M. (2006) "Absent Qualia and the Mind-Body Problem." *Philosophical Review* 115, 139–166.

Tye, M., and P. Bradley (2001) "Of Colors, Kestrels, Caterpillars, and Leaves." *Journal of Philosophy* 98, 469–487.

Valberg, J. J. (1992) *The Puzzle of Experience* (Oxford: Clarendon Press).

Vision, G. (1997) *Problems of Vision: Rethinking the Causal Theory of Perception* (New York: Oxford University Press).

Williamson, T. (1990) *Identity and Discrimination* (Oxford: Blackwell).

——. (2000) *Knowledge and Its Limits* (Oxford: Oxford University Press).

Wittgenstein, L. (1921/1961) *Tractatus Logico-Philosophicus* (London: Routledge and Kegan Paul).

Woodruff-Smith, D. (1986) "The Structure of (Self-)Consciousness." *Topoi* 5, 149–156.

Yamamoto, T., and S. Ueki (1980) "The Role of Central Serotonergic Mechanisms on Head-Twitch and Backward Locomotion Induced by Hallucinogenic Drugs." *Pharmacology, Biochemistry and Behavior* 14, 89–95.

Zeki, S. (1990) "A Century of Cerebral Achromatopsia." *Brain* 113, 1721–1777.

——. (1991) "Cerebral Akinetopsia (Visual Motion Blindness): A Review." *Brain* 114, 811–824.

——. (1993) *A Vision of the Brain* (London: Blackwell Scientific Publications).

Index

www.ingramcontent.com/pod-product-compliance
Ingram Content Group UK Ltd.
Pitfield, Milton Keynes, MK11 3LW, UK
UKHW041839190726
13854UKWH00002B/617

9 780199 981137